PRAYING TO THE ALIENS
GARY NUMAN

PRAYING TO THE ALIENS

An Autobiography by Gary Numan

With Steve Malins

ANDRE DEUTSCH

First published in 1997 by
André Deutsch Limited
106 Great Russell Street
London WC1B 3LJ
www.vci.co.uk

André Deutsch is a subsidiary of VCI plc

A catalogue record for this book is available from the British Library

ISBN 0 2339 9205 7

Typeset by Derek Doyle & Associates
Mold, Flintshire.
Printed and bound by
WBC, Bridgend, Mid-Glamorgan.

Contents

This book is dedicated to Gemma, my best friend, my most fierce ally and my wife.

Introduction

Trent Reznor, Nine Inch Nails – 'After hearing Gary Numan's "Cars" on the radio, I knew I wanted to make music with synthesizers.'

Marilyn Manson – 'I was always into his apocalyptic fiction lyrics. He pioneered electronic dance music.'

Beck – 'I don't care what anyone says, I love Gary Numan.'

Afrika Bambaataa – 'Numan was so spooky, so spaced out and it sounded like the future of music to me.'

Saffron, Republica – 'What's party politics when you're talking genius. He's so cool, all that alien stuff was just brilliant.'

In the '90s there's already been too much hype about too many revivals. It seems that every artist who has ever had a hit is dug up by rabid fans in the media who push, cajole and gush until their hero receives a critical pat on the back or returns to the charts. So it's odd to find myself turning from a fan into a more active role in Gary Numan's career in the last two years by putting together the covers album *Random*, and working with him on this book. My only excuse is, three years ago, I realised big American acts such as Beck, The Foo Fighters, Weezer, Smashing Pumpkins, Nine Inch Nails and Hole were either covering Numan's songs or citing him as a major influence on their own music, and no one else seemed to notice or acknowledge the fact. At the time I was working as a feature writer at *Vox* magazine and I proposed a piece on Numan.

Given my out-of-the-closet status as a plains clothes 'Numanoid', my idea was instantly dismissed. Faced with this resistance I decided to get my hands dirty. The result, two years later, was *Random*, a double CD which featured 26 artists including Kenickie, The Orb, Dubstar, Dave Clarke, Damon Albarn from Blur with Weezer's Matt Sharp and St. Etienne. For all my enthusisasm, I was extremely aware that most 'tribute' albums are poorly packaged, earnest and reverential, often adding little of value to the original recordings. However I saw *Random* as an opportunity for the artists to be experimental and imaginative without the pressure of commercial restraints. This was the spirit of *Random*, to make a witty, accessible, eclectic pop record for 1997, sprawling across all the sub-genres of electronic music – synthesiser pop, hip hop, techno, ambient, trip hop, industrial, neo-gothic, disco, P-funk, avant garde, lo-fi and the plain weird. Thanks to the support of Beggars Banquet, in particular Steve Webbon who backed me all the way, *Random* is a rarity amongst tribute albums – it was actually very well received by the British press.

Now I find myself the so-called 'ghost' writer for *Praying To The Aliens*. I found a publisher, structured the book and gave Gary the odd rap on the knuckles for writing too much. Otherwise this is mostly the artist's work, bar the introduction which gives me the opportunity to express a positive tilt on his story. I have my reasons for liking Numan's music, which have nothing to do with nostalgic yearnings for my swaggering walks along Rugby's High Street in black nail varnish and Max Factor 28 panstick some 16 years ago.

One of the biggest problems for the media is that Numan has never been on firm, 'authentic' ground as a songwriter. Whereas the likes of Oasis and Paul Weller slot into a classic pop lineage, Gary Numan was not a fan of '50s or '60s pop music. However in the early '70s he latched on to Bowie, Marc Bolan and to a lesser extent Lou Reed and Mott The Hoople. The disposable 'flash' of glam was attractive, but more subtly, the freakish and individualistic personas of these artists struck a chord with this doleful introvert. Numan had been writing short stories since the age of four, and as he took his material more seriously he started to flesh out his lyrics with ideas stolen from sci-fi magazines and authors such as Philip K. Dick and William Burroughs. The surreal scene settings, bizarre characters and futuristic themes of these novels offered oblique, otherworldly locations for him to express his own feelings. Although David Bowie stole freely from the same sources, Numan created his own unique style. Bowie's synthetic chill on his *Low* album is a combination of restrained passion and cocaine-fuelled paranoia, but Numan has none of his ironic, layered detachment. Like Bolan, he's in love with the idea of being a 'pop star' but he sings with all the frailties of a boiler-suited Morrissey. These qualities were already in evidence in the pop-punk of early Tubeway Army who signed to Beggars Banquet in 1977.

As a punk he was a complete fake, but he adopted the image to get a deal and work out what he wanted to do next. Not that he was alone. By the time Tubeway Army trod the boards of punk clubs The Vortex and The Roxy, most of the initial idealism of the movement had long since vanished, but few people were ready to own up to the fact. Encouraged by the support of Tubeway's bassist Paul Gardiner, the young singer followed his instincts. According to Gardiner 'The band was hardly off the ground when Gary came for the audition. Three or four people came but I was the only one who wanted Gary in the band. The others couldn't see his difference, but I thought he was exceptional, playing guitar like nobody else ever did at that level in 1977. I was convinced from first hearing that he was going to get somewhere.' In retrospect, some of the early three minute Tubeway Army singles 'That's Too Bad' and 'Bombers' stand up well against their contemporaries, because of their pop suss and the urgency of recording over 20 songs in a couple of days.

It was at one of these frantic sessions that Numan stumbled across a synthesiser. He certainly wasn't the first to fall in love with the Moog's fat, burbling analogue sound but his approach was different. Brian Eno had briefly enjoyed fame in Roxy Music as a fully-fledged low-tech star, but he had long since moved into more ambient territory with his mixture of studio strategies and DIY instinct. Apart from their one-off 'novely' hit 'Autobahn', Kraftwerk's exploration of flawless, machine-made pop hadn't made much of on impression on the High Street, and even David Bowie was seen to be retreating to more esoteric ground with his Eno-produced *Low* and *Heroes*. Furthermore, these were well established innovators rather than a 20-year-old from West London, who was signed to a small indie label. Numan was virtually alone in seeing the possibility of being a 'synthesiser star' and, much to the critics' anguish, he achieved success almost overnight.

In late 1978 Beggars Banquet released Tubeway Army's self-titled debut, mixing electronics with post-punk guitars and solid, no frills drumming by Gary's uncle, Jess Lidyard. The only other member of the band at this stage was Gary's best friend Paul Gardiner, but their record label refused to let Numan take on solo status just yet. Although the garage electronics of Tubeway Army was briefly championed by Radio One DJ John Peel, Numan was in a hurry to get back into the studio. He recorded *Replicas* in three days at Gooseberry Studios in London, utilising a stark synthetic sound for most of the tracks, punctuated with more guitar-dominated songs. The album's first single 'Down In The Park' announced this radical change of direction but no one believed the alienated, rhythmical drone of the follow-up 'Are "Friends" Electric?' would elbow its way past the likes of ELO and Squeeze to the number one slot. Within weeks Numan was posing on *Top Of The Pops* in harsh white light, bringing a touch of showbiz camp to the clipped, motorik repetitiveness of the song. From that moment on he was simultaneously branded 'hero' and 'villain'.

When 'Cars' and *The Pleasure Principle* album both topped the charts in autumn '79 he put together a complete package of song, promo video and aloof stage image which act as a catalyst on a new wave of suburban no-hopers who achieved fame through their own synth pop styles. Phil Oakey from The Human League repeatedly pointed out his kinship with his critically reviled contemporary. 'Numan said, since World War Two, society's meant to be great, but, in fact, I'm scared of society, so scared that I just want to get in my car and shut my doors. And that was brilliant, it meant something and it made sense alongside what we were doing at the time.' In the '90s Dubstar's Steve Hellier traces British synthesiser pop back to Numan, whom he describes as 'the godfather of poppy electronics.' In some cases, such as Depeche Mode, Numan's success encouraged them to switch from guitars to electronics. In others, notably The Human League, Soft Cell and – oh dear – The Flock of Seagulls, he opened up the market both in the UK and the

States, where 'Cars' was a hit in 1980, long before the second English invasion in the early '80s.

Furthermore Numan's music influenced a new form of black American music, hip hop. One of the genre's innovators, Afrika Bambaataa, was still enthusing about the Englishman in the late '80s. 'There are still more Europeans I'd like to work with, Kraftwerk and especially Gary Numan,' he told a disbelieving British music press. 'His early cuts from the Tubeway Army days were wild, but some people couldn't get into it. I was a DJ and played it all, particularly when 'Cars' came out and there were blacks getting ecstatic on it. The beats were there but the singing was so weird, so gone, so off, people were freaked. It was spooky, so spaced out and it sounded like the future of music to me.' The Beastie Boys are also Numan enthusiasts, recently running an interview with him in their own *Grand Royal* magazine. This year one of the leading figures in British hip hop, The Underdog, informed *Vox* magazine; 'Electro and hip hop wouldn't have existed if it hadn't been for Gary Numan.'

Numan also played a significant role in the birth of techno, with pioneering black American DJs dropping his name into interviews. Their own underground status meant that few journalists noticed at the time, but the genre's high profile in the '90s has carried Numan more visibly into the dance and mainstream press. The recent *Random 2* album of techno remixes grew out of the original project, simply because the large number of DJs who wanted to contribute justified a CD on its own. Dave Clarke, one of the leading lights in British techno, recently commented on the impact of 'Cars' on his own music. 'It was the first seven-inch single I ever bought. Gary Numan had more influence on me than Kraftwerk ever did – he's the dark side of electronica.' The Orb's Alex Paterson also regards Numan as 'miles ahead of his time, especially for a white person from west London. I'm not only the only DJ who understands the rhythms he was trying to get together back then, even if he didn't fully comprehend what he was doing.'

In his book *Industrial Revolution*, journalist Dave Thompson further underlines Numan's impact by claiming he was 'crucial to the future development of the industrial-electronic scene.' Nevertheless his detractors consistently attacked him as 'pretentious' and 'bombastic,' ludicrously claiming that he had no influence or importance in pop music beyond his initial unit-shifting, teen appeal. To be fair he was often freakishly wooden on stage, an articulate but unworldly young man shoved in front of sold-out theatres through his own success. He also had a self-destructive habit of saying the wrong thing at the wrong time, which journalists pounced on, despite the fact that most of them were a lot older and wiser. As for his self-styled, theatrical 'images', they ended up inspiring both British and American comic book creators. Jamie Hewlitt and Alan Martin, the inventors of the female anti-hero Tank Girl, revealed to the *Daily Telegraph*, 'Tank Girl is about all the things we're into – youth, culture, '70s retro, things like Mad comic, Tiswas and Gary Numan, things we spent our youth paying attention to because it was good.'

Over the next two years, Numan scored more hits including Top Ten singles 'We Are Glass' and 'I Die You Die', as well as a third number one album *Telekon*, which featured an increasingly opulent sound built out of synths, piano, strings and guitar. Then he took the wind out of his pop career by announcing his intention to give up live performances, making a melodramatic, emotional exit with three lavish Wembley Arena shows in 1981.

Nevertheless the period 1981–1994 was as turbulent, action-packed and strange as everything that had come before. New albums poured out, often bright, instinctive and forward-looking but too heavily stylised for the changing times. When baggy and aci-eed were at their height, Numan's wound-licking, moody pop songs were so out-of-vogue he seemed to belong only in his own little world. Yet this was preferable to the other option of raving up his material and incorporating smiley faces into his stage sets. Numan's original problem of an inauthentic, art-glam rock lineage also loomed large, as he simply made his albums up as he went along, stealing ideas from a wide range of sources and re-arranging them with no heed to current fashion. Interestingly many of the artists on *Random* commented on his unorthodox and diverse songwriting as they stripped away Numan's style to the bare-boned compositions. If he'd engaged more fully with the British music industry he might have been able to stand firm and communicate some of his off-the-wall ideas successfully, but instead he retreated into self-pity and a lack of confidence about the value of his own material, fatally allowing his critics to dominate with their pot-shots at this reclusive, isolated figure. For his hardcore following, this perversely strengthened his appeal as a cult artist who was 'different' from the prevailing chart acts. Numan fans Shampoo told *Melody Maker*, 'We thought he was just so cool. He's so different from everything else you hear, you can really hear the Gary Numan sound.'

Even so, against all odds, the picture of Numan as universally hated by the media isn't true. The *NME* conceded his 1981 album, *Dance* was 'his cleanest and most responsible homage to Brian Eno,' described the jazz-electro of 1983's *Warriors* as 'attractive' and opened their review of his 1987 compilation album, *Exhibition*, with the irony-free, gob-smacking line, 'the official *NME* line for 1987 is that Gary Numan is fab.' *Q* applauded his late '80s albums *The Skin Mechanic, Automatic* – a logic-defying collaboration with Shakatak's Bill Sharpe – and *Metal Rhythm*, commenting on the latter, 'it seems he stays ahead of the crowd by communicating something, even if it's unattractive, rather than the ever popular nothing at all'. Other publications such as *Melody Maker* and *Smash Hits* have been surprisingly supportive over the years, while overseas Numan's standing has always been considerably more credible than it ever has been, or ever will be, in the UK. It's tempting to speculate what an organised, ambitious record company could have done if they'd built on these flashes of positive criticism in Numan's most hostile territory. However for most of the mid-to-late-'80s and early '90s he was on his own label, which by his own admission, often struggled to sell their founding artist, let alone anyone else. As a result his passion for aeroplanes increasingly grabbed the headlines at the expense of his music, offering further ammunition to his critics despite his achievement in making himself one of the country's top aerobatic pilots.

Although barely noticed by most people, 1994 was a turning point in his career. In addition to the wave of American artists covering his material, British pop artists Damon Albarn and Pulp's Jarvis Cocker helped to change the climate in Numan's favour by referring back to him as an unlikely English pop icon. On the UK dance scene, Tricky and various DJs also started name-checking him in interviews. Furthermore, Numan set his own agenda by recording his darkest album in years, 1994's *Sacrifice*, and vowing to continue in this direction for the foreseeable future. The growth in the States of electronic-based, heavy, alternative rock, led by Nine Inch Nails, has made Numan relevant again. Trent Reznor admits he was turned onto synthesisers after hearing 'Cars', while Marilyn Manson, who has covered 'Down In The Park' on an EP, recently commented in the *Guardian*, 'Numan? He pioneered electronic dance music.'

At 39, Numan's life and 20-odd albums of private, instinctive tech-noire pop suddenly possess a very contemporary twist. Technology, dance music, aliens, alienation, pre-millennium tension, ghost stories and machine-based thrills are part of day-to-day life and peak-viewing entertainment more than they were in 1979. Perhaps just as importantly for a man with a passionate commitment to showmanship, Numan's story is full of extreme highs and lows, with nothing much in between – the tale of an improbable and imperfect pop star who, for 20 years, has fulfilled an entertainer's primary role of dividing opinion and never being boring.

My thanks to Patricia Bush, Mary and Brian Malins, Bernard MacMahon, Caroline and Koulla, Sally, Alan and Alice and everyone at Q.

Foreword

Fans expect contradictory qualities in pop artists. They want you to be special, to be different somehow to 'ordinary' people, they want you to be mean, moody and magnificent. They want you to be larger than life. But they also want you to be approachable. They want to be able to talk to you. You therefore have to be 'different', strange, mysterious, larger than life, and yet approachable, easy to talk to and sympathetic to their own nervousness. I am none of those things all the time and, to be honest, only a few of them at any time.

No one thinks about this balancing act between real life and fantasy before they become a musician. It's not an easy thing to get right and fans are occasionally disappointed. I once lost a fan that I'd been speaking to the previous evening because she said I was 'nice. I didn't want him to be nice'. You can't really answer that can you? I think she wanted me to glow moodily in the dark. Or something. After a while you stop trying to be all things to all people. It's one of the many lessons that you learn about fame. Be yourself. I leave all the play acting, all the pop star stuff for on stage. Off stage I'm still Gary Webb, technology freak, music fan, pilot and family man.

Writing a book such as this has been a strange experience. I had no idea that I had done so many things, and had so many secrets. But the story of your life must be truthfully expressed or it has no reason to exist at all. The amount of luck, good and bad, that has come my way is incredible. I have done things that have made me very proud and others that I am deeply ashamed. I've made some good decisions and some incredibly bad ones. Being forced to remember these things has been a learning experience as much as anything. Until I started to write this I'd always been too busy with what's ahead to ever look back very far. It was as though I was looking at my life clearly for the first time.

Inevitably an autobiography comes from one person's very distinct perspective. I've always been an outsider on the music scene, right from the early Tubeway Army days when I skirted around the edges of late '70s punk. I don't know enough about other musicians to offer a context for everything I've done. I convert sounds and atmospheres from imagination into music, occasionally made contemporary by my enthusiasm for one or two current acts. My relationship with changing technology has also been a constant influence on my life and musical direction.

I write this as a new chapter in my life opens up before me. My wedding, a new record deal, a new level of recognition for the work I've done over the years and a new career perhaps to add to my ongoing obsession with music. The immediate future is as uncertain and as exciting as anything that has happened to me before. I hope I can thrive on this insecurity. I still have a long way to go.

CHAPTER 1

Praying to the Aliens, 1958-70

I was born Gary Anthony James Webb in the Chiswick and Hammersmith Hospital, London, at 10.30 pm, 8 March, 1958. I wasn't the main reason my parents decided to get married, but I was beginning to form my own little fingers as Dad slipped the wedding ring on to my mum's hand. My mother was about six months pregnant, not that I could tell when I looked back at pictures of her from that time. When I hold those photographs I wish I could have been there in a more tangible way, I was so near and yet so far. My mum, Beryl Webb, née Lidyard, a former dress-maker, was just 20 years old and I was to be her only child. My dad, Anthony David Webb, was just a year older and working as a paint sprayer. A former ammunition storeman with the British Army (albeit on National Service) and a merchant seaman, Dad was, is, and always will be, a shining example to me of all that is decent in a human being. He's hard working, ridiculously honest and extremely faithful. Although I share some of these character traits I have to work harder on them than my dad and we have often failed to see eye to eye. We do have a very different outlook on certain aspects of life, but because of my admiration for him I have always gone to him first if I was ever unsure about things. I've inherited other sides to his personality which are more of a mixed blessing. We can be grumpy, awkward and opinionated. These have often got me into trouble. Our honesty means we would both rather die than cheat at games. We also possess a perfectionist streak which is a real double edged sword. If we make a mistake when we're driving it bothers us

1

for days. Physically I feel more like a clone than a son: the silly shape our mouths make when we're angry, everything, down to the shape of our fingernails. My mum comes from a very close family and has done everything in her power to make the Webbs a strong unit. She has made her life revolve around us all, my dad, my adopted brother John and me. She would stand up to the devil himself if he threatened nothing more sinister than to flick my ear. She also has tremendous courage and determination. Since she was diagnosed with cancer I have never known someone go through so much suffering with so few complaints. She was put onto a powerful anti-cancer drug, which has kept her alive, but has forced her to endure every single known repercussion that the drug can inflict. She does so without a grumble. If I had a tiny fraction of her strength I could take on Mike Tyson. She is a great listener and has probably heard more confessions than the Pope – sometimes from virtual strangers. She also has a memory that would make an elephant seem forgetful, especially if it concerns someone who hurt any of us, in any way. Because of her devotion to her family, my mum makes 'getting even' almost seem like a way of life and yet, as long as you've done nothing against her clan, she is, genuinely, one of the friendliest, happiest people you could ever wish to meet.

I'm quite hermit-like in many ways but my mum is terrible. She trusts no one. She doesn't really have many friends outside the family, and even those are kept at arm's length. I can't remember the last time anyone went round to my parents' house for dinner; in fact I'm not sure if anyone ever has. They go out, meet people when they're out, and then they go home. That's probably why I've been something of a loner, I've inherited it from them. I have always been just as happy on my own, more so actually, than when I'm around people. For all of my mum's mistrust, she has a brilliant knack of getting people to like her. She's just so likeable, she listens to everybody and people tell her all their problems. No one seems to realise she keeps them at a distance. My dad doesn't seem to interact much at all. However, they are both madly keen on country music and line dancing and this has opened them up slightly in recent years.

If it sounds as though I was spoiled then you're right, I was. As an only child, until my adopted brother arrived seven years later, I was spoiled rotten. But I was never allowed to stamp my feet and have a tantrum. That sort of behaviour saw me sent straight to bed with no tea. I was spoilt by the time they had for me, the warmth that they surrounded me with, the care and concern they have shown me every minute of my life. I do not believe that anyone could have had as loving a home as mine and I doubt I will ever come close to paying back a fraction of the debt I owe them. I love them with all my heart.

When I eventually appeared my parents were renting a room in a bungalow in Ashford, Middlesex. They were forced out, after my mum was told by the landlady 'You're washing the walls so often you're wearing the paint away'. Cleanliness is one of mum's obsessions. After that they moved into another rented room. This time the landlord was a slimy old man, who would go out of his way to catch a glimpse of bare female flesh. He was so creepy that, after a few weeks, my mum could stand it no longer and so they moved into yet another tiny room. It wasn't too long before my parents arranged with one of dad's brothers, Lional, to share a rented house, 45 Ravensbourne Avenue, Stanwell. We had the upstairs and they, with their two boys, lived downstairs. I would fight regularly with my two live-in cousins, Clive, who was a couple of years older, and his brother Garry. It was in this house that I was cured of bed wetting. My parents bought a device that comprised a box with a loud buzzer and a red flashing light on top. Out of this box came two crocodile clips that were fastened onto a sheet which looked like a strip of Bacofoil. If I had an accident in the night the bloody thing would go off, buzzing and flashing. I would wake up with such a start I doubt more than a drip ever reached the mattress. I was cured in no time. It was either stop wetting the bed or die of sleep deprivation, as far as I could make out.

My dad was allowed to use his works van outside working hours and most of my earliest recollections are of sitting between the front seats on the engine cover, driving off to the seaside. I was put there because it was the warmest place. My dad was out doing three or four jobs a day – driving lorries, buses, coaches, mini-cabs, anything he could get. He worked constantly, tirelessly. (Although I wasn't aware of it, he would come home in the early hours of the morning and look in on me.)

Even at such a young age, I was aware that he was out working when all my friends' dads were back at home. Money was extremely tight but dad was determined to work all hours to get us out of the tiny hovels we were forced to live in. He was determined that we should have a better life than he had had as a youngster. My dad's background was quite hard. My mother tells a story about when she first started seeing my dad, as a teenager. She went round to his house and was sitting in the front room waiting for him. Suddenly there was a tremendous crash and my dad and his brother John, fighting wildly, literally came through the wall, which was basically a sheet of asbestos.

A few years later we moved to a new council house in 53 St Annes Avenue, Stanwell. This time it was all ours. Lional had the next house along, number 55. The playing fields of my first school, Town Farm, ran along the back of our garden. I was, surprisingly, a good little fighter as a youngster and had many scraps on the playground. Calling me 'Spider Webb' was always good for a clout. However, my idea of an acceptable fight never got beyond the point where you stopped as soon as someone cried or got a bloody nose. I hate violence, it disturbs me even to watch it on TV. Not fictional Hollywood violence, but news items on football matches, that kind of thing. The pleasure some people seem to derive from it completely escapes me.

I was bright at school, so they tell me. I was also part of a special national child development survey, set up to follow the lives of all children born in the UK between 3 March and 9 March 1958. I was often taken away for special interviews, exams and medicals designed to build up a picture of my natural abilities and how they were then affected by upbringing and environment. I loved being part of the survey. It helped me understand why my dad was working so hard to change our circumstances. It also made me feel special. My mum used to tell me that it was a survey for gifted children – which wasn't true but boosted my self-esteem even further. The only other person from that survey group who became famous was Andy Gibb. My parents were delighted when the survey exams revealed that I had an unusually high IQ. This meant very little to me at the time, other than the knowledge that they were very proud of me. When I was 11 one of the essays I was asked to write by the survey concerned what I thought I would be doing when I was 25. I wrote that I would be a famous musician, which surprises me now, as I was far more interested in aeroplanes at the time. I guess like all children I had a different fantasy for each day of the week. On that particular day I was obviously dreaming of being a pop star. I enjoyed the extra exams. In fact I used to enjoy all the school exams and I could never understand why the other kids used to get so nervous and upset about doing them. I had no real problems at school, not in the infants and juniors, although as a child I was very shy, which made it hard for me to take part in many of the school activities. I had no intention whatsoever of standing up in front of anyone, for anything.

Apart from the odd flare-up I didn't get into too much trouble. On one occasion I overheard yet another boy calling my cousin Garry 'Spider Webb'. The insults against us Webbs rarely got more creative than Spider. I hit this boy in the face and laughed my head off when he opened his mouth to cry and his sweet, a Fruit Spangle, fell out, neatly broken into two pieces. I soon stopped laughing though, and began a wild dash for my life as his overly large and much older friend came bearing down on me. My legs were going like pistons and my Wellington boots struggled for grip as I blasted out of the school gates. I couldn't believe my luck when I looked up and saw Dad waiting for me, for he rarely came to the school at lunch time. I launched myself into the car without so much as a hello and then kept my head down as he tore this poor boy off a strip. Safe and secure I was driven home, beaming from ear to ear.

When I was growing up my parents never used to talk about money being 'their' money, it was always 'our' money, an attitude I took into adulthood when I started to earn a living. Every penny I make is for the Webb family, not just for my own use. I remember Mum getting her first job at a soft drinks factory at 15 pounds a week, and Dad jumping up and down with glee because we had so much money all of a sudden. By this time I was eight and my dad had worked hard enough to enable my parents to buy their own house by the time I was eight. For the next ten years 615, London Road was to be my home.

I would go to mum if I suffered any emotional upsets and wanted to be sure of a sympathetic response. My dad would tend to give a 'Get a grip of yourself' style advice on matters of the heart although, quite often, that's exactly what was needed. I had a good understanding of who to talk to depending on what kind of advice, or comfort, I was looking for as a child. I still have very different conversations with each of my parents, which is, I think, quite typical of families. In the past I've often been ridiculed for being so close to them but I owe them so much, I couldn't imagine distancing myself from them in the hope that it would sell a few more records or make me look better in the eyes of some people. I have a good circle of friends, especially now, but I count my parents as friends as much as anything else and I enjoy their company. I also value their advice. In fact my dad has managed me since 1979 and my mum has run the Gary Numan Fan Club since it first began, so we are linked in business as well as in blood. I wouldn't want it any other way. It could be four o'clock in the morning with me fast asleep but, if the phone rang, whatever the problem they might have, I would get up without thinking about it, jump straight into my car and be off.

Although I'm the first to admit I was spoilt, I was brought up to be well-mannered: don't eat with your mouth open, don't talk over people, that kind of thing. Nothing too heavy or strict, I never felt oppressed by rules and regulations. I was always made to feel important but I was never allowed to get away with any bad behaviour, especially outside the home. I always knew who was in charge.

Meanwhile, one of my earliest birthday presents reflected an awakening interest in machines and technology. It was the fake control panel my dad made for me, consisting of a wooden box with lots of holes drilled into it. He'd filled the holes with dials and switches. For years I used to sit there with it on my lap. I could make that control panel be anything I wanted. It was a racing car, a boat, an aeroplane or a spaceship. I was only a little boy, flicking these switches up and down in my bedroom, but in my mind I was somewhere else, I was an astronaut, a test pilot, a racing driver. That was one of the best presents I ever had. I have always loved machines and gadgets. I enjoy pressing buttons, moving levers, flicking switches and making things happen. When I first started to learn to fly I used to like moving the flap lever because I'd look back over my shoulder and see these great big bits of metal on the back of the wing slide out. I love technology, especially big powerful machines, and I think this passion of mine began with that first wooden control box.

A new interest in guitars was also based on my new fascination with technology. I remember seeing The Shadows on TV at a very young age, about four I think. I liked their guitars because they were electric, and I thought it was really cool having switches and buttons and dials. Their shape was also appealing, it looked so hi-tech and futuristic compared to acoustic guitars. They had a scratch plate on the guitar so, when Hank Marvin played, it used to glisten and shine under the lights. My mum and dad bought me a Spanish acoustic guitar when I was four and I would tie a bit of string to it and pretend it was a lead. It was to be another four years or so until music began to become a real interest, though.

I had another early machine-based thrill when my parents took me for an aeroplane ride when I was about four. It must have taken them months to save the money. We went to Fairoaks airfield where, about 20 years later, I would keep my own aeroplane. I thought I was just going to watch aeroplanes fly, maybe get close to one, and that was exciting enough, but they walked me out to this small Jodel Cecille. The pilot opened the door and, to my unbridled joy and amazement, we climbed in. The motor took a few attempts to start but soon we were soaring through the sky. It was an unforgettable experience. Probably the first interest I had outside of my immediate surroundings was in aeroplanes. We lived close to Heathrow Airport and my grandparents' house was directly under the approach path to one of the runways. On certain days aircraft would fly low over their garden and I would sit still for hours, watching. I'd lie on my back on the grass, wait for the roar and then these huge machines would appear and thunder overhead. You could see right up into the wheel wells. Even now I get excited when they come over low. I love them – the sheer size of them, the shape, the power, the speed, I think they're beautiful things.

When I was seven my parents adopted an eight month old baby – John. I loved him from the second I first saw him. My brother John Webb was actually born Donovan Webb and he was really my cousin. Unfortunately his father committed suicide a few months later and his birth mother was, to put it kindly, unfit to look after the children. She didn't want them at all, if truth be told. We adopted Donovan, renamed him John after his dad, my dad's brother, and so we became four. We did have to fight to keep him,

7

as his birth mother became awkward and kept changing her mind. John's health was very poor when we got him. He had skin sores through neglect and had been wearing the same nappy for days. To this day he still pays a price for what he suffered in those first few months of life.

John and I formed a fantastically close friendship as children but I also had mates of my own who have stayed with me for life. Living on the next street along to London Road were the Robson brothers, Garry and Nicky. They were my enemies for a while and we used to fight all the time. Just kids' stuff, really. One day I was arguing with Garry about something and we got into one of these silly pushing matches where nobody really wanted fight, so we both started giggling. We became best friends from then on and both Garry and Nicky remain my oldest friends. I don't see them that much any more, they both have successful careers and families, but it's as though time has stood still whenever we speak. One of our favourite games was to tie Airfix aeroplane models to bits of string, which had already been secured to a nearby tree, set fire to the models and watch them burn as they slid down the string towards the ground. Garry Robson was in my first ever bedroom band a few years later. It was just the two of us really, he would slap the back of his acoustic guitar, as though it were a set of bongos, and I would strum mine. I wrote the songs but Garry did the singing because I was far too shy.

At school my stage ambitions were non-existent. Every week a class had to give a service. My mum helped me miss most of them, but once in a while they were unavoidable. The school had these big sheets with the words of the hymns on them. My job during this particular service was to lift over the pages so that the rest of the school could read the words to each hymn in turn. Standing on that stage, even with such a simple and non-performing task as page turner, was a nightmare for me and I was shaking with nerves. It all went horribly wrong. The paper clip marking the pages fell out and I turned over to the wrong one. Everyone laughed, I went red, got myself into an even deeper muddle and then found that the sheets were actually quite heavy and I was just too small to turn over the number needed to get back to the right place. A teacher had to come on stage to help me. Although I was only eight years old a life on stage did not seem to feature in my destiny at all.

The first time I took an interest in music beyond the technology was when I went out to buy a Monkees album. However, at the shop I saw a Jim Reeves album that my mum wanted and so I bought that. I had been saving up for some time for my Monkees album and so, when I brought home a record for my mum, she thought I was so sweet she cried. The Monkees were the first pop band I liked without being influenced by the tastes of my older cousins and uncles. I was in the Monkees fan club for a while and I used to get the monthly fan club magazines. We even had a band in our street called the Monkey Juniors. We would mime to Monkees records in people's houses for two shillings a show. I was Mike Nesmith, the guitar player. He used to have a green bobble hat, without a bobble, and my mum made me one just like his. There was always a bit of friction in the band because my friend Chris Buxbaum, who was Davy Jones the singer, would snatch up a guitar and mime along whenever there wasn't any singing to do. This upset me no end, because I was the guitar player and he would always grab the guitar during my guitar solos. We split due to musical differences – when he stole my solo once too often. That, however, was my first genuine experience of performing, albeit in someone's living room. I was sad when the real Monkees split up. It was quite a big thing at the time, a big part of my young life, but within a week I'd forgotten about them. It was a lesson in the fickleness, and therefore the dangers, of a young audience.

In my final year at Town Farm we sat for our Eleven Plus exam and I passed. I'm told only seven other pupils from my class got through, so I guess I did well. I don't remember being particularly aware of the importance of education at the time, it was just another exam. My parents were delighted, though. This was a major deal to them. This was me on my way to a higher level of education, the academic road to success. I was one of only four pupils in the school that year to be allowed to study from the highest level maths book on the curriculum, the legendary 'green' book. I've read that my old junior school teachers thought I was 'rebellious and yet did very well, and did so naturally, in his own way and without being particularly attentive'. They said I was a 'frustrating boy to teach'. That I didn't like to be 'guided'. That I had a 'determined streak, a vivid imagination' and that I was 'strong minded and very worldly'. I honestly don't know where those opinions came from. I thought I was fairly quiet and just got on with things. I'm glad to know that I made an impression on my teachers at such a young age, I just wish I'd known about it then. I left Town Farm feeling very ordinary, and very nervous. I was off to grammar school and I was not looking forward to it.

At the age of 12 I set our house on fire. I was of course forbidden to play with fire but it held such a fascination for me that it was one of the few things I was ever disobedient about. My dad kept his car in the back garden and we had big sliding doors, which were open, and long, flowing curtains. I was in between the glass doorway and the car with a kitchen bowl filled with water and a model of the German battleship *Bismarck* floating in it. I had just watched the film *Sink The Bismarck* and so I was attempting to re-enact the moment by setting fire to my model. My friend Gary Stevenson was with me, although he was more interested in burning things than re-enacting historic battles. I had a tin of model aeroplane motor fuel and I was squirting that, in a long jet, onto the burning model. I thought it looked incredibly realistic as the flames leapt into the air. They also leapt back up the jet of fuel and set the car on fire. I screamed, threw the can away and quickly put out the fire on my arm. Unfortunately the can had sprayed its fiery contents all over my dad's car, and into the house, where the curtains were beginning to catch rather nicely. Luckily the fire on the car went out of its own accord but the curtains were really getting going. I turned to Gary for help, but he was crying and no good for anything so I made the brutal decision to rip the curtains from the rail and get them outside the house. I probably saved the house from burning down, which was pretty cool for a youngster, even though I'd accidentally started it in the first place. My feeble excuse for the near disaster was accepted but not, I think, entirely believed. My dad had a model of an outboard engine for a motor boat which was actually a cigarette lighter, so I said I had been innocently demonstrating it to Gary when the wind blew the curtains onto it, setting them on fire. 'Honestly Dad'. Being able to lie on my feet and think up ridiculous but vaguely plausible excuses in the heat of the moment was to save me from many a severe punishment at grammar school.

CHAPTER 2

I'd Love to be a Man, 1970-74

I started grammar school in 1970 at the age of 12. I knew a few people from the junior school who were also going, and my cousin Clive had been a pupil there for about three years already. I hoped he would be able to look after me. I was more than a little scared of being bullied and it was quite a long way away from where I lived, a car ride away, which made my feelings of isolation and vulnerability all the more acute. The school itself seemed massive and it was very daunting. I was, like many children when they first go to secondary school, more concerned with getting through the day than with what being there could mean to my future. I felt totally overwhelmed. The first year I was in the Alpha class and I was reasonably quiet, I just got on with things. I was something of a dreamer but not disruptive in any way. I soon found the rhythm of life at the school and quickly realised which pupils and teachers to avoid wherever possible. I began to learn the rules and how to break those that were not too strictly enforced. Overall, I settled in reasonably well. My main classroom overlooked the distant airport and I would sometimes lose myself, gazing at the aeroplanes as they came and went. Not surprisingly, I was often told off for not paying attention. It was in the second year that things really began to go wrong.

I've spoken a lot in the past about my difficulties at grammar school. I was shy and hated having to ask questions to begin with, which meant my inhibitions were sometimes interpreted as arrogance. But this wasn't the main problem. Nothing is worse than a

11

teenager who thinks he has all the answers. I was that idiot. I resented the authority of the teachers and I began to listen to them less as I realised school could not help me become a successful musician. Mixed with this was an increasing desire to make my mark, to misbehave, namely to rebel in the only way open to a schoolboy. Add to that a growing awareness, and keenly growing interest in sex, and you have a very destructive mixture. I began to show off badly, and believed that to do homework was a sign of weakness, a sign of accepting the authority of the school. I became a complete lad and I cringe now at the thought of it. Musically, though, I was slowly beginning to get myself together.

The first electric guitar my parents bought me was so old it didn't even have a conventional jackplug. It had one of these really old double point things which you just couldn't get any more. They also bought me a tiny amplifier. I think the whole thing cost about £15, which was a lot to us. The neck was so thick I could barely get my hands around it, it was a huge thing and I was still young and small. I remember feeling a bit disappointed, although I never said so, because it was shaped with only one horn. In those days what I really wanted was a Stratocaster-shaped guitar with two horns. Still, it was an electric guitar, and it was mine.

After that I bought one with two horns from a shop called Bandbox near Staines railway station. Then I got what I thought was a genuine Gibson Les Paul which came from a shop in Shaftesbury Avenue and cost £37. The man in the shop said, 'It's a genuine Gibson, mate.' He told me the reason why it was so cheap – ten per cent of what a Gibson should cost – was due to a manufacturing flaw which meant the Gibson emblem wasn't engraved into the neck. I was beside myself with joy, a real Gibson, for only £37. I went home with this black thing and I loved it. It didn't sound that good though and I could never work out why, until I discovered that it was just a very cheap Gibson copy. I was morti-fied at the news. I had told everyone I had a Gibson Les Paul so I must have looked such an idiot.

I was really into my guitars and to this day I prefer it above all other instruments. I had a few effects pedals and I began playing for hours every night. It was all I did for years, I rarely went out. I had Burt Weedon's guitar book but I couldn't get to grips with it. I couldn't get my fingers to go where they were supposed to, so I made up my own tunes because I couldn't play anybody else's. I knew the basic chords, because my cousin Richard had taught me those, using his old, short-necked Rickenbacker. I would go over to his house a lot when he was still a kid, living at home with his mum. He was very good to me, very patient, because I must have been very irritating – this little kid going, 'Do all that feedback stuff, Richie.' He was brilliant, a proper hippie, into peace and love and he always had time for me even though I was seven years younger. He fostered my interest in music more than anyone and is probably the main reason why I got into it so deeply.

I became a huge T-Rex and Marc Bolan fan in 1971 when I was 13. I loved the music and I also liked Marc's image. He was quite possibly one of the best pop stars this country has ever had. I never saw him play live, unfortunately, simply because it never occurred to me that I could go to a concert. In fact I didn't start going to concerts until I was 16.

My enthusiasm for the image conscious T-Rex coincided with growing interest in clothes. My mum always made sure I had good clothes. Whatever was fashionable I would have it, although she always got me something that was a slight variation. If a black crombie coat was in, I'd have a check one. I also got my ear pierced when I was 14 in a shop in Staines High Street. The view around school at the time was that, if you had your right ear pierced, you were gay. I had my right ear pierced, as did the two friends who went with me, because that was where the man put it. I began to colour my hair when I was in the grammar school, which got me into trouble on more than one occasion. My natural hair colour is a light brown, mousy affair and it doesn't do anything for me at all. I started to put auburn rinses on it when I was about 14, so it would go slightly different shades. It wasn't enough to get me expelled, just enough to irritate the school. That wasn't the original reason for doing it but my coloured hair did become another symbol of defiance.

I was always a bit of a loner and spent a lot of my time in my bedroom. When we moved into the London Road house I had all my aeroplane models in there, on the shelves and hanging from the ceiling. As I became more interested in music I took all the models

13

down and converted the room into a stage. It was quite a big room and one side was covered with twelve-inch mirror tiles. I had disco lights put in the corner and I would pull down the blinds, put a record on, the lights would flash and I would become all of my heroes rolled into one. I was gigging man, I was happening in that room. All my friends would come round and we'd be in the band together up against the mirror. I was anyone I wanted to be, a great guitar player with the finest shapes, or a cool singer with girls falling at my feet. I spent most of my teenage years up in that room, miming away. No one was allowed in unless they knocked on the door first, just in case I was throwing a shape. I still loved aeroplanes but by now what I really wanted out of life was to be a pop star. I wanted to be famous. But I wanted to be famous my way, I wanted to be a particular kind of star.

I started writing songs when I was 13: a kind of semi-poetry, with a few easy chords. I'd been creating stories and poems on and off all my life. I used to love writing essays at school even when I was very young. I wrote pages and pages of stories. I didn't dream of being a writer, I just saw it as fun. As a child I was a big science fiction fan, so a lot of my stuff was very sci-fi influenced. I also read *Lord Of The Rings* as a teenager and it remains my all-time favourite. I was very keen on the Saberhagen *Berserker* books and my imagination was inspired by *Stranger In A Strange Land* and *Dune*. I wasn't always very literary in my selected reading. If a book had a really cool spaceship on the front cover I'd buy it. I loved one called *Swordships Of Scorpio* which was part of a whole series of *Scorpio* books. They were a mixture of sci-fi and fantasy warrior stories. None of the characters had guns, they all had these monstrous swords and armour which made them look like humans in alien survival suits. My stories were always about wanting to be something more than I was. Pure fantasy. I also wrote stories about what it would be like to be a famous pop star and a lot of my ideas for stage shows were subsequently developed from those early ramblings. I'd write down how I imagined the stage sets would look and what I would be wearing.

For a while I harboured boyhood dreams of being a racing driver. My dad has a keen interest in motor sport and he bought a go-kart, a 210cc Villiers, when I was in my teens. We took it to a track at the back of Blackbushe airfield the following weekend and he had a great time on it. Then he let me have a go. I was still too young to drive so I just went as quickly as I could with it in second gear. It didn't go that fast and after about three laps the constant high revs blew a hole through the engine. After that Dad got me a little kart of my own. I was a typically fearless teenager as I raced around at 80 mph. For a while I took part in proper races, even held a junior novice licence, but we didn't have the money to buy a good enough kart to be competitive, so I used it mainly on practice days and would race whoever was in front of me. I had one fairly big accident where I went in to a sharp right-left-right combination much too fast. I went off at the first right, hit an embankment, flew across the track, pretty much airborne the entire way, into the next embankment and then up a short hill. I came to rest at the top with bits of the kart spread all over the track and the front wheels hanging over the edge of a reasonably large drop. My foot was still hard on the accelerator. I was convinced that I could get it back on to the track right up until the moment that the engine came apart. I still love karting.

I must admit not all my technology-driven hobbies were quite so cool. I was an unashamed plane spotter when I was a teenager. I'd regularly travel to the airport with some of my friends, normally to the Queens Building at Heathrow, and watch the aeroplanes. I could spend hours just watching them taking off and landing. My respect for the skills of airline pilots was unrivalled as a boy. They had the ability to make these huge machines go wherever they wanted and I thought that was something truly special. I even had a little book of aircraft registration numbers and I would tick them off when I spotted the aircraft concerned.

Around this time I joined the Air Training Corps, the Air Cadets, but found it very disappointing. We spent too much of our time marching up and down. I was in 94 Squadron, Feltham, Middlesex and it was actually quite violent, which was the last thing I had expected. I had thought that everyone would be an aviation fanatic like me and we would just live and breathe aeroplanes once a week. It seemed that most of the boys joined cadets just to get out of the house. My total flying time in over a year was only 15 minutes – one trip in a Chipmunk light aircraft. As it turned out, the Cadets had very little to do with aviation and so, after a year, I left. I've still got the uniform somewhere. I used to get threatening letters saying the military police were coming round to pick it up, but they never did. I did go for a Duke of Edinburgh's Bronze award while I was in the ATC which was great fun. I was, at 13, a year too young to enter but I lied about my age and went anyway. We actually had a practice run in our local area before the main test itself, but this was made less than authentic by my parents, who popped up about every hour or so with ice creams and a lift in the car. There were no such luxuries in the real test, we had to hike across the moors in groups of three or four, camp out overnight and then find our way somewhere else the next day. I loved it. We had the heaviest rainfall in the area for over 50 years one day and a heatwave the next.

I'm not sure I became strong-willed at secondary school, but I was argumentative. I really started to kick up in the second year. I was very bored, very dreamy and always wanted to be doing something else. I found grammar school frustrating and often irrelevant. I don't remember ever going on a single class trip the whole time I was there. If only they'd taken us to the *site* of the Battle of Hastings, it might have actually meant something. It was very, very book-intensive and incredibly boring.

I began to slide down the slippery slope between making my mark and throwing it all away. If that was the start however, the third year really saw me getting into my stride. My behaviour, and therefore my academic performance, was so bad, that I was made to do the year twice. Throughout most of the year I had been on special report, I was almost a permanent fixture outside the headmaster's office and I managed to interpret that, as *cool* somehow. The ultimate punishment that the grammar school possessed was a thing called Headmaster's Detention, known to the pupils as Bods Own. Bods Own meant staying behind for an extra hour on a Tuesday. If you didn't turn up they gave it to you again, and so on. I stopped going almost immediately and so they kept giving it to me again, I wouldn't go again, and on it went. Authority without teeth was no authority at all.

My parents were desperately disappointed in me. They felt I was throwing away a major chance to improve myself and do something worthwhile with my future, but they were still very protective. My mum went to see the headmaster once after a teacher had reported me about a particular incident. The headmaster criticised me in a way my mum found offensive. His desk had drawers both sides and he was sitting with his fingers tucked inside them, so Mum kicked the drawers and took all the skin off his knuckles. My parents were very supportive when anyone else was around, but I was made to feel the full wrath of their feelings at home and was told, in no uncertain terms, to buck up my ideas. They really did try to sort me out and put me back on track. My fourth year was actually my third year again and I spent it in the worst class – 3B, with all the other rejects. The headmaster came round to us at one point and said that in his 27 years of teaching he'd never come across a class as bad as this one, and that I was the most unruly pupil in it which, at the time, I considered a huge compliment. The most badly behaved pupil in 27 years of teaching, what a stupid thing to be proud of. I wore that comment like a badge of honour, like a medal around my neck. What an accolade, what a twat...

As soon as I was in there with all the other troublemakers I thought I was special, we all thought we were special. We did whatever we wanted because we felt it was expected of us. We disrupted the entire flow of the school. I lost my virginity when I was in that class. We had a party at one of the girls' houses, which backed on to a river, where her dad had a boat tied up on the water. I ended up there with a girl from the class called Julie Cooper. On the other side of the cabin was a friend of mine with another girl. I hadn't done 'it' before but I'd manufactured a fine rumour that I was not only very experienced but bloody good at it as well. The moment of truth had arrived and I was scared, very keen but definitely scared. At least there was a table between us and the other couple, so there was privacy, after a fashion. I was only able to get her skintight jeans halfway down her thighs, so her legs were shut, clamped tight together. I must have been going at it for five or ten minutes before I realised I wasn't even 'in'. I pretended it was my technique and was endeavouring to go those final few inches when a mob of giggling friends climbed onto the deck and started rocking the boat from side to side. It keeled hard over and I fell off Miss Cooper and ended up on the wet floor. I thought the bloody boat was sinking at first until I saw a dozen beaming faces at the windows. I think I got

17

it right eventually, but to this day I'm not entirely sure. I do know it didn't last long. The other couple were still at it when I left so I felt more than a little embarrassed. However, afterwards I felt everyone could tell that I was now a man of the world. I'd done 'it', there had to be something different about me. Somehow my mum did know, because she started buying me big boxes of Durex, saying, 'I think you'll be needing these'. She was great, I think she was proud of me.

Sex was a key feature of our class parties, of which there were many, and a great deal of sharing went on. No one was really attached to anyone. It was an amazingly free and easy period, especially considering we were still pretty much children. I saw and took part in things that would still be considered outrageous in the midst of the more depraved rock star parties that were to come later. We were all between 14 and 15. So much for the innocence of youth.

Not surprisingly 3B also had a violent reputation. The fights were usually classroom against classroom – mainly us against everybody else. We made these things called Tolly Whackers which were magazines rolled up very tightly, with a length of string along it, sellotaped together. They were very hard. You'd put a bit of a string around your wrist and go round whacking people with them. Things could only get worse. Some of the boys started dismantling desks so they could put the metal strip from the end of the desk inside the Tolly Whackers. Then one victim got knocked out in the sandpit and it all ground to a halt. Just as well really, as it had begun to get far too violent for my liking. People were getting hurt and that was never the appeal for me. I just liked being unruly, I didn't want to harm anybody.

I had most of the traits of a rebellious teeanager, but I didn't get into drinking. I have never drunk, not even wine or shandy. I have never smoked either. I've never known the questionable delights of falling into the gutter on top of my own vomit. I tried lager a few times but I couldn't get past a few sips without feeling sick. I tried vodka and Bacardi mixed with Coke but I didn't like that either. When my friends were going out to pubs, sneaking in and developing this taste for alcohol, I was on tranquillisers. My school troubles had meant that I was referred to a local child psychiatrist, and then a leading London psychiatrist, and I was prescribed Nardil and

Valium for a year. It was supposed to keep me calm, tame down my temper and help with my apparent 'depression'. I wasn't depressed, I was bored shitless. The peer pressure to drink and to smoke was very powerful and many people did things that they didn't really want to so that they could fit in. I didn't want to fit in particularly, I didn't care about that at all. I wanted to be the odd one out, for I knew my own mind; I was stubborn and clear about what I wanted. If someone said to me, 'You've got to have a lager otherwise you can't come to the pub with us', I told them to piss off. I did not and do not bow to the opinion of the many, if I believe it to be wrong for me. I have my own views and, rightly or wrongly, I follow my own path.

The temper, or whatever it is, is something that I'm only now, at 39, beginning to get on top of, and it has caused me a great deal of humiliation, embarrassment and regret over the years. I wind myself up very easily and I seem to explode without much provocation. I see nothing worthy or interesting about this whatsoever, although at one point, when I was at school, I saw it as another example of my difference from everybody else. I would have uncontrollable rages, I would break objects, scream, do any number of things. At first my behaviour was just dismissed as youthful temper, but eventually the psychiatrist put me onto drugs to keep me calm. I was zombied out for the best part of a year when I was 15. When these fits of temper do occur, far more rarely these days, I do not know for sure what I'm doing. It's like an inner battle that is beyond my control. I rant and rave and generally behave in quite an appalling way, and all the time I'm ashamed and embarrassed and unable to do anything about it. It can go on for several minutes and, when it's over, I'm so tired that I just lie down and sleep like a log. The psychiatric help was worthless, so eventually I just got on with things and worked on myself, but I was often a very difficult person to be with. Still am at times, apparently!

I have been left a small legacy of concern about my mental health because of those early troubled years. Not very often, but sometimes, I worry about my state of mind. I wonder if it's quite the way it should be. It has conjured up one or two very strange experiences. I've never had an out-of-body experience where I died, floated off and saw myself but, one day, I woke up inside this bubble. It's very difficult to explain, but I felt as though the world had suddenly ceased to be and this bubble I was in was the entire existence of everything. It was real enough to make me think I'd gone mental. I knew that the world was still there, had to be, but something in my head suddenly shut it all off from around me and I had no idea of how to get out. I was completely awake but I couldn't see anything. I tried to push through this layer, which was almost a physical thing, like a membrane, until finally the world popped back. I was badly shaken by the whole thing since I have a hang-up about pains in my head. Every headache reminds me of the time a schoolfriend of mine went home to find his dad had died. This poor man woke up with a headache and it turned out to be blood leaking in the brain.

Becoming an airline pilot was still running a close second to being a pop star, but I completely abandoned my pilot ambitions after a careers lecture in class one day. They were going through all the various job options and then said, 'All of those of you thinking of being a pilot, only one in a thousand succeed, so we suggest you try something more sensible.' The grammar school had about a thousand people in it so this sentence stopped me dead. I wasn't the brightest in the school and, given that advice, the pilot idea seemed very unlikely. I felt that if I was going to do something that was essentially down to luck I might as well drop school and go for the big one. As it turns out the careers lecturer was wrong. It's hard to become a pilot but nowhere near as difficult as he suggested.

Schooling no longer seemed to have a use for me. My behaviour got worse and I was suspended for a while and then put on 'Special Report'. I was given a form to take to each lesson for the teachers' behavioural reports. If you had a week of good reports they were supposed to take you back off it. Our games teacher was very anti-me and gave me my only bad report of the week. It was the last lesson on a Friday afternoon and I honestly hadn't done a thing wrong, I just wasn't any good at football. That kept me on report until I was expelled at the end of the year.

I saw grammar school as offering a service. It was there to give us an education and our parents paid for that service. It was supposed to prepare us as young people for the world. When I left school I didn't know how to write a cheque, didn't know what insurance was really for, didn't know anything about car mechanics. Useful everyday things were missing. Learning about rock strata is fine up to a point, but not something you call on very often. I think there are practical things we should have been learning. Things to do with the world we were going out to face. General education, valuable though it is, has little practical use in everyday life. When I was 15 years old, in a grammar school physics class, we made a little electric motor. It was a bit of plastic with some wire wrapped around it stuck between two magnets. Excellent, that was really going to serve me well as I headed off to face the world! The sum total of my woodwork manufacturing at the grammar school was two things. One of them was a pencil sharpener, which was a piece of wood four inches long by one and a half inches wide, with a hole drilled in one end so you could hang it on the wall, and a piece of sandpaper glued to it. The other, supposedly an oil tanker model, was another square piece of wood with one end sharpened to a point. The other end was a vague curve and then the bits you chopped out to give the impression of tanks were stuck on the back to make the bridge and funnel. Four years of grammar school woodwork education resulted in those two objects. In metalwork we ended up making bottle openers. When I read about schools having problems with discipline and order, I can't help wondering if the pupils are as bored as I was at school.

Finally the school expelled me, and my girlfriend Shelley, and so I went to Stanwell Secondary School. I arrived with a chip on my shoulder the size of a planet. I got into trouble the first day I arrived. I sat in seats reserved for the fifth year or something silly. I was punished, which seemed a bit harsh given that I was a new student, and this incident got me off to a very bad start. I was very anti the school from day one, and I think they felt similarly about me. On another occasion I was at assembly and I didn't have the right sort of shirt. It had to be a plain blue shirt and I didn't have a clean one that particular morning. I did find a blue one with little black stripes which, with the best intentions, I wore to school. They pulled me up in front of assembly and gave me a lecture about it. One teacher said to me, 'What kind of a state do you look?' I was actually dressed quite well, since it was a fairly expensive shirt, albeit not quite the right colour. The man talking to me was wearing worn-out

21

loafer shoes, trousers hanging on the floor with the ends frayed, an old tweedy jacket with worn out leather patches and a grey shirt which wasn't ironed. I said, 'Fuck me, look at the state of you.' I got caned for that. Some teachers believed in working you harder by belittling you if you got it wrong. Typical, I thought. They expect you to behave as adults and they treat you like children. In one class we were all asked to write a story and I did one about being famous, as usual. My teacher got me to stand at the front and read it out as an example of how not to write a story. I thought that was a very poor way to teach. Everyone preferred me so luckily the whole thing backfired on her. I didn't get expelled this time but several canings later, I was invited to leave. By now my parents had given up on me ever having a decent education. It must have been a terrible disappointment to them, since they had been so proud and optimistic when I passed the Eleven Plus exam. For my part I was sure that music was my future and equally sure that education would play no part in it. All I wanted was to get out of school and get on with it. My parents, however, made one final attempt to get me an education. They sent me to Brooklands Technical College in Weybridge to study a five O Level course in Maths, Music, Sociology, English Language and English Literature. Once again I was to prove a bitter let-down to them.

I still didn't see the point, I was going to be famous. I was also getting more and more interested in girls and so, rather than respecting the more laid-back approach to education that the college offered, I just stayed away. Not from college, from the lessons. I spent all day in the common room talking to girls and playing table football. I had tried briefly to get involved in study but it hadn't gone well. I had a disagreement on day one with the maths teacher when he wrote some binary figures on the board and then smugly said that no one would know what it meant. I was actually very familiar with binary and so gave him the answer. He said I was wrong and embarrassed me in front of a class of complete strangers. He was a bloody liar. I was right and he knew it, but I'd stolen his opening line to a new class. That was my first and last maths lesson at Brooklands. Music was similar. We were asked to write a four-part piece of music for piano. I took mine in and, after the teacher had played what I thought was my very pretty little piece of music, I was told that it was not acceptable because my sequence of notes was considered unattractive in notation terms. I argued that it sounded fine but was told that that didn't matter, my sequence of notes was not acceptable. I found this hard to take, for surely the whole point of music is how things sound, not how they're written. I later learned from a band member, who himself had a degree in music, that one of my best-selling songs would have failed a musical degree exam for that same reason, the sequence of notes used is considered unacceptable in academic circles.

After a while the principal wrote to my father to find out if I intended to return to college. This came as a shock to my dad, because he was taking me to the station every morning to catch the Weybridge train. I was out before the third term began. My schooling ended without my gaining any qualifications at all. Even more upsetting for my parents was the fact that I hadn't actually sat for a single exam. My attitude towards school is something that I have regretted ever since. I see nothing good about the way I behaved, the way I rebelled and the way I let my family down at all. Strangely, I am now a knowledge junkie, and I try to learn as much as I can about anything and everything.

CHAPTER 3

Tubeway Days, 1974-78

The first band I ever went to see in concert were Nazareth who played at the Rainbow Theatre in London in 1974. They'd had a single out called 'This Flight Tonight' which I liked, although I didn't know any of their other songs.

It was an interesting night. I was fascinated by the sheer size of the PA system and the volume was incredible. One strange thing happened, though. During one of the songs the guitar player would hit a particular note which fed back and every time he did so I fell over. It was as though that note, played that way, was connected to an 'off' button in my sense of balance. La la la went the song, weeeeeh went the guitar, down went Gary! I actually liked the support band Silverhead more than Nazareth. One of the reasons why was because the frontman, Michael Des Barres, had double-jointed elbows and he could bend his arms back the wrong way. Not all the way of course, but enough to leave a lasting impression of gross weirdness. I also loved their music, in fact I've still got their album *Sixteen And Savaged* although I don't think I've played it in the last 20 years.

I had a few friends at school who were interested in being in a band and, because my mum and dad were pretty cool about the noise, we usually ended up messing about at my house. I had a guitar and speakers so it was easier for us to play music at my house anyway. I still wasn't singing at this stage. Garry Robson was the vocalist in one of those early bands. The fact that we never set foot outside my bedroom with an instrument didn't seem to matter, *we were in a band*. Another friend from school, Gary Stevenson, of

24

Bismarck-sinking fame, is now a highly successful and talented record producer. We used to mess about on guitars together. I remember Gary had a seemingly overwhelming desire to get his willy out at the slightest provocation; breathing was normally provocation enough to whip it out and show it to the world!

Until I was 15 I was forever sitting at home talking to anyone who would listen about how I was going to be famous, without ever actually doing anything about it. I was drifting along as though someone with a red book would one day knock on my door and say 'Gary Webb. This is your life'. It was my dad who eventually said to me, 'How are you going to make it unless you get off your arse and actually do something about it.' This came somewhat out of the blue and I was momentarily shocked. He'd always gone along with my grandiose fantasies before. After the initial hurt and feelings of parental betrayal had died down, I realised that he was right of course and so began my assault on the ladder of success. Bottom rung first, no need to be hasty. Stage One of the master plan was to scour the local papers and the back pages of the *Melody Maker*, looking for bands who needed a guitarist.

Eventually, after just one audition, I joined a band called Crimson Lake. One of the band members played his Fender Stratocaster guitar left-handed like Jimi Hendrix, but he only had three and a half fingers, which is a bit of a disadvantage if you're a lead guitarist. I went out and did a few gigs with them at working men's clubs and weddings. I think they only took me on because I had a good guitar. My parents had bought me a Gibson 'Gold Top' Les Paul after I'd responded to Dad's pep talk. My mum and dad were totally behind me from the moment I started to make a serious attempt to become involved in music as a career. They started putting their money into music, which was particularly impressive because they didn't have a lot. My dad was still working as a British Airways baggage handler at Heathrow airport and they had a hefty mortgage. They did, however, have some savings and they began to dip ever deeper into those. To be honest, and he'll be the first to admit it, my dad doesn't know a good song from a punch in the face and he didn't have any idea whether I was talented or not, so he was purely motivated by love – trying to give me every possible opportunity to pursue my dreams.

After Crimson Lake I joined a band from Twickenham called Black Gold who were on the same type of circuit. Working in these kinds of bands can be soul destroying. You're playing other people's songs, stuff like 'Tie a Yellow Ribbon' and 'Route 66', the audience aren't fans, quite often don't want you there at all and are only too happy to tell you why, and you're getting paid crap money. Meanwhile you're all kidding yourselves that you've got a career in music and that the big break is just around the corner. The only way the big break is just around the corner for 'wedding' bands is if the MD of EMI happens to frequent the local British Legion or Darby and Joan emporium.

I might be wrong but I'm convinced I also auditioned for The Jam in 1976, just before the punk thing happened. There was an advert in the *Melody Maker* saying something like 'lead guitar player wanted for three-piece'. I put my guitar and amp into the car and headed off to a terraced house in Woking. When I arrived I was met by two men and taken up a narrow flight of stairs to an upstairs bedroom. The main man was a slightly unusual-looking bloke and the other one looked tired and strained. Neither of them wanted me to use my trusty 'fuzz' effect on the guitar. I was therefore buggered immediately, because I could hardly play without it. Not surprisingly they said, 'We'll let you know' and I never heard from them again. A year or so later while watching *Top Of The Pops*, I recognised the main man as Paul Weller and the tired man as the bass player Bruce Foxton. He was easy to spot because he had the same somewhat exhausted expression and spiky David Bowie style haircut, although not in Bowie's glorious Technicolor but in a rather naff shade of brown. They still didn't use fuzz.

By this time I'd caught up with the whole Bowie thing and was a big fan. I think I was 16 when I bought his *Aladdin Sane* album. I also started going to a gay club in London's Poland Street called Louise's. A group of us would travel up on the train to Louise's, or to another London club, Crackers in Wardour Street, where we persuaded the management to let us have our own David Bowie night. The gay club was great, it was the only place you could go without being beaten up if you looked a little out of the ordinary. My whole concept of what looked good and what didn't was turned upside down on those nights. I saw things I hadn't even imagined.

My dad taught me to drive in 1975 when I reached 17 and my parents bought me a Morris Marina estate car, quite a new one at that, which was an incredible surprise. I dread to think how difficult it must have been for them to have saved the money for such a good car. They wanted me in something safe rather than an old banger now that I was about to start driving. I passed my driving test at 17, first time luckily, and being able to drive immediately opened up a whole new world.

The first Bowie concert I went to was at Wembley Arena on the Station To Station tour in 1976. I dressed up for the event, dyeing my hair orange with gold sprayed in the front. It looked a bit crap. I had the wrong hair to have a David Bowie cut, since it was too fine. My mum would cut it into spikes but the hair went flat immediately and I refused to put hair lacquer on it. I was also wearing a waistcoat with Gitanes cigarettes in my pocket, even though I didn't smoke. I was like one of those American punks who don't quite get it right. We actually started a small riot. About a dozen of us had gone along and we were all very up and excited. We got everyone else on their feet by pointing at people and embarrassing them until they stood up. Bit by bit we worked through the crowd until the whole of our stand were on their feet. Then I shot off. I went down to the front of our section, straight over the railing, hung off the edge and dropped down. Everybody followed. It was magnificent. It was also on page six of the *Daily Mirror* the following morning – Riots at a David Bowie concert. In the end I made it to the front, holding one of those glowing green sticks which they were selling at the gig. I threw it at him as he was playing 'Jean Genie' and it hit him squarely in the chest. He picked it up and danced with it. Up to that point it was the greatest moment of my life. I was almost beaten up by the road crew whilst trying to retrieve the stick after the show. They threw it to the wrong person and I could not contain my disappointment. I became slightly 'verbal' and was hastily bundled outside by my friends with cries of 'it's okay, he's mental'. A few years later Bowie, and large entourage, turned up at a Human League gig at the Nashville Rooms in London. I was standing on a chair at the back and couldn't resist touching the top of his head as he walked past. The next time I saw him things were slightly different.

When I was 17 I got beaten up by a gang in Soho. Strangely

enough it was right outside the building that, years later, would become such an important part of my life, WEA's offices. I was wearing very tall Dr Marten style boots which ended just below my knees, white jeans which I'd splashed with red paint, a shiny black bomber jacket and my Mick Ronson 'Slaughter On 10th Avenue' T-shirt. I also had orange hair. I was walking with my girlfriend, Jo Casey, towards the Marquee club in Wardour Street to see a band. I'd just looked around to say something to Jo, who was fiddling with a camera strap, and when I turned round again the punch was already on its way. Smack, straight into my face. There were about five or six men, all in their early 20s I guess, not that I had much time for looking around, and they all steamed in. I'd always been scared of being beaten up, and wondered what it felt like, so I couldn't help thinking, 'Oh, so this is what it's like'. Everything was coming in fast but it didn't hurt very much, I guess because your adrenalin's flowing. Feet and fists were coming at me from all directions. My face, stomach, genitals, all took a good hammering until I saw a small gap appear between the men surrounding me. I shot forward and tried to make a run for it but I ran straight into a parked car that I hadn't seen, and fell over the bonnet. I looked up to see one of the men stabbing a sharpened umbrella spike at my face. I managed to turn my face away but the spike went into my ear, ripping the inside as he twisted the spike and pulled it out again. It felt as though the inside of the ear had been torn out. There was blood everywhere. I ran over the road to what I'd always thought was a police station, because I'd seen lots of policemen come out of there in the past, but it turned out to be some kind of a gym. I stumbled to the reception counter and asked if it was a police station. When the attendant said no I just seemed to run out of ideas, I couldn't think what to do next. I laid my head down on the reception counter because it was hurting badly by now and I noticed that blood was pouring all over the counter and running off in streams onto the floor. I started to go a bit whoozy at the sight. The attendant asked if I wanted an ambulance but I said no. I didn't mean it, I didn't know what I was saying really. I don't remember much about the next few minutes but eventually two policemen arrived along with an ambulance. They took the details, the few that we had, put me in an ambulance and sent me on my way. Jo came in the ambulance with me. We arrived at a hospital, I was stitched up and swiftly shown the exit. I ended up in an unfamiliar part of London, a long way from my car and badly shaken. No one had asked if I had any money to get a bus or cab back to the car, we were just abandoned at the hospital door. Luckily Jo was together and so, with her help, I made my way back to the Marquee club to find the security of my friends. I hadn't been there long though when I began to feel pretty sick, the various thumps that I'd taken were beginning to throb from top to bottom and I wanted to go home. As we left the club I couldn't believe my bad luck when another football-scarf-clad moron walking opposite called out to his mates further up the road that they should 'Come and give this weird-looking fucker a kicking' and pointed at me. Luckily, depending on your point of view of course, they were already giving some other poor unfortunate a kicking, and so couldn't be bothered. My would-be assailant decided to help them rather than kick me on his own – clearly a brave man – and ran off. By the time I arrived home my face was puffing up nicely and I looked a bit of a state as my mother opened the door. My dad was a little disappointed that I hadn't got in at least one punch. So was I, to be honest; it might have been a futile gesture but I would have felt a little better.

The council estate in Stanwell had been pretty rough but I'd always managed to avoid anything too unpleasant. There wasn't a lot of money around but pretty much everyone had jobs. It was still quite violent, though. Not long after I passed my driving test I got hijacked by a group of men whom I knew well enough to say 'Hello' to, although they weren't mates at all. They made me take them to a nearby town and they were just looking for trouble. They had wooden sticks and drill parts which they'd stolen from a building site and whenever they saw one or two kids, and I mean kids, they would tell me to stop so they could beat them up. I couldn't understand the pleasure they would get from that. Yet they were really happy, laughing and giggling about the ways in which they were going to hurt complete strangers who were doing nothing worse than waiting for a bus. I wouldn't stop. I kept finding some reason why it wasn't possible. I pretended that I'd seen a police car, that I didn't hear them tell me to stop, anything I could think of. They quickly realised that I was being awkward and so they gave up on beating up people in the street and tore up the inside of my car instead. After a while they made me take them home and left me to go my own way.

I went to a football match once. I'm not a football fan but, for a week or two, I thought I ought to be. I went to see Chelsea play Manchester United in London. After the game we walked back to the train station and were horrified to see that not a single blue and white scarf was anywhere to be seen. Thousands upon thousands of Manchester United supporters, as far as the eye could see, and the two of us with our Chelsea scarves tucked up our sleeves. The United fans were so friendly, too friendly in fact. I'd been told that the one thing they hated more than Chelsea fans was Manchester United supporters from London. We couldn't win, we were doomed. They kept trying to talk to us but we daren't open our mouths. We nodded, smiled, chuckled and laughed at all the cockney wanker jokes. We did what we could to stay alive. How long can you not answer someone before he gets suspicious? It was nearly half an hour before we saw another Chelsea scarf.

A year or two after we moved away from the estate I met up with three old friends – in fact one of them was my cousin. We went out for the evening and they started picking fights with people – one person at a time of course. I was disappointed in them. These were ordinary blokes, or so I thought, no problems, no real money worries, nothing to cause them to hate the world and the people in it. They had no reason to be angry, so I just couldn't understand why they wanted to hurt people. They enjoyed it, it was as simple and as sickening as that. I had a huge argument with them and they had the cheek to call me a coward. Obviously four of us onto one little passer-by was courageous in their eyes.

Another time I went to a club and one of the people I was with picked a fight with someone. This act of bravado came from one of the wimpiest people I knew, but because he was with a large group he suddenly became brave. I told him to leave it, the man had done nothing, his girlfriend had been a tad mouthy but the man had done nothing. That simple fact didn't wash with my friend though, he was determined to be 'hard' and tried, rather pathetically I must say, to give this poor man a thump or two. Unfortunately it turned out that almost everyone in the club was a friend of this man's. They came flooding out onto the street after us, summoned no doubt by the trouble-making girlfriend who had stirred up the stupid affair in the first place. She must have been very happy with the outcome. Brave to the last my friends ran for their lives towards the car park where, once again, my long-suffering car was waiting to take us to safety. No braver than them, but far more sober, I was already there trying to open the doors with trembling fingers. My wimpy friend who had started the fight was run over by a passing car but managed to keep going. Justice, I thought, but only for a second. I opened the doors of the car and in piled about eleven people. I tried to drive out of the exit but the other gang, which to my horror I noticed numbered at least fifty, had blocked it. I reversed the car and made for the entrance barrier. A hail of bricks and other missiles came at the car, the side windows were smashed as was the windscreen although, luckily, it didn't shatter into the car. Not until I drove through the entrance barrier anyway, then suddenly we found ourselves covered in broken glass. With my hands at the wheel I got the worst of it, my face and hands were cut in dozens of places. We got away though. When we arrived back I drove around the various houses, dropping people off, and was disgusted when only one man offered me any money towards the damage done to my car – and he only offered a fiver. It was the last time I went out with any of my old estate friends.

One of the most violent and unpleasant stories I've ever heard came from one of my fans who was knifed. These animals held him to the ground and slashed his legs and back with a Stanley knife from top to bottom. He needed several hundred stitches. They just opened him up. There was absolutely no reason for it, it was one of those so-called random acts of violence and apparently they were laughing all the time. We live in a country where we're not allowed to defend ourselves. Call the police they say. Yeah right. So what do you do? Protect yourself and hope the police don't catch you or just hope that nobody attacks you?

For a while, after I first became successful, I carried a small aerosol canister of CS gas with me. On one occasion I accidentally released a tiny squirt of it into the air, about 18 inches away from my face. It was extremely painful, my eyes burnt, I couldn't breathe, it was horrible and lasted for a good ten minutes so I do understand why these things can't be made legal. I carried it knowing that I could get into trouble for having it but, considering I was regularly getting threats of all kinds, including death threats, I thought the extra feeling of security it gave me to be worth the risk.

In late 1976 I went to see the Sex Pistols at Notre Dame Hall, London. I really liked the Pistols although musically I didn't associate them with many of the other punk bands. I remember one of The Damned said they thought the Pistols were a complete cop out because their music wasn't really fast, like it was supposed to be if you were a punk. Well, I didn't like that fast stuff. When the Sex Pistols came out I thought they were an aggressive rock band. I was never a big punk fan, to be honest. I didn't like the aggression of the audiences and I didn't like the music much. I would be there pogoing with everyone else, but I always felt I was doing it because I was supposed to. I liked the fashion for a while. I'd seen the Pistols crowd in Lousie's on several occasions so I was already well into the way they looked.

In 1977 I started a punk band with some mates. Punkish anyway. We only did a few gigs, one of them at the same club in Wardour Street in London that used to have the Bowie night. For the first gig we were called 'Riot', for the second gig we changed the name to 'Heroin' and for the third, and last with me in it, we were called 'Stiletto'. When the band first got together I was the only one who had written any songs, and the only one who was interested in writing songs, so I became the front man, vocalist and songwriter. I also played the guitar. The drummer was an old school mate called Kenny Bishop and the bass player was a David Bowie lookalike called Henry Sabini. We had another guitar player, Neville Nixon. Neville was a coke fiend. He could hardly start a conversation without a line of coke. Not long after it first got together actually, the band began to get a bit funny with me about things. They thought it was a great laugh being in a band but they didn't want the bother of writing any songs. I was happy, I didn't go out much anyway and I loved shutting myself away to write. It's hard to imagine jealousy existing at such a small level but it did. They began to complain that we weren't doing any of their songs which, considering they hadn't finished any, was a bit strong. They then said that they didn't want me doing all the singing. I said fine you can sing your songs but they wanted to get someone from outside the band, to sing everything.

32

That bothered me a great deal. One day I went along to a rehearsal in Chelsea and when I got there I was surprised to hear someone else singing. A weird couple of hours followed with this man and me trying to outdo each other by both shrieking into the one micro-phone at the same time. It was obvious that devious plans were afoot but, these were my mates, so stupidly I really didn't think much more about it. A few days later things became a bit clearer.

We were all supposed to be going to the Rock Garden in Covent Garden to see a band. I drove round to Kenny's house to pick them up, and was surprised to find that they'd already gone ahead. When I arrived at the Rock Garden I saw some of them walking towards me so I walked over and said 'Hello' and they all turned around and walked the other way. Not one of them would talk to me. For a long while I thought it was some kind of wind up. Any minute I expected them all to start laughing and things would be okay. Then one of the girlfriends came up and said they didn't want me in the band any more. I was stunned, it was so gutless and pathetic. Not only was I out of the band, I was out of the entire circle of friends. I began to hear all kinds of stories about things that I had supposedly said and done, all lies. They changed their name yet again and started calling themselves Mean Street. I actually went to see them at one gig. I thought they were shit.

In summer 1977 I answered an ad in the back of the *Melody Maker* for a band, The Lasers, who were looking for a lead guitarist. I wanted to stay in the background and get more experience at just being in a band so the idea of being a guitar player in somebody else's suited me for a while. When I went along to the audition for The Lasers I met Paul Gardiner who was on bass and another man on rhythm guitar. I can't remember his real name, but his stage name was Wayne Kerr. Get it? The drummer I don't remember at all. I took to Paul immediately and, thanks to Paul's insistence, I got the job. I didn't mean to do it but I got more involved in the band's direction than I should have done, considering I was the new boy. During one of the early rehearsals I mentioned that the name was a bit clichéd. Everyone was called 'The' something, why didn't we come up with something a bit different? They asked for suggestions so I read out a few of the names of chapter titles that I had for some of the short stories I'd been writing off and on for a few years. When

I mentioned the name 'Tubeway Army' they all said that was the one. The name came from a spate of violent incidents that I'd read about several years before in the newspapers, where gangs were running onto trains on the underground and then, when the train stopped, they'd get off, beat up anyone who happened to be standing on the station and jump back on the train as it pulled out. This is also why there was a drawing of an underground train on the artwork for our first single, 'That's Too Bad'. After the name was decided I said, 'All your songs are by other people – The Beatles and some punk covers. Why don't you do some of your own stuff?' They said they didn't have any songs of their own actually finished and so I said 'Well, I have a few I did with this other band'. So, by the end of the first rehearsal, we were called Tubeway Army, we were doing all my songs and I was singing. It was Paul's idea that I become the singer. He had been doing the vocals up until then but he seemed to think that I had a more distinctive voice. I didn't realise at the time, but the other two had actually taken Paul to one side and tried to persuade him that I was going nowhere, they didn't like my songs, my voice or my 'pushy sense of purpose'.

A few weeks later I was hanging around a Covent Garden punk club where I noticed, with some irritation, Mean Street were booked to play. I was trying to get gigs for Tubeway Army and so went inside to see what I could drum up. An hour or so later this particularly seedy man at the club, I was never sure if he was the manager or the owner, was trying very hard to get me to sleep with him in return for giving us the gig. I thought 'This is a bit heavy', so I was talking fast, trying to get the gig on a vague and empty promise. At one point he shut me in his office and closed the door. I had only just turned 19 so it was all a bit traumatic and scary. I wrote a song about him many months later called 'Kill St Joy'. The song title has a certain, but hidden, connection to his name. I told this man the whole story about Mean Street and he thought it would be fun to put us on the same bill and not tell them. It was fun actually. They were very upset. They talked to me just enough to let me know that I had let them down somehow. I just thought 'Fuck the lot of you'. We didn't play very well but we were miles better than Mean Street and I watched them slide quickly into oblivion from thereon.

Tubeway Army went through a number of different line-ups in a relatively short time but whoever came in or went out it was always Paul and me. Paul and I left the original drummer and rhythm guitar player, but we kept the band name and became a three-piece with my uncle, Jess Lidyard, coming into the line-up on drums. From the very first time we met, Paul seemed convinced I was going somewhere and was happy to come along and be guided by whatever I wanted to do. He wasn't weak, far from, it was just that he believed I had a clear idea of what I was doing and where I was going and he wanted to be a part of it. I find it hard to put into words how important it was, at such a young age and at such an early stage of my career, having someone see me the way Paul did. It boosted my confidence and encouraged me to take my own path, with him always just a step away.

I was still trying to make Tubeway Army sound like a punk band at this point, but I couldn't quite get it right. We always had a more melodic batch of songs than the real punk bands. I was always a semi outsider in the punk scene, what with my uncle on drums and a guitar style which was more rhythmic than discordant. I played guitar, still do come to think of it, with this very chunky style, using big dampened power chords with a few noises and slides thrown in. I think my brother was more of a punk than me. He was eleven years old and he used to call himself Johnny Silver, spray his hair silver for the night and join us on stage for a song he'd written called Lucky. He was a star.

During this period I went to see Mick Ronson at the Rainbow Theatre in London's Finsbury Park and Iggy Pop on his '77 tour. I thought Iggy's *The Idiot* album was brilliant. Bowie played keyboards at those shows attempting, rather too obviously, to look like a mere band member. Lou Reed was good as well. Tubeway Army used to do a punk cover of the Velvet Underground song 'White Light, White Heat'. I also thought the American singer Jobriath was excellent, if a bit off the wall. Jobriath was often dismissed as a David Bowie copy, something that would come to haunt me in years to come, but I thought he was great. After the Ronson concert I was hanging around outside the stage door with a few other people when someone put a knife to my throat. A gang of locals had come along for some fun, it seemed. This man mumbled something completely unintelligible and then, much to my relief, walked on. I also went to see Queen at the Rainbow and was very impressed after the show when they allowed everybody by the stage door to go to the dressing rooms to get autographs signed. It was the first time I'd ever seen a big band take that much trouble to please their fans. It was a lesson to be remembered. Unfortunately the only thing I had on me that could be signed was a five pound note. I had to use it for my train fare home.

Unlike most of the true punk bands I didn't write protest songs about wanting to change or destroy society. I didn't want to change it, I wanted to use it. My songs were more often than not escapist or personal. I became very interested in the science fiction writer Philip K. Dick when I was 15 and still at school. I came across his book, *Do Androids Dream Of Electric Sheep* and I thought it was such a brilliant title I had to read it. The film *Blade Runner*, which is based on it, is a great film but there is so much more in the book. As well as Philip K. Dick I'd read some George Orwell, J.G. Ballard, Asimov, Saberhagen, who wrote the *Berserker* series, and many others. I also started reading William Burroughs. You can read one page of Burroughs and the scrambled text will leave you with little more than a feeling, sometimes a picture, but very rarely any kind of continuous story. It was great for filling you with an onslaught of imagery but horrible if you just wanted a simple tale to follow. He writes by literally cutting up pieces of writing and throwing them together in a haphazard way to create something entirely new but accidental, the infamous cut-up technique. I've read that David Bowie has also used this approach extensively. However, I have never used it for my own writing. I prefer to write things that mean something to me rather than make random connections of phrases or words. However, for much of the eighties, whenever I got stuck for a line I would read a page of Burroughs and wait for the images to pour out, hopefully sparking off a train of thought in my own mind. To be honest I probably relied far too much on Burroughs for far too long.

Burroughs' entire life seems to have revolved around drugs. Although I've had very little to do with drugs over the years, I've not been entirely immune to the temptation. I have many drug references in my songs and not all of them are taken from third-hand experience, or inspired by Burroughs' imagery. I first took speed when I was

18 or 19, in the form of little tablets called 'Blues' which were actually diet pills. I used to get so nervous before going on stage that I was all but physically sick. The nerves were so bad I was finding it hard to imagine how I could ever have a career in music. Someone suggested I try 'Blues' at one of our gigs. He said it would give me confidence. To me that sounded like the perfect treatment for my nerves and so I began to take them off and on for a while.

There was a club in Reading where all the minor punk bands played regularly and, after one Tubeway Army gig, I went off with a girl from Oxford who had her own flat, and a child, I later found out. I crammed into a car along with some other people who had been at the gig. Everyone was on something. On the way to her flat I was a bit worse for wear, I'd taken too many 'Blues' and was losing the plot quite badly. At one point I fell out of the car, couldn't get up, was crawling around in the gutter and kept asking someone to get me orange juice because a man at the club had told me that it took away the effect. It didn't. It was a bit scary, not exactly hardcore drug taking but it frightened me enough to make me wary of dabbling with drugs again. I didn't try anything else in those days, although there were always drugs around. I already knew a few coke addicts and there were other people I knew who were deeply into heroin. I didn't feel I had to be a strung out junkie myself to write about a scene where, for some people, drugs were a part of their everyday life. I got most of my information by just being around it. I've never tried heroin or LSD, I have no interest in these whatsoever, but I have tried cocaine and Ecstasy on rare occasions, although not for many years now.

In my songwriting, at that time anyway, I was writing about my experiences and those of people around me. I wrote a song called 'Mean Street' which was about being let down by my old friends. Another early punk song, 'Positive Thinking', was inspired by a situation I ended up in with Paul Gardiner. Although Paul usually went along with my ideas he was also swayed by other people and I'd have to work a little to bring him back to my way of thinking. The Positive Thinking man was one of the worst. We did a gig one evening at a local Scout hut where all these 12 year old kids were spitting on me. At the end of the show Paul said, 'I know how we can make it, man. It's all down to positive thinking. I've met this bloke and I'll take you to see him because he wants to manage us. He can make us famous.' We drove round to this man's house, went in and it was like an opium den. My dad had come with us. The room was full of smoke and there were people lying on the floor, sitting on cushions, totally wasted. Mr Positive Thinking was sitting against a wall like some guru, surrounded by people listening to his thoughts on life. It was like something out of a Beatles film but on a housing estate in Hayes. I asked him what his idea was for making us famous and he said, 'If you think positively about something, and I mean really, really positively, then it will come to you because you're putting out vibes of positivity. Everything will come to you like a magnet.' My dad said, 'You're talking crap aren't you? Truthfully, you're out of your face and you're talking bollocks?' Mr Guru was unsure, 'No, no ... well I am, but what I say is true, look what it's done for me.' I said, 'Very impressive, I've always wanted to live in a drugged stupor in Hayes with no food and no money.' About halfway through the conversation Paul started to giggle. He'd finally realised it was all nonsense. In the end this Mr Guru sent us away because, as he said, 'You guys are bringing me down with all your negativity.' I wrote the Positive Thinking song as much as a reminder to Paul about the dangers of listening to idiots as anything else, but he took it well and we laughed about it for years afterwards.

For a short spell I was employed by a neighbour fitting air conditioning. It didn't last long. I had a bit of a fight with one of the other fitters (he punched me, I hit him with a hacksaw) and, in the end, I got fed up with scrabbling around on building sites.

I then started work at an air freight company called United Marine (1939) Ltd. I was officially an export clerk but I was mainly driving a fork lift truck, loading and unloading the lorries. The manager there was a Bowie fan and he would bring in his Bowie bootlegs which we'd dance around to as we worked. He used to let me bring my guitar and amp into work and we'd play when things were quiet, which was most of the time. We also set up race tracks in the warehouse using pallets as markers and would then have fork lift truck races. This was a great laugh but then I got moved to the import clerk office, which was in a big building in the main part of Heathrow airport's cargo centre.

Being an air freight import clerk was dullness beyond compare.

People in offices seem to get sucked into the most petty-minded behaviour. I worked in two or three offices and they were all the same. I remember in one job my telephone cord was resting very slightly on the desk of the man who sat opposite and he threatened to punch me unless I moved it. Another man said he was going to slash the tyres on my car because I'd thrown one of my bits of paper into his waste basket. Part of my job was to operate the computer terminal, typing in the details of every import. That information went to a customs computer via on-screen forms which randomly checked the entries. Details about goods and duty rates were entered, that kind of thing. I was never any good at it. I got blacklisted once because I accidentally undervalued something by one million yen. Customs put a black mark against me, which meant all my stuff was checked thoroughly for a few months because they didn't trust me.

The only good thing about United Marine was that we weren't very busy for most of the week. I spent much of the time writing reams and reams of poetry. I would scribble the poems down and when I got home, type them all out neatly using an old typewriter. I didn't go out that much. I was just sitting at home typing out poems and writing songs. Eventually I had a row with the manager at United Marine and was sacked.

The job I went to after that one, again as an import clerk, was for a company called Mercury Air Freight. My workmates at Mercury would never let me go out with them at lunchtime because I had red hair. I went home for lunch one time and found the front door of our house wide open. I called my parents from a nearby phone box and they arrived to find that we had been burgled. The only two rooms the thieves had gone into were mine and my brother's. They had stolen all of my guitars, some of my clothes and smashed whatever they didn't want. My Gold Top Gibson was taken, along with a chocolate-coloured Fender Stratocaster. I went to court to look at the men after the police caught them and was amazed to see one of them wearing my clothes. They got community service and a suspended three month sentence. I didn't get my guitars back. I actually lasted a year at Mercury, even though I was still a very poor clerk, but my money stayed the same for the entire time I was there. I was taking home £18 a week.

After failing dismally as an import clerk I got a job as a courier, picking up and delivering parcels for a company called A and B Cars in Ashford, Middlesex. I sold my car and bought a miniature Honda van, the first of the micro vans, because it could carry more weight. Unfortunately, about a week later, I got the sack.

I then went to work at a W.H. Smith's warehouse near Heathrow where things were relatively free and easy. You spent a week on the lorry, driving stuff to and from the airport, then three weeks in the warehouse. One of my duties at W.H. Smith's was to drive the fork lift. This meant it was also my unofficial duty to accidentally damage as many boxes of chocolates as necessary, so that they were taken off the shelves and put into the canteen choccy bin. I was particularly good at this but ate so much chocolate while I was there that I've hardly eaten any since. It completely ruined my taste for it. We also used to take it in turns doing the daily chip run, but they soon stopped sending me. I would go out in the lorry and keep driving until I found a chip shop which didn't have anyone in it. I could be gone for an hour and a half, sometimes more. If there was someone in the shop I'd end up getting tongue-tied because I didn't like talking in front of people. I began to build up a real phobia about being around people, asking for things in public, which in many respects, I still have. Then I end up doing what I do for a living – it's hard to understand. I'd worked at W.H. Smith's for a few months when we were having a break and talking about what we wanted to do with our lives. One man wanted to be a football player, another a pilot. It was a real transitory place, nobody was there for a career, apart from one man whose life ambition was to be the warehouse foreman. I was quite surprised at this because I'd always had very lofty ambitions and I couldn't understand someone wanting so little out of life. When it was my turn I said I wanted to be a pop star and this man just went berserk. It was so bad other people stepped in and calmed him down because he was set to give me a hiding. We'd started out as mates, strangely enough, and after this he wouldn't speak to me. He said I was stupid and that I didn't live in the real world. The man who wanted a career as a pilot already had a private licence and one day he got some of us together and took us off to Blackbushe airport in Surrey, Camberley. We flew in a little aeroplane to the Isle of Wight. On the way back we hit some bad weather and it got a bit hairy, so we had to turn round, but it was good fun. It fired up my old desire to want to learn to fly.

My parents paid for the band to demo three songs, 'That's Too Bad', 'Oh, Didn't I Say' and one other whose name escapes me, at the cheapest studio we could find, Spaceward in Cambridge, on 16 October 1977. It was all punky material because I mistakenly thought that record contracts flowed like water for that kind of music. I soon found out that it wasn't quite that easy. We made up some cassettes and a friend of the band's took it around to lots of record companies but everyone turned us down, absolutely everyone. One man actually threw the tape out of the door and told him to fuck off. Then Paul Gardiner wandered into a record shop in Ealing, Beggars Banquet, to trade in some old second-hand albums. He started talking to the man behind the counter, Steve Webbon, and mentioned that he was in a band but that we weren't having any luck. Steve said the shop's owners, Martin Mills and Nick Austin, had just set up their own small label and we should give them a tape. In those early days I was more comfortable letting Paul do the talking, he could talk easily and confidently, telling anyone who cared to listen, and many who didn't, how great we were and about all the things that we were going to do. It was Paul's enthusiasm and persistence with Beggars – he badgered them constantly until they listened to the tape – that finally made the wheels creak into motion. When Martin Mills eventually listened to 'That's Too Bad' he liked it, but he wanted to see us play live. They got us a gig at a club called 'Vortex' in Wardour Street supporting one of their other bands, The Doll, who had a small but loyal following. I found gigs like this quite difficult and I learned to appreciate just how hard it can be to play as a support band. Most of our previous gigs had been in places where none of the bands really had a following and so we were all either ignored or applauded in equal amounts. Supporting a band with a following of its own, even a small one, was far more intimidating. The audience really just want you to get off as soon as possible so that they can watch the people they've come to see. I've never lost my respect for support bands and I have always made sure that people who support me are looked after and get the time they need to perform well. I don't mess with their sound or equipment and I will abandon my own sound check to make sure they get theirs. Anyway, that night, things

41

went quite well for us. Beggars said I had a command of the audience, which was nice of them, but there weren't really that many people there to be in command of. About 50 people and a prostitute in the corner trying to drum up some business as I remember. I was terrified as usual before going on but when I walked out on to the stage the nerves just vanished, as they always did. Martin said later that he thought everything about me was magnetic during that performance, although he didn't say it to me at the time. I was a skinny kid, with a strange voice and an unusual guitar style, more bizarre than magnetic. I didn't feel particularly magnetic or commanding. The gig also saw the band debut its new drummer, Bob Simmons. My uncle Jess had played on the recording session for the 'That's Too Bad' demo but had since left the band. He felt that we were on course and I think he wanted to get back to playing stuff that was more to his taste. He played in his own band, Shadowfax, which had a far less aggressive style than Tubeway Army.

After seeing us play live Beggars were now interested in signing us. They agreed that 'That's Too Bad' was the most commercial track and sent us away to remix our rough original at Manor Studios in Oxfordshire with a sound engineer friend of theirs called Nick Glossop. It was my first visit to a high-quality studio and I was amazed at the level of equipment. It was packed with every gadget you could think of. I was told that another reason for us getting the deal with Beggars was down to the fact we not only owned our own instruments but we also had a good PA system and a van. Thanks once again to my mum and dad, who by now had pretty much spent their entire life savings on the band. To find out that you're going to get a record contract, to me anyway, was like winning the lottery. I felt as though I was halfway to fame and fortune already. I think many people who are newly signed feel that way, which is probably why so many people become disenchanted with the way record labels treat them and their music. The record deal itself is merely the first step in what could be a very long road. With Beggars I was happy. I knew that they were a small label and that big money promotion was not really possible, so I was just glad to have a deal. It had a lovely family feeling to it and I used to spend a lot of time up there just hanging out. The head office was at the back of their Earls Court shop and Paul and I would regularly go up to the local burger bar with Martin Mills and talk about the future that was in store for us. Beggars Banquet in those early days had a great atmosphere. Everyone was in it together, from Martin down to me, and we were all young, keen and desperate to succeed. I worked at W.H. Smith's up until the day that 'That's Too Bad' was released, 10 February 1978, with 'Oh! Didn't I Say' on the B-side. It sold for 69p. I can remember seeing a copy of the sleeve for the first time, holding the finished record in my hands. It was a dream come true, an unforgettable moment. It was released on 7-inch vinyl and came in a picture bag. I played it again and again, I found it hard to take in just what it was. It was my first record, I was on my way.

'That's Too Bad' sold about 4,000 copies, which was an encouraging start for Beggars but a quite amazing thing for me. I thought about how many people used to be in the assembly hall at my grammar school, about 800, and how big that group of people had looked like. The record had sold to five times as many people as that! I was jumping off the ceiling. It had no publicity behind it and the press didn't seem to like it much; they thought I was a Billy Idol lookalike as my hair was bleached white by now. The really big mistake I made with that record was the name I chose for myself. I didn't want to be called Gary Webb. I wanted something that had a more interesting sound to it but I couldn't find anything suitable. On that first single I was called Valerian, Gary Valerian actually, although only the surnames were printed on the sleeve. I wanted to be spacey and mysterious, so I also wore a silver suit I'd bought in the King's Road, London, which made me look like an extra from a low budget sci-fi film. It may not have been the best look around but it was ours and ours alone. Valerian is actually a flowering herb, and the name of a Roman Emperor. With the release of the single I also started to take the lead more when it came to talking to Beggars about the band. I started to hassle them about gigs and recording plans instead of Paul. I was always very clear about the things I wanted to do and even more clear about the things I didn't. I'm sure that this must have been irritating to Beggars at times.

I have never thought of myself as particularly clever, or gifted, and yet I have always believed I would be successful. It's a strange meeting of conflicting personality traits, and one that causes people like me to appear erratic at best and out and out weird at times. I live in permanent turmoil, possessive and fiercely protective of my work and yet constantly unsure of its worth. I was once categorised by Ray Coleman, a most excellent man and gifted journalist, who wrote my biography way back in 1982 as: 'Shy, cocky, hard, soft, cruel, kind, infuriating, neurotic, obsessive, introspective, worried, jokey, enthusiastic, nervous, creative, imaginative, up, down, articulate, bright, opportunistic, aggressive, depressive, compassionate, dispassionate, sulky, highly strung, fair and yet very human.' That sums it up nicely.

Encouraged by the sales of 'That's Too Bad' Beggars agreed to a second single and also agreed to pay us a little retainer. It wasn't much, about £15 each a week, I think. When I left W.H. Smith I signed on the dole. At my dole interview I was asked what jobs I wanted to try for but I explained that I was in a band and that I wanted to be a pop star; in fact I wrote down on the favourite job column of the form, pop star. The dole man was very nice about it and said, 'We don't get many vacancies for pop stars so you're on your own with that one.' The money from Beggars wasn't enough to live on but a normal job was out of the question. I needed to be at Beggars, I needed to be out and about, pushing the band forward, not stuck in a warehouse.

We carried on getting a few gigs here and there. Mainly we were used as the support for another Beggars act at the time, a hard core punk band called The Lurkers, whose guitarist came out with the legendary question during one sound check, 'Where's me noise?' Supporting The Lurkers was okay. We were gaining experience bit by bit, but the problem was that I didn't like the violence, the spitting or the music. The most prestigious place that we played at was the Marquee club in London's Wardour Street, a stone's throw away from where I'd been beaten up, but that was still with The Lurkers. We supported The Adverts at the Cambridge Corn Exchange when it was still a spit and sawdust place. We also played the Royal Hotel in Luton, which was a very violent gig. We were the only band on and there were glasses flying through the air from the moment it started. Looking back on it we must have done quite a few gigs, as many as 30, although they seemed few and far between at the time. I absolutely hated live work for a long time, not so much being on stage as the build up to it. When I first started I desperately wanted the gigs and would go out and try to get them. However, from the moment I was told, 'OK, you've got the gig' I would start to dread it. I no longer took my little blue confidence builders and, although I was never actually sick, I would be retching outside before we went on. I was so nervous I was unapproachable. My dad, who was at nearly all of the gigs, would say to me, 'Why are you doing it, if you hate it?' Once I was on stage, though, I was all right and as soon as the gig was over I felt so relieved, I was on cloud nine. The nervousness was something I was just going to have to get on top of.

I began to have problems with Nick Austin, the other owner of Beggars Banquet. Nick believed that we were the commercial, acceptable face of punk and we had many arguments about the direction I wanted to go in. I was already convinced that punk had had its day and I was looking to take the band elsewhere. I didn't really know where but I knew I didn't want to be part of the dying dinosaur I felt punk was fast becoming. Nick was not sure about this at all, although Martin seemed more willing to go along with my vague plans. Nick was to be a fairly constant thorn in my side. At one point we weren't talking to each other at all. What others saw in me as decisiveness, Nick saw as arrogance. The way I saw it, punk was a fad, a passing fashion, not a way of life, and it was winding down. He wanted to tie me down to a sinking ship and I absolutely was not going to let him do it. Without Martin and his remarkable intuition fighting in my corner, and Steve Webbon, I would have been buried.

Another man was introduced to the band by Martin. Steve Hedges was an agent working for the influential Bron Agency. Steve also liked the band when he saw us play live and this reinforced Martin's faith in us. We went back into Spaceward on 7 March for three days to record some more demos, the week I turned 20. I loved the place, it had all started there. It was a little homebuilt 16-track studio and the people there were very helpful and enthusiastic. Bob had left, so my uncle Jess was back helping out on drums. Most of the songs were from our live set, but I was writing so much stuff at this point that I had stronger material almost immediately so I wasn't keen on releasing any of it. None of these recordings were released until years afterwards, when

Beggars pulled them out of a dusty cupboard somewhere and released them as an album called *The Plan*. Meanwhile Tubeway Army's line-up continued to change. Jess left again and Barry Benn came in on drums. We also added a second guitar player, Sean Burke. This was one of the first real problems I had with Beggars Banquet because Martin Mills kept saying to me, 'You're wasting the second guitarist. You're both playing the same things.' I tried to explain to him that that was exactly the point of having him there. I didn't want to have two guitarists playing different things, I wanted twice the power on the same riff. I was in search of power. I wanted us to be louder, heavier and raunchier than before, more than anyone else. I think Martin was expecting us to start playing counter-harmonies, like Thin Lizzy. That wasn't my idea at all.

On 15 April 1978, we went into a proper studio, The Music Centre, Wembley, to record our second single, 'Bombers'. Beggars insisted we use a producer, a man called Kenny Denton, and I went along with it. I was just happy Beggars were committing themselves ever more deeply to the band by investing more money. 'Bombers' cost a bit more to make, about £1,500, which was a lot for Beggars, but it sold about the same as the first single. I had yet more arguments with Nick Austin about the arrangement of the song and the lyrics. I was also beginning to realise that my new band members were as deeply entrenched in punk as Nick was himself. We began to argue within the band, although it was always Paul and me against Sean and Barry. Beggars were disappointed with the sales of 'Bombers', especially after putting so much money into its recording. Meanwhile, I began to realise that the attitudes of the public were changing. I became convinced that people were hungry for old-fashioned stars again. I used to flip through the magazines and papers and I noticed that band members were being pulled to the front of photographs, and magazines were interviewing one member only rather than the whole band. It seemed to me that people were fed up with the anti-star stance of the punk bands and were looking for pin-up poster heroes once again. I didn't want to be in a punk band. I wanted to be a pop star. I didn't want to be an anti-hero, I wanted to be the man on a poster on someone's bedroom wall. I wanted all the things I'd seen my heroes have. I wanted huge stage sets, the money, the fame, the life, everything. I just didn't know how I was going to get it.

Our first headline gig was at the Hope and Anchor pub in Islington and it was a big deal to me at the time. I was deeply embarrassed when only three people turned up to see us, and they were all from Beggars, including Martin whom I was desperate to impress. I'd hoped that we might pull in some of The Lurkers' followers, but not one turned up. We obviously hadn't been impressing their fans very much. It takes a lot of will power and ego-stifling to go on stage when it's a poor turnout. Especially in front of your record company!

We carried on gigging for a while until we played the White Hart pub in Acton, London in July '78. It would turn out to be the last gig Tubeway Army ever played. There was a mix up on the billing, The Skids should have been headlining and we were supposed to be the supporting act, but the poster had it back to front so they went on first. The Skids were a really good band. Then we went on and about three or four songs into our set a huge fight broke out in the crowd. The gig actually got reviewed in one of the music papers and gave me something of a slagging. First of all they said I was a Billy Idol lookalike, again. They also said that the difference between me and Joe Strummer was that he would have known how to handle the fight – he would have stopped, dived in and sorted them out apparently. What I did was keep on playing, trying to keep as many people interested in the band and as unaware of the fight as possible in order to minimise it. It didn't work though, the fight just got bigger and more out of hand until the pub landlord pulled the power. I was appalled at the violence. As soon as the gig was over I decided I was never going to play in pubs again. We would become a studio-based act, and build up a following through our records.

After that gig things also came to a head with Sean and Barry. They were more convinced than ever that punk was here to stay, so we decided to go our separate ways. Paul stayed with me. I heard that Sean and Barry started up another band some time later, called Tubeway Patrol, but I don't think it got anywhere.

Later that month I went back into Spaceward with Paul and Jess to do our first album for Beggars. It was not going to be a punk album as such, but it was still very much guitar, bass and drums. It's a difficult thing to explain but I had sounds in my head. More than that, I had a picture, an image, a feeling almost of how I wanted to go, but I hadn't come close to realising it with the band. It was so vague, I couldn't put it into words yet it was there nonetheless. When I arrived at the studio the previous band had left behind a Mini-Moog synthesiser and so I asked if I could have a go before it was collected by the hire company. I had never seen a real synth before and, to be honest, had never really thought about them very much. Although I liked some electronic music I still associated it mainly with pompous supergroups, like Yes and ELP. To me they conjured up visions of disgusting, self-indulgent solos that went on for half an hour. Pressing that first key changed my life. Luckily for me it had been left on a heavy setting, which produced the most powerful, ground-shaking sound I had ever heard. I realised immediately that this was what I had been looking for. It had the power I had been in search of and when I played my simple guitar riffs on it it sounded like nothing else I had ever heard. If it had been pre-set on a horrible, tinny, bleep sound I probably wouldn't have given it a second thought. It was one of those pivotal moments when luck shines down upon you, and you are awake enough to recognise it. For me it was a real eureka moment in my life. As I've said there was some electronic music I liked, I had a few Kraftwerk albums, but they had a clinical feel to them that didn't fit with my musical direction. I'd liked some of Brian Eno's music, but again it was a long way from where I wanted to be. I've still got some old Eno albums actually, but I do think he crawls up his own backside at times. He's extremely clever at putting sounds together, a very talented man, but I think you can go into a studio and do something creative without having to use those bizarre motivation techniques he seems so fond of. Just go in and write some bloody songs, mate. I love writing music, I don't need to be psyched into it. Just open up your mind and see what comes out. Eno had also worked with Ultravox, who had been closer to where I wanted to be, musically. I was a big fan of the band but it hadn't been raw enough or heavy enough to make me see what synthesisers could do for me and my music. In many ways the answer to my vague ideas, the picture in my head, had been staring me in the face for quite some time and I just hadn't seen it. My desire for a more powerful sound had stopped me from seeing the potential that the synth had. Until now.

I did what I could but I wasn't really happy with the results of those sessions and I was eager to get back in and add more electronic sounds to the songs. I had also started writing yet more new songs on an old piano that my mum had bought for me for £20 as a late birthday present. From the outset these songs were written with the synth in mind. I couldn't play the piano, I had no idea what any of the notes were called, but did the best I could to come up with material that I hoped would breathe life when I converted it onto the synth. Beggars cautiously allowed me back in to Spaceward on 23 August to do extra work on the album. This time, I was allowed to hire a Mini-Moog for the entire session, and when I returned to their offices, I was an electronic act. Beggars were less than pleased to begin with, especially Nick, but they began to come around.

I enjoyed being in the studio. It was almost like playing with my old control panel. I was fascinated by every gadget, every knob, button, switch and fader and I wanted to learn how every one of them worked. I loved it everytime someone would say to me 'You can't do *that* with it', because I would try to find a way of doing exactly *that* with it. I worked constantly to find new ways of creating sounds, of using effects, of doing everything. I felt that by some freak chance I was working with sounds that nobody else had stumbled across. I became slightly obsessed with getting the album out, quickly. I was terrified that other people would come along and put out this sort of music before my album was released. I was convinced that electronic music was going to shake up the world. The album was still credited to Tubeway Army but it felt more like mine than ever. I had wanted to go solo but Beggars were keen to keep the name, because they felt that to abandon it could lose the small following that we had built up with the two punk singles.

I've sometimes been credited with starting the electronic music revolution but I didn't. Many people have used synths before I did. The only thing I take credit for was the way in which I put together a package – the sound, the lyrical content and the look – which all fitted and made sense. Ultravox were definitely ahead of me and I saw them a number of times, but I think the band, and John Foxx in particular, made a huge mistake when he went on TV singing 'Hiroshima Mon Amour' in a Hawaiian short-sleeved shirt. He should've been a big star but he blew it. He didn't make the pieces fit properly. Later he tried to make better use of image, to present things cleverly, but he was already too late. By then I'd already done the things he tried.

All that was still a year or two away. That first album, called simply *Tubeway Army*, was released by Beggars on 24 November 1978. It was released as a special limited edition of 5,000 on blue vinyl and has since become better known as the Blue album amongst the fans. I also changed my name to Numan just in the nick of time and so this album credited me as Gary Numan for the first time. I'd written the music and lyrics, produced it, played guitar and sung. I was very proud. I really believed I'd come up with something new. Not original, I do not believe originality can exist in music any more. It is impossible to know what a song is without having heard one and, as soon as you've heard one, it's impossible not to be influenced by it, if only by a tiny amount. To know what a verse is, a chorus, a bar, a chord, is to be influenced to a degree by what has gone before. All we can have in music is variation. I've been criticised for admitting my influences yet all musicians have them. For a band to come along and say 'We are completely original' is absolute rubbish. It amazes me that I've been criticised for my openness and honesty about this and yet the artistic arrogance and bare-faced stupidity of these originality-claim ego-heads is still praised.

The name change to Numan was again something that Beggars didn't see the need for and Steve Webbon tried hard to convince me that it just wasn't necessary. I was convinced that the chosen name, when I got it right, would be another vital piece in the big machine. To me a career is just like a machine. All the pieces have to fit together and work together perfectly or else the machine will tear itself apart. It's one of the main reasons why I've always been so involved in every aspect of what I do. Not because I feel I'm great at any of these, but only I know what I'm trying to achieve, only I know where the machine is heading. Rightly or wrongly, I prefer to put it together myself. Anyway, I was looking for the hundredth time through the phone directories in the back of Beggars office when, in the middle of the Earls Court edition of Yellow Pages, I came across the name Neumann. Exactly *what* it was is hard to remember, it may have been a plumber or a kitchen appliance company but whatever, it was the name for me. The only problem was its German origins at a time when David Bowie was working extensively in Berlin. I didn't want to look as though I was adopting any of his German influences. To get round this problem I dropped the 'e' and the extra 'n' and so ended up with the N U M A N spelling. I thought it was the perfect name for a new and unusual style of music. It was the right length, two syllables, which was something I had been keen to stick to, had an alternative meaning and yet remained an everyday name. I felt that in the context of a pop career the name would take on a life of its own somehow, it would sound more effective than Webb although it was also a well-used name. The spelling made all the difference.

As I've said, I was very happy with the Tubeway Army album. I very rarely write songs about ordinary things and this album was a clear indication I looked at things slightly askew. 'Everyday I Die' was one of my favourites on the album and originally that was also going to be its title, but Beggars had been keen to call it 'Tubeway Army' in an attempt to establish the band name. 'Everyday I Die' is about masturbating and it underscores a constant theme in many of my earlier songs, of alienation and a retreat from hurt emotion into a cold detachment. I was a young and emotionally over-sensitive young man when I wrote these songs and it was my way of coping, as much as anything else, that encouraged me to write about my lack of feelings and detachment. The truth, of course, was the complete opposite.

Another song, 'The Life Machine', was concerned with the thoughts of a man on a life support machine. He is separated from his body but cannot leave because of the machines he's been plugged into. He watches those around him at his bedside, and as time goes by, their feelings of love and anguish turn into something else, something more like impatience and hostility. All he wants is to die with dignity. 'My Love Is A Liquid' is very off the wall. I was reading about cloning and genetic engineering and I imagined a time in the future when you could go into a shop and buy these dehydrated children, in powder form, which you make into babies by masturbating into a bowl. Similar in a way to the way in which we add water to dehydrated potato to get mash.

'Jo The Waiter' was named after a girl, Joanna Casey who was my first love, or as close as you can get to it at that age. The lyric deliberately suggests that Jo is a man. A line about Valium boys with painted eyes is about me. I don't know where I got it from, but I had a bottle full of Valium so I zombied out a bit, feeling sorry for myself, until my dad gave me another one of his famous kick-up-the-arse talks. A lot of the stuff I wrote was sexually misleading. I wrote into the songs a great many things with bizarre implications: that I was bisexual, a drug taker, a devotee of weird sex, violent, cold, unfeeling. In most of them I would use the words I and Me, transplanting myself into them as the central character. This was my imagination turning me into a more interesting and unusual character than I'd ever felt. I was a skinny little man, with no real worldly experience, still living in a small room in my mum and dad's house. I didn't go out much, didn't socialise well and had a fierce ambition that was often misinterpreted – or accurately interpreted – as stubbornness, self-righteousness and arrogance. I was moody, volatile and carried that haunted look of the driven youth like a warning sign. I was a man on a mission. Anyway, Jo Casey left me, for the second or third time, broken-hearted yet again, and then I actually found her underneath a friend of mine in a car park one night. I was very cut up about it and a lot of that hurt was woven into my music. His betrayal as much as hers.

My songs were often a rambling, disjointed mix of things. 'Somethings In the House' from that first album is a good example, 'Listen To The Sirens' is another. I wrote a lot of 'I'm an alienated young man sitting in my room, lonely, hurt and misunderstood' type stuff. In many ways, it was an exaggeration: by nature I am very insular and a bit of a hermit, however, I wasn't surrounded by white walls and a stark white light bulb, I was in my bedroom with my record player and my dog. In a song called 'My Shadow In Vain' there's a line 'One hand on the handle of the mad/sane door'. I did have problems as a kid. The fact that I was sent to a child psychiatrist by my school proved that I was a little disturbed but to make matters worse, I was fascinated by my own problems. I used to read a fair number of psychology books and identify with mental problems because I wanted to be different. There was one condition that really struck a chord with me, the Disembodied Self. I remember little about it now, but it was something to do with people consciously adopting different personalities. I used to do that. For a year or so at school, between 14 and 15, I would wake up and decide what personality I would have that day. One morning I'd sit up in bed and think, I'm going to be funny today, and I'd go to school and I'd be very witty and tell jokes which I usually couldn't remember. Then I'd wake up the next day and decide I was going to be weird and moody. In my head I was thinking, 'what an interesting boy I must be', everyone else was probably thinking, 'what a wanker, you never know what he's going to be like from one day to the next.' Whatever cold self-image I was creating through my lyrics, I was actually extremely sensitive to everything. Bob Geldof once said in an interview that he wished he could be more like me because criticism just rolls off me like water off a duck's back. It made me smile when I read that. He couldn't have been more wrong.

CHAPTER 4

When The Machines Rock, 1979

I hassled Martin to get back into the studio as soon as possible. My head was so full of ideas it was exploding and I was desperate to get going again and record the new songs I'd been working on at home. Martin booked us into Gooseberry Studios in London's Chinatown and there, to begin with, we demoed three new songs, 'Me, I Disconnect From You', 'The Machman' and 'Down In The Park'. Beggars were pleased with the new tracks and so Paul Gardiner, Jess Lidyard and myself put the *Replicas* album together in the little basement studio, which you reached through a trap door in the street. I still didn't own any synthesisers so we rented a Mini-Moog again, plus the mighty Poly-Moog. There was also a Roland SH2000 keyboard in the studio with a big hole drilled in it so that they could keep it chained to the wall, to prevent it being stolen, I guess. Gooseberry was mainly a reggae studio – 16-track, home built and very cheap and so I was surprised to see an in-house synth. We recorded the album in five days and then took another three to mix it. I played all the guitars and keyboards and did the singing, Paul played the bass and Jess the drums. Most of the songs were written on the upright piano that my mum had bought for me. I couldn't really play the piano so I used to make up my own chords. If they sounded right, fine, that would do. Then I memorised the positions of my fingers. I still had no idea about tuning to a constant pitch at this time. I could tune my guitar within itself, and I could tune the band to each other, but I had no idea that A-440 existed.

It wasn't until the third album that I learned about constant pitch. Before then I used to adjust the E-string on my guitar until it seemed to be about right and then tune everybody else to that. I was amazed at how close those first two albums were to A-440 when I subsequently realised my mistake and went back to check them.

The album has many of my guitar roots showing through it but it also marks a much clearer path towards electronics. The first album had been a guitar-based album that had had electronics welded onto it. *Replicas* was an electronic album from the very beginning.

The lyrics on the *Replicas* album are still quite personal in a few places but they are mainly science fiction based. It's often been said that I'm a tech head, sci-fi fan who writes doomy songs about space ships, robots and aliens, but *Replicas* was my only fully-fledged sci-fi album. Most of the songs are linked and are about the degeneration of humanity, the isolation of the individual, and I put myself into them, lots of 'I' and 'Me', so that I could place my own young, alienated feelings amongst the more storyline based sci-fi stuff. Those feelings are absorbed into the general theme behind the album which, lyrically, was loosely converted from a collection of short, connected stories I had been writing off and on about a future city scenario.

For instance, the talking bits in 'Are "Friends" Electric?' are absolutely personal. They're about two specific women. The S.U. line in the song is a reference to Su Wathan, who worked at Beggars Banquet. We had an odd little arrangement for a while, which I was far too immature to deal with or understand. The 7.4. mentioned at the start of the spoken part applies to the 7th and 4th letters of the alphabet – G.D. a woman called Gail Deal. She was an ice skating instructor and one of Su's friends, who slept with me one night and then wasn't interested at all after that. It was the first time someone had done that to me and I got pathetically hurt, but in a chauvinistic kind of way, I'm ashamed to admit. I had a lot of growing up to do. *Replicas* is filled with images of decay, seediness, drug addicts, fragile people and the abandonment of morals. The bisexual allusions are partly based on encounters I had with gay men, most of whom were much older than me, who had attempted to persuade me to try things. I was never interested in gay sex, never felt the slightest bit tempted, but the seediness of those situations left an impression which I used in songs for years afterwards and certainly used on *Replicas*. I knew of some school friends though, one in particular, who had cruised men a bit, mainly to get things out of them. A ticket agent, for example, used to bribe young men into having sex with him by getting them tickets for anything they wanted – concerts for the most part. In the songs I exaggerated these experiences, invented some others, set them in a scary, futuristic scenario and wrote about them as if it was all based on first-hand knowledge. I hinted at all kinds of things, I was taking limited experience and turning it into dark entertainment.

Although the songs were based on a series of short stories, I hadn't resolved the ending. The stories were flawed but some of the basic ideas and imagery, when converted into songs, worked quite well. I set the stories in the not too distant future. Cities have become isolated from each other, worlds within a world. The actual city that the stories revolved around had given control over to a machine created specifically to sort out the near anarchy that life had become. The machine decided that the cause of the problems was humans themselves, and so it set about ridding the city of people, with only a select few being aware of and involved in the scheme.

The machine realises it can't just kill everyone, it would be destroyed by rebellion long before the job was completed, so it develops a quota test. The quota test is a method of assessing people's IQs and anyone who falls below a given level is supposedly taken away, re-educated and made a better person. However no one ever comes back, they are killed. The quota tests' level of acceptability is raised periodically, so the machine systematically gets rid of all the weakest people first and then moves on to eradicate everyone. By the time people fully grasped what was going on, they would be too few to put up any meaningful resistance, and the final annihilation would be swiftly carried out. The tests were administered by the Grey Men, the image of which I used on my fifth and sixth album sleeves. The songs are filled with characters from the stories, sometimes used as song titles, sometimes just as part of a lyric.

The Machmen are Terminator-type creatures, machines with a cloned human skin that go to form a super police force. The only way you can spot them is by the difference in their eyes – they have a horizontal bar across the eye, instead of a circular pupil, which you can see on the back of the *Replicas* album cover. This was put together some time before the Terminator films were released, so I had a big interest in the ideas put over in those films. I don't find the concept of man and machine being linked fanciful at all, not perhaps like terminators, but in some way. In many respects it's already happening now. I was just writing about it in a highly exaggerated way.

The 'Friends' in 'Are "Friends" Electric?' are similar machines but they provide services, as opposed to being the law. You can call for a Friend to play chess with, or indulge your most obscene sexual fantasies, or anything in between. No one else will know because they all look the same. As anonymous as a plain brown package. The governing machine has imposed a curfew and no one is allowed out after dark. The walls of all the city buildings are light-sensitive and glow as soon as it reaches dusk, which means there are no dark corners to hide in. In the stories I visualised some parts of the metropolis in great detail. I had certain parts of streets and buildings where I would write about things that happened. No one is allowed guns but one of the characters in it has an old rifle, passed down secretly from generation to generation. He's one of the people who fights against the machines and he goes underground to where the Crazies live. They aren't actually crazy, they realise what is going on and so hide where they can and fight back as best they can. The machine puts out propaganda against them to alarm the other, more gullible, citizens.

The Crazies come out at night because, for one thing, they don't pay any attention to the curfew. They scavenge for food and equipment to maintain their survival. Much like the gladiators of Roman times, the machine has created a spectacle for the chosen few to keep them amused. It has created specialised killing machines located in the main city park. They're also light-sensitive and activate when it gets dark. All captured Crazies and other law breakers are put into the park, which is actually a prison. Very few people survive more than one night, no one survives two. The machines are programmed to commit all sorts of atrocities – rape, murder, torture – against anyone they find. The chosen few, however, the administrators and so on, are allowed out at night and their favourite hang-out is a club, Zom Zoms, which overlooks the park. From this vantage point they can watch the machines at play, purely as entertainment.

On the album sleeve I'm representing one of the Machmen. The whole black image came after I'd seen someone in a night club, dressed in black clothes, almost military in style, and looking very sinister. Although I have always thought that pop stars should some-how be larger than life, that showmanship was a vital part of the whole package, the image still felt like a prop to me. I used it as a support for my lack of confidence, something to hide behind, as much as for trying to enhance my appeal to a hoped-for audience. I used it to bring the album characters to life but also to paint myself as a character, not really as me at all. If you dress up like a pop star it makes it easier to pretend you are one, or even to be one if success comes your way. If you can make yourself feel like a pop star it makes it all the easier to get up on stage and perform. Put the image on, put the make-up on, and it doesn't matter whether you've sold a million records or a few thousand, you feel much more like you belong there. It was to me, still is in a way, like dress-ing up and playing cowboys and Indians. The imagination is given a small but effective helping hand. My images have helped me over-come my shyness and inhibitions on stage, they've helped me develop an on-stage persona that is anything but shy and nervous. On stage I'm full of arrogance, confident, at ease and very much in charge of the evening. Without the images I would have curled up in the corner and shrivelled away.

Some people took one look at the black clothes and white hair and, while I was busy trying to be a cold androidy type person, they thought I was pretending to be an Aryan Nazi figure. To make matters worse I was once asked why I was so keen on image and I tried to explain to the journalist how image can be useful and why it can have such a powerful effect. A particular image can be very useful for getting over a particular feeling or message. I used the Nazis as an example – they were terrorising people and they looked terrifying, it was a perfect combination of image going with func-tion and it must have had a devastating effect on the victims. I couldn't have picked a worse analogy as my chosen image was so

58

similar in many ways to the Nazi image. I was very stupid and naïve but the *Replicas* look was nothing to do with Nazis at all. For me the album was all sci-fi, machinery and robots, just fantasy stuff. It was fun, I didn't take it seriously, it was, as I've said, all based on an incomplete sci-fi story and I certainly never saw, or intended, any connection with Nazis or extreme right wing politics. I had no idea people would analyse the way I looked at that level since I didn't think anyone would be that interested, but then I didn't think it would go to Number One in the chart either.

I was concerned about how the image would be interpreted on our 1980 German tour of Berlin, Hamburg, Düsseldorf and Munich. To my horror some of the local German press not only made the connection between my image and the Nazis, but they also selected a photograph which looks as if I'm giving a Nazi salute. I have a particular gesture when I'm singing, where I punch the air, and when freeze-framed it took on a horrible new meaning. This was a real shock as I didn't wish to offend or ignore the feelings of the German fans. However I defend the right of any artist to take their ideas from almost any source. We're making music at the end of the day. As for this particular political taboo, if I'd been born 40 years earlier I would have fought the fascists with my heart, body and soul.

Meanwhile, the black image and my own avowed patriotism were also interpreted as evidence that I was racist. I don't have a racist bone in my body. I was so concerned about this in 1982 I wrote a song, 'War Songs', where I say, 'I don't remember if she's black or white/this is the heart', to make it clear that I only care about whether someone has a good heart. I also light-heartedly refer to myself as Vera Lynn in the song, a figure who's obviously closely associated with British patriotism. I'm, rather obliquely as usual, trying to make the point that because I love my own country it doesn't follow I'm a racist. We've allowed right wing groups to hijack the Union Jack because we've developed a guilt complex about our own patriotism. Of course, I recognise the dangers of nationalism but there's nothing wrong with taking pride in your own country and culture. Also a lot of my strongest feelings on the subject were expressed in 1982 when I was living in America and feeling somewhat homesick. My fervour reached rather eccentric levels at times.

One day, I was missing home quite badly and for some reason, there is nothing quite so patriotic as an Englishman abroad. I was in bed with a famous groupie who later sold her stories about me to the press and we had the TV on quietly in the corner of the room. Suddenly the British national anthem began to play, along with a picture of the Union Jack waving in the wind. I was stark naked as I stood up on the bed for the entire anthem, saluting Queen and country.

Back in 1979 I was seeing Magenta De Vine, years before she became a TV presenter, on and off for a few months after I finished *Replicas*. She was a friend of Su Wathan's, or at least Su introduced me to her. I was a bit intimidated by her because she was older than me. I thought older women were quite scary because they were far more experienced than I was sexually and I was a very unworldly 20 year old. I don't know if she is actually older than me but I thought she was at the time. Early on I was told that she was into heroin, although I never saw her taking it. She had her own place in London, I thought that in itself was pretty cool, and she shared it with the drummer from The Clash. It all seemed exciting enough to me for a while.

In the spring of 1979 we released the first single off the album, 'Down In The Park'. To this day it remains one of my favourite Numan songs. It achieved what I wanted from the moment I thought up the first line. It was haunting yet powerful. It was also quite unusual for the time. Our sales almost tripled, up from 3,000-4,000 to 10,000, so we were obviously doing something right. On the B-side was another song from the *Replicas* session, 'Do You Need The Service', which was written from the perspective of a 'Friend'. When *Replicas* came out in April, it sold about the same as the single, and we started talking about doing a headline club tour. I remember being told that the song was number 198 in the Top 200 chart. I thought that was amazing. It meant that only 197 singles were doing better than mine and, considering how many singles were put out each week, and how many more bands there were that never made it into the Top 200 at any time, I was doing bloody well.

Although I thought *Replicas* was a big step forward musically, I had no expectations of it becoming successful. At best, I thought I would be able to headline The Marquee club with a good crowd. That would have been a triumph for me at that stage. I hoped it was going to give me a degree of musical credibility, and that maybe I'd be credited with being at the forefront of a new form of pop music. I was quite calculating about that aspect of the release. There's a song on the album called 'When The Machines Rock'. It's an instrumental I put on the album specifically because I wanted to make the phrase 'Machine Rock' my own. I wanted to ensure that was how this new movement would be labelled by the press and that the label would always relate back to me, no matter what bands they were talking about. This scheme failed dismally because they called it everything but machine rock. I also felt that the time was right for a solo synthesiser star and I was more keen than ever to drop the name Tubeway Army and put the album out as a Gary Numan album. However, *Replicas* was still credited to Tubeway Army because Beggars now wanted to build on the sales for the first album, so keeping the band name was very important to them.

The Radio One DJ John Peel was very supportive towards Tubeway Army at this stage. He'd played tracks from the first album and we did a three-track session for him on 10 January 1979, which he broadcast a week later. They were quite raw versions of 'Me I Disconnect From You', 'Down In The Park' and an instrumental 'I Nearly Married A Human' performed by Paul, Jess and myself. However Jess didn't want a full-time career in music and I therefore needed a new drummer. There was also no way I could play both keyboards and the guitar live, so I knew I had to get some more people in.

We auditioned for extra musicians in a rehearsal room below Beggars Banquet's Fulham shop. Paul Gardiner was still in the band and Jess helped with the drummer auditions. They were really quite simple. I would play a synth, the parts to 'Are "Friends" Electric?' and 'Down In The Park', and these people had to play along using a kit that we had provided. Jess decided who was the more capable drummer. One man turned up in concrete-encrusted work boots who could barely clap his hands in time let alone play drums. Another man who came along said it wasn't a fair audition because the songs were too difficult. Well, I don't think any drummer in the world worth the name would consider those songs even vaguely taxing, let alone too difficult, so he didn't get the job. When Cedric Sharpley sat down to play, it all came together. He had a tremendous style, very powerful, very solid but with a lot of tricky stuff going on. As soon as Cedric played things sounded right. He was very impressive and Jess said to me immediately, 'He's the one'. I also needed two keyboard players but only two turned up, so they were both in. Chris Payne was one of them and he arrived in Wellington boots, looking like a farmer with a big moustache, a scarf and a flat cap. He could play though. I had already set the synths up and again I used the same two songs as the audition. Chris later confessed that he'd never played a synthesiser before in his life, but he completely fooled me. The other man was French and I think he was very short-sighted because whenever he played the keyboards he would lower his head until it was about two inches above the keys. He wasn't that great but as no one else had turned up I had no choice. When we had the first rehearsal this French man spent the whole day in the toilet being sick and he was terrible. He couldn't actually play at all, so I had to let him go. I decided I would have to keep looking after all. Meanwhile Ultravox had split up and their keyboard player Billy Currie was out of a job so luckily, a little later, I got him in the band. I was a big Ultravox fan and I was really quite in awe of Billy for a while. I had no idea how successful I was going to be in just a few months' time, and so I still thought of Ultravox as a fairly big band. I saw him as the synthesiser expert and myself as a young pretender, so to have him in the band was amazing. However, I still needed a guitar player.

Shortly before 'Are "Friends" Electric?' was released as the second single from *Replicas* I sang on a Lee Cooper jeans TV advert. Somebody was playing the first album in my publisher's office and a man called Ronnie Bond, who was putting together the music for the advert, heard my voice and decided it suited his ad. He rang up Beggars and asked if I would sing on it. It was his music and lyrics, I believe, although I don't know that for sure. I was paid £40 to sing it, then the lyrics were changed and so I received another £40 to do it again. To get £80 for a few hours' work seemed like big money and I thought I'd arrived. I was a professional, I was actually being hired as a singer. I later realised that I'd been turned over slightly, because I wasn't paid any kind of a repeat fee and £80 was far too low for a buy out. I didn't know that at the time though and I was very happy with things. In the late '70s a number of adverts had spawned hit singles and so I asked if the music from this ad was going to be released. His answer was dismissive and arrogant and I was made to feel really small in a studio filled with strangers. The advert went on to become highly popular and when I became successful soon afterwards, they got in touch with me to ask me if I'd sing on the track, as it was now being turned into a single, called 'Don't Be A Dummy', after all. I even got a message from the managing director of WEA (Beggars had since signed a licensing deal with them at the start of 1979) which said he'd consider it a personal favour if I were to sing the track. I said no, that man had made me feel two inches tall when I'd asked about it being a single and I wanted nothing to do with him or it.

'Are "Friends" Electric?' came out on 4 May 1979. I loved the song but I never expected it to be a hit. It was over five minutes long because it's actually two different songs put together. I had the main verse and chorus part but I couldn't think of a suitable middle 8 for it. I also had a ballad that I couldn't quite work out a conclusion for. One day I was playing parts of 'Are "Friends" Electric?' and then went straight into the other song and was amazed to realise that they fitted together perfectly. Those two unfinished songs became the five minute long 'Are "Friends" Electric?' The main keyboard melody was also different at one point. One day when I was playing it back on my piano, some time before it was recorded, I hit a wrong note and thought it sounded much better so I kept it, even though it was actually a bum note. Bizarrely I've sometimes been hailed as a genius for writing that song but it has always struck me as ironic that it was finished by bolting two separate, incomplete bits together and that the main hook was actually a wrong note. So much for genius.

Someone at WEA came up with the idea of putting it out on a picture disc. Picture discs were a very new thing in those days and serious record collectors were buying anything that came out in picture disc format, often without even hearing the song. They pressed 20,000 picture discs, twice as many as the previous single had sold in total. I didn't get paid any royalties on picture discs, so I can't say that it was a great risk on the label's side, but nonetheless it was a big move to make for a relatively unknown band. The plan worked well and it sold enough to get the single into the Top 75. If I had been pleased with number 198 imagine how I felt being in the Top 75. It was all happening fast, very fast. Soon it would dawn on me that it had all happened far too fast.

I had been very excited about the John Peel Radio One session but our first TV appearance was something else again. On 23 May we played on the *Old Grey Whistle Test*, where we did 'Down In The Park' and 'Are "Friends" Electric?' I had been watching the show for years, I loved it. I had seen so many great people appear, and now I was going to be standing in the same studio, maybe even using the same dressing room, sitting in the same chair as these big stars. I was literally going to be following in the footsteps of my heroes. It was the biggest thing to have happened to me in my life. It was a major opportunity and I intended to make the most of it. I worked out every move the night before in front of a mirror. Every glance, every hand gesture, everything was pre-planned. This was not only done in a search for the best performance, but because I had no idea what to do with my hands. I had never performed without my guitar before and I genuinely didn't know where to put my hands. I therefore had to choreograph my movements. That's why I looked like Pinocchio, totally wooden and completely unnatural. I stared forward throughout the whole performance, give or take the odd sideways spasm, since I'd decided it would be a mistake to look into the camera the whole time. I'd seen lots of bands on TV who, as the shots went from one camera to another, would always be looking directly into it. Then of course they'd miss it sometimes and appear foolish as they stared meaningfully into the wrong one, only to switch, too late, to the right one two seconds later, which was always a bit sad. I had made up my mind long before that, if ever I had the chance to be on telly, I'd just perform and let the camera move around and pick up whatever I was doing. I still think it's the best way of doing it. Most of the pop artists in the late '70s smiled all the time and looked sickeningly happy, which I found very naff and resolved to avoid. The subject matter of the songs dictated the way I would perform but the cold, alienated stare was as much nerves as image. Whether people loved it or hated it, we did look different.

Before the show fire inspectors came round and tried to set fire to the drape that we had placed around our drum riser which annoyed me a bit. I was nervous enough as it was without some pompous, self-righteous official trying to set fire to my drum riser. With only minutes to go before our slot one of the TV cameras, whilst being wheeled around on a long arm rather too enthusiastically, hit my PA stack and knocked it over. Annie Nightingale, who was hosting the show, laughed and so I delivered her one of my most withering stares. I think it was actually more a nervous laugh than a lack of concern on her part. I got to know her a little in the years that followed and she was really quite nice. The performance itself went pretty well, although I was a million light years away from being an accomplished performer. The most incredible thing about the day, though, was being told that we also had a slot on *Top Of The Pops* the very next day. Before that though, and the morning after the *Old Grey Whistle Test* went out, I signed my very first autograph for a road sweeper in Hogarth Road, Earl's Court, London. They say you always remember your first kiss. I don't, but I do remember my first autograph request. Su Wathan was with me and we laughed and giggled our way up Earl's Court Road so much people thought we were loonies and kept out of our way.

Top Of The Pops. Oh dream come true, kill me now and send me to Heaven, my life is complete. I couldn't believe it. *Top Of The Pops* had been a part of my life for as long as I could remember. Just being on it was to have made it, as far as I was concerned.

Getting onto the programme was one of those huge strokes of good fortune that go hand in hand with every success story. At that time *TOTP* were running a feature on the programme called 'Bubbling Under', featuring a band whose single was outside the main chart but showed significant movement. I'm told that, in that particular week, it was between Tubeway Army and Simple Minds. Someone has since said that it was the name that swung it for us – they thought it was a more interesting name. I don't know if that's true. We were bubbling under that week and so we were on. Whoever decided to put 'Are "Friends" Electric?' out on a picture disc was the person responsible, as much as anyone else, for my subsequent success. Sadly, I've never been able to find out who it was, which is surprising because everybody else began to say they'd discovered me. I think my dustbin man claimed to have discovered me at one point.

I expected the people at *TOTP* to be quite awkward for some reason but in fact they were excellent and went along with my ideas completely. I told the set designers I didn't want any of their flashing, coloured lights, I just wanted white light, and a lot of it, on the floor to try and make the presentation stark and different. I had seen white light used very effectively by people in the past at various concerts and I was sure it would work equally well on TV. I was surprised the *TOTP* people let me have it, as the programme had a clear visual identity of its own. They said it made a change for someone to show an interest in the lighting and they were pleased to have some new ideas. I had the band dress in black and I told them there was to be no looking at the camera unless it was appropriate, no smiley faces mouthing Hello Mum. I wanted everything about the way we presented the song to express its theme, the atmosphere. All the pieces had to turn together now or it would be a waste of an opportunity. I was determined not to blow it the way I thought Ultravox had blown it. This was the chance of a lifetime. I may have been very calculating about the look of the performance, about the image, about everything really, but I was more terrified than you could possibly imagine when the time came to do the song. The pressure of the scale of the opportunity was heavy on my shoulders, the realisation that so much could hinge on the next few minutes. The simple fact that, despite my being very much in charge of things, I was shy, lacked inner confidence and still didn't know what to do with my hands was lost on most people around me. The beginning of a lie was being born. I have often likened my success to putting my hand out and grabbing onto a fast express train as it roared, unexpected and without stopping, through the small village station I was standing on. This was the moment I first saw the train come hurtling around the corner, heading straight for me. I stuck out my hand, grabbed onto something, held on by the tips of my fingers and was dragged away, everything a blur, breathless, frightened and excited. Doing *TOTP* also gave me the opportunity to give my old friend Garry Robson a place in the band, as miming guitarist, so that he could experience *Top Of The Pops* with me. After that first *Top Of The Pops* appearance we went to a club called Blitz, run by Steve Strange, to celebrate. Strange would only let me and Billy Currie in because the others 'Didn't look good enough'. He made the others stand outside in the rain while Billy and I tried to persuade him to change his mind. He wouldn't, so we all left. He spoiled what should have been a major celebration and I was very angry about it. On the other hand, though, 'Are "Friends" Electric?' was selling up to 40,000 copies a day and the excitement of that level of success would take more than Steve Strange's little quirks to dampen down.

Our music was, if I say so myself, quite different and we really were like nothing else around at the time. I'm not saying we were better, I don't believe we were, but we were different. Sometimes I watch those *TOTP* rerun programmes now and when it comes to 1979 the charts were just full of 'You Can Ring My Bell' and all that other disco, smiley-faced bollocks. I think we were a breath of fresh air. I wasn't the first to get into synthesisers but I was the first to become a household name. I took the full force of the venom though. As door opener for a new, and in many areas, extremely disliked style of music, I was media enemy number one. They sharpened their poison quills and came at me with a savagery that I think is only now being acknowledged as undeserving and totally unnecessary. The anti-synth feeling was running high amongst the press, though not the public. The Musicians Union even tried to ban me and my synthesiser music at one point. They said I was putting real musicians out of work.

I was definitely of the opinion that people either loved me or hated me. I was surrounded by extremes on both sides and I actually thought it was the best way to be. If I couldn't have a really nice review then I'd rather have a really bad one, hurtful though they were. I'd rather have no stars than three out of five. To be a star you have to arouse something extreme in people, whether it's good or bad, and only then are you really starting to get through. To not make much of an impact at all, to be merely 'all right', was not good enough, *is* not good enough. I want that extreme. It's what separates those that last from those that don't.

We performed 'Are "Friends" Electric?' several times on the *Top Of The Pops*. The song went to 48, then to 27, then to 20. When it reached number 20 I thought that it was over because its progress had slowed down considerably. It was picking up virtually no radio airplay, something that was to become a peculiarly Numanish phenomenon, unfortunately, and so I was beside myself the following week when it went up again to number 13, then to 7 and then to number 2 and finally, incredibly, to number 1. A few weeks later the *Replicas* album joined 'Are "Friends" Electric?' at the top of the charts and so I had the rare distinction of having my first hit single and album top the charts at the same time. I was 21 years old and everything I had ever dreamed of had come true. I was a pop star. I was that one in a million.

It was Martin Mills from Beggars Banquet who rang me at home and said, 'You've done it, you're number one.' When I put the phone down I leapt around the room for a bit. There was an over-all feeling of tremendous satisfaction and pride, but in many ways it was also an anti-climax. I knew I was number one and the joy of that cannot easily be put into words but in an everyday sense noth-ing had altered. I was still living at home, I still had the same car, I still didn't have any money, my day to day life hadn't changed at all. I went back into the front room and carried on watching the telly. I was smiling, though. Things were soon to change, perhaps more than I wanted and certainly more than I was prepared for. For all my studying of the music business and my so-called cool calculating approach to how I wanted to do things, I was completely unpre-pared for the realities of fame.

I was immediately unsure of my next move. It wasn't supposed to have happened now, not this soon, I had a lot of learning to do, I had a lot of experience to acquire before reaching this level of success. I didn't know it at the time, I thought I was taking things in my stride, but I was floundering badly. So now I'm a pop star, what am I supposed to do? I'm supposed to be mysterious maybe so I'd better not smile. I'm supposed to be what? I started living the life of a liar the day I got that phone call. I felt completely the wrong man in the wrong job. I just didn't feel natural, didn't feel at ease at all. In many ways, and I've said this before, becoming famous is like losing your virginity. It isn't how they say it's going to be. It's not what you expect at all. You have to take in and accept a whole range of new sensations and experiences, sorting out the ones you like from the ones you don't. You learn how to avoid the things you don't like and enjoy the things you do. At first it's something of a let down. You feel naked, exposed and very much a beginner. You have to learn how to do it and the only way to learn how to do it is by doing it, there is no shortcut to experience. The only difference is that when you become famous quickly the whole world is watching you as you struggle to learn, hopelessly out of your depth, and all the time pretending you know exactly what you're doing. There's also a terrible pressure attached to being number one so early in your career, because you can only go down from the top. You can chug along as a nearly-man all your life, but if you make it big people are willing you to fall. You get more insults and spiteful pisstaking when your records do less well after you've had a number one, than someone whose records never got into the Top 10.

The money didn't come in until quite a long time later and even then my idea of wealth was very unworldly. When I was younger we always used to go to a camping site in Weymouth and the rich people, or rich to us at any rate, had big caravans on the hill. So when I first got famous that's what I thought of as an extravagance. I went back to the campsite and rented a big caravan. Simon Le Bon went off to Montserrat, I lived in a caravan for a week. In many ways it takes as much time to understand and appreciate money as it does fame. I sometimes read stories about Lottery winners whose idea of how to spend their millions is to put an extension on their terraced house. It's easy to laugh at so limited an understanding of what can be done, what can be enjoyed, but it's also hard to explain how long it can take to fully grasp what you have when you first come into serious money.

I did do some stupidly naff things when I became famous, settling old scores mainly. I wanted to revenge myself on all the friends who had turned against me, mainly the Mean Street crowd. It had only happened a year or so earlier and the memories were fresh and still painful in my mind. I went round and slept with their girlfriends, which was easy all of a sudden. Amazing how being on the TV does things for your looks. I couldn't get them all, but I had most of them. It was shallow, childish and not something I look back on with any pride but, at the time, it was excellent. I didn't even like any of them, these girls had been as much a part of it as the men. Revenge makes us do some very petty, small-minded things I'm afraid.

Beggars Banquet wanted me to do a club tour, but I was very much against the idea. I wanted to go out with a big show, something truly special. I wanted my shows to be events that people would talk about not just the day after but for the next year. That's how I'd always imagined it. They had actually started to arrange dates, which made me furious and I refused to do them. I thought when and where I played live was not something that was their decision to make. There were big rows, especially between me and Nick Austin, as usual. I had many ideas for the shows but it would take time to put them all together. I didn't know who to go to, who could turn my ideas into reality. Steve Webbon backed me up, as he often did, and so the tour was put on hold.

On 25 June John Peel transmitted a second session which we had recorded the day after our first *Top Of The Pops*. This time it was with the new band, including Billie Currie, and we played early versions of three new songs – 'Cars', 'Airlane' and 'Conversation'. We'd actually started demoing the next album back in April at a tiny studio, Freerange, just off the Strand in London. We kept some of the demo material, such as the weird viola part on the song 'Complex', because we couldn't recreate it when we went to a bigger place, Marcus Music. The studio was, equipment-wise, a huge step forward but it was still in the process of being built and there was scaffolding everywhere. Billie Currie and Chris Payne played quite a lot of strings on the album, although I messed around with the sound so they turned into this weird pitch-bending wail in the background. I still played most of the synths and concentrated on a very rich, layered, Poly-Moog sound. I wanted to experiment a little, by making the album without guitars, except for the bass guitar, just to see if I could do it and make it sound acceptable. It wasn't intended to be a great artistic statement although I did feel synthesisers were, to this new form of music, what guitars had been to most of the musical styles that had gone before. They provided an opportunity for people without any great musical training or ability to make pop music. You could rent them fairly cheaply, record them in little studios and they would sound incredibly powerful. It was the garage guitar band concept but without guitars. In some ways, though, I was making a statement. I was making sure that everyone was aware that this music was capable of standing up on

70

its own, that it didn't need to lean on guitar riffs to succeed. It was a pointless gesture in many ways. The album would probably have been much better if it had had some guitar on it. We were actually working in Marcus Music throughout the time that 'Are "Friends" Electric?' and *Replicas* went to number one, so they were incredibly vibey sessions.

The album was to be called *The Pleasure Principle* after a Magritte painting of the same name had caught my eye in a book. It had been written in about eight weeks, which meant that I had written and would soon have recorded three albums within twelve months. All the songs on *The Pleasure Principle* had one word titles, just to be different.

Lyrically *The Pleasure Principle* is a mixture of ideas. The track 'Metal' is pure science fiction. One of the images in it actually came from an advert for Castrol Oil. Their slogan used to be Liquid Engineering so I stole that and put it into a song about a robot's desire to be human; 'And I'm frightened by the liquid engineers'. Another line in the song, 'If I could make the change, I'd love to pull the wires from the wall', was a play on the sex change wishes of some human beings in relation to the machine's desires to be human. 'Complex' is more personal and describes a situation where a girlfriend had let me down. It also has another, entirely separate theme, about the fickleness of fans. When I wrote the song I was not successful, but I was beginning to see small signs. 'Complex' voiced my early concerns about the way fans can come and go, some time before I actually had any.

The song 'M.E.' is sung from the point of view of the last living, for want of a better term, machine on earth. The people have all died, the planet is laid waste and its own power source is running down. I used to have a picture in my mind of this sad and desperately alone machine standing in a desert-like wasteland, just waiting to die.

'Films' is pure paranoia, my dislike of everyday life and the dangers I saw lurking in every stranger's face. Despite the title, it's not about movies – the 'actors' in the lyric are people, the 'show' is life. 'We're so exposed' is me being outside, walking down the street, and the 'scenery' and the 'set' are the city around me.

'Observer' states that I'm on the outside looking in, that I was

71

watching the world rather than being a part of it. Fantasy stuff really, but it was very much the way I felt at the time. 'I could stand here for days, I could stand here for hours. I could stand here for a lifetime watching you and waiting always'.

'Conversation' tries to outline how I expected fans to be like when I had them. I had already started to get a little fan mail, after the first album, and some of it made me wonder. These early fans seemed to want me to be exclusive, they wanted to be into something that no one else knew about. They seemed close to having a go at me with every letter that came in, their support appearing fragile, to say the least. The three main letter writers all wrote to me after the success of *Replicas* and all slagged me off in the most offensive way for 'selling out' – whatever that meant. This was the same album that they had been praising only weeks before. All this was to give me a deep suspicion of 'fans' for many, many years to come and was to cause a fair degree of misunderstanding between us for quite some time.

The last track on the album, 'Engineers', was inspired by a short story, written by Philip K. Dick probably. It's the story of men who spend their entire lives working underground. All the roads are actually conveyor belts, but on a massive scale running all over the world. These engineers keep them running and feel very bitter because they live in darkness, never coming to the surface or being allowed to use the roads themselves.

The album cover is a parody of the René Magritte painting, *The Pleasure Principle*. In the painting a man is sitting at a desk, with his body turned towards a small rock to his left, on the edge of the desk. He's wearing a business suit and instead of a head there's white light coming from out of the neck. The reason why I'm looking at a glowing pyramid is that it just happened to be lying around the studio and I thought, that looks cool. I came out with loads of rubbish about the pyramid being the strongest shape and so on at the time but it was nonsense. I was asked endless questions about my thoughts on pyramid power. I just liked the shape, but I had no pyramid allegiance whatsoever. When people asked me questions in those early days I often felt obliged to answer. I thought I should know about anything and everything that they asked me, which was a mistake. On many occasions I would try to bluff my way through questions until I could figure out what they were talking about. I was trying to recreate the vibe of the painting with the bland business-suited man so I let my hair go brown. Another mistake looking back on it. As for the clothes, I told the photographer, I wanted a businessman type of suit and, bizarrely enough, one of Mean Street turned up with it. He was working for a hire company or some such thing. The world can be a surprisingly small place.

On 24 August 'Cars', the first single credited to Gary Numan rather than Tubeway Army, was released and quickly went to number one. I think 'Cars' is probably the best pop song I've ever written. In many ways it's quite possibly the only pure pop song I've ever written. It has a very simple lyric but people still got it wrong. One man in America wrote a really long review, examining every line and coming to the conclusion that it was all about me coming out of the closet and admitting that I was gay. No, not at all. It's about me feeling safer in a car than walking down the High Street. It's about the way I think of the modern motor car more as a personal tank. I can always drive away at the first sign of trouble. I was very pleased with the promo video, my first, because I thought it went perfectly with the image, the style of music and the song. I also had black hair by now.

The Pleasure Principle went to number one in the charts in September. This was also at the top of the charts the same time as the 'Cars' single, which meant I had another double number one. According to the *Guinnsess Book of British Hit Singles* this was only the tenth time in the history of British music that such a thing had happened so that was cool. It also meant I had three albums in the Top 40, as *Replicas* was still there and the Tubeway Army album had been re-released with a new sleeve. It now had a black and white shadow drawing of my face, taken from the 'Bombers' Single cover, the idea of my old friend Garry Robson. It's been the Numan business logo ever since.

My first tour kicked off at the Glasgow Apollo on 20 September 1979. All 16 dates were sold out, including two at Hammersmith Odeon, and yet I lost £60,000 on the tour because of the staggeringly high cost of the stage show. The design was based on how I imagined the buildings would look in the *Replicas* stories, skyscrapers with walls that glowed when it got dark. No one had used light panels before, so we had them custom made. I wanted a wall of light but the problem with that was, if we used conventional lighting methods, it would blind people, so there had to be a way of diffusing the light to stop that happening. We came up with the idea of perspex panels with lots of light bulbs behind them, which would diffuse enough so you just saw an overall block of light. It would look very bright but not so much that people had to look away when they fired up. Then we put black lines across the panels to make them look like glowing white strips. I kept up the pyramid theme, which was also in the 'Cars' video, by incorporating a triangle of light at the back, above the drum riser, and using it as a kind of logo. We also created two pyramid robots, Huey and Duey. We nearly lost one when it went off the stage, but luckily, it got itself stuck before it fell off completely and the road crew managed to rescue it. They had radio-controlled motors underneath built on a frame and a technician drove them from the side of the stage. Each of the robots had a light inside, so the top part glowed. I also had the PA painted white, which made the whole set look much bigger. The PA company charged me for this colour change and then billed me for the cost of painting it black again, so I wasn't too happy when I saw the PA again, still white, a few months later at Hammersmith Odeon with another band. That's one small example of how we started losing money unnecessarily. My dad, who took over my management during the tour because I didn't have a manager and we didn't trust any of the people who came along to offer their services, was against us spending so much right from the start. However, I'd had these big dreams since I was at school, and now I was playing the role for real, so it was really hard for him to say No, you can't have this and you can't have that. Dad was also aware, despite the big bowl family policy with money, that this money was generated by me and he felt awkward telling me that I couldn't do what I wanted with it. From my point of view I didn't see the huge amount of money pouring out as a problem. I was too lost in realising dreams to see past my nose. I thought the money spent on the tour would make me an even bigger star. The shows would be so spectacular that even the press, clearly hostile towards me, would see the light. The idea of losing £60,000 meant noth-

ing to me. A few months before, losing 60p would have been difficult to recover from and now, well, what on earth did I think I was
doing? It was, I suppose, the folly of youth, the innocence of the
dreamer.

It was so exciting to watch the whole set light up for the first
time. We rehearsed at the Roxy in Harlesden, London. By now I'd
been to many gigs, big arena concerts included, but I thought this
one of the best things I'd ever seen. I would wander around backstage because I could, because I was actually allowed to be there. I
had a pass with my name on it. I would see my name written on
flight cases and it felt good. Everything there, every person, every
piece of equipment, was there because of me. I have never lost that
feeling of how special it is to be doing what we do. To this day when
I'm walking around backstage and I see everything plugged in and
all the technology behind it, just realising it's all there because of me
makes me feel good. I still get a kick out of it. Back then it was
amazing. I went up to all the different keyboard positions and
looked out, loving it. Then, when you hear your music coming out
of a big PA system for the first time, well, it's stunning. That's what
I expected being a pop star to feel like. I was loud, big and lit up like
a God. I was larger than life.

The whole idea behind such an extravagant stage show was that
every night should be an event, not just a concert. Whether it was
the music or the lights, there was something there to entertain
people. I still think it's the best way to do it. It is a tremendous feeling. I hate it when bands become successful, start playing in bigger
venues and have little more than a few coloured lights scattered
around the stage. I couldn't short-change the audience that way, it
would make me feel really cheap. I worked with Alan Wild, the
lighting operator, long into the night, every night, to ensure that
every single beat of every single song was as full as it could be. I
wanted the shows to be a non-stop onslaught of surprises. I wanted
it all to be spectacular.

Walking out on stage at the first Glasgow Apollo gig was very
scary. I could hear the fans going crazy long before we went on. I'd
never been on stage without a guitar before, and now I was being
thrust into the big league and I had to deliver. I remember walking
out and I had no idea what I was going to do when I got to the

microphone. The fact that I didn't dance around and wasn't full of expression was part nerves, part lack of experience and part image. Some of the things the press said about my stage performances, although they missed the point completely in many respects, were not far from the mark in others, I was very wooden, moving awkwardly and without any real flow. It was certainly individual but I'm not sure it was any good. I moved like Jarvis Cocker only with less humour. I knew I had a lot to learn about stagecraft and I felt awkward for some of the tour. Then again, it might have looked a bit weird if I'd come out all loose and thrashy like I am now. Although I look back on those early shows and cringe slightly when I see myself on video, it worked for the audience. Glasgow was coming apart at the seams. You could actually see the balcony moving up and down on what I assumed were hydraulic dampers as the fans danced along to the music. It was genuine pop hysteria and it was everything I'd ever imagined. People were fainting, girls were screaming and crying, people were dressed up like me, same haircut, same clothes, they copied my movements, such as they were, they mimicked my stare, my posturing, everything. It was a truly amazing experience.

Both I and the band were dressed uniformly in black. I had the people with me who played on *The Pleasure Principle*, plus a new guitarist called Rrussell Bell, who could play a very chunky style like mine. It's all about dampening the strings and it's not difficult but, to my amazement, a lot of people couldn't do it when they auditioned. Orchestral Manoeuvres In The Dark supported me, which didn't do them any harm. The Skids were my first choice, because I felt I had an allegiance to them after my last Tubeway Army gig, but they couldn't do it. My next idea was The Normal, because I really liked their single 'TV OD/Warm Leatherette', but the main man Daniel Miller was setting up Mute Records at the time. Funnily enough I saw Depeche Mode in a tiny club a few months later and tried to sign them to Beggars Banquet, but Mute had already got there first. OMD were very good and the tour pretty much launched their career into the big league as well.

During the tour Billie Currie started to talk about getting Ultravox back together and I was all for that. It was a bitter disappointment to me later, after Ultravox reformed and achieved some notable success, to see them slag me off in the press. I sang their praises for a year and I always acknowledged them as an influence at a time when I was one of the biggest artists in the world, and after they had been universally written off by the media. Their new singer, Midge Ure, started running me down in the press, claiming that I'd only praised Ultravox because I'd stolen all their ideas in the first place. This was not only untrue but extremely uncharitable. I felt, with some justification, that I had been instrumental in getting them back into the public eye and to read Midge's comments, especially as he hadn't even been in the band when I was a fan, was upsetting to say the least. He also said that the only reason I had big light shows was to hide behind the lights and they didn't need them because they were in touch with their fans, or some such crap. They went out on tour a few years later with a decent light show themselves and then he said they did it because they owed it to their fans. I never understood why he said those things – but I've not forgotten it. Perhaps some people are able to shake off these things and don't worry about it, but I can't leave them alone. I make it very personal. I'm trying to get over that but it's in my nature.

It had always been my intention to try and create a much friendlier atmosphere amongst the bands than seemed to exist at the time. I thought that if we all acknowledged each other, said a few kind and complimentary words about each other, everyone would benefit. The problem of being hostile towards other bands is, in my opinion, stupid as well as unnecessary. You run the risk of alienating people who might well have been into your music, if you go around rubbishing other bands. It took me some time to get into Bowie when I was a kid because he had said some unpleasant things about Marc Bolan. If we could paint a picture of friendship and mutual respect it would not only create a more pleasant atmosphere, but it could also well encourage some cross band, less partisan support, from the public. It seemed to me that we would all do better by supporting each other. I poured out praise left, right and centre but saw nothing coming back my way, which was disappointing. I would telegram messages of congratulations to newly successful bands, to try and foster a warmer relationship between us all, but it never really went beyond my own efforts. I eventually got fed up with reading some fairly horrible comments from people

I'd praised, congratulated or otherwise acknowledged. Well, not so much fed up as well and truly fucked off, actually. Adam Ant was one of the very few people to ever acknowledge a message and he turned up at the studio one day with a bottle of wine. He knocked it over and spilt the lot on the carpet, but I was grateful to him for the gesture nonetheless.

Initially my mum and dad followed us from venue to venue in their car. At one point I said to them, 'This is stupid, you might as well come on the bus with us.' So they did and that was when my dad took over as my manager. Obviously he had a lot to learn at first, but he took to it like a duck to water. Meanwhile, my mum started looking after all the band's clothes on the tour, just to keep them clean and ironed. If she hadn't done it, I would've had to hire someone, so it made sense to me and she became the tour wardrobe mistress. Having my parents around surprised a few people, but I couldn't have cared less. I needed the jobs that they were doing to be done by someone, so why not them?

On that first tour, which I called 'The Touring Principle', I had to be given a police escort in and out of many of the venues because there were so many people going crazy. In Newcastle there were people dropping off the balcony and climbing on the PA system to get on to the stage. It was so exciting, the places were packed. The security was swamped at every gig, so the road crew would line the front of the stage in an attempt to keep people back. The minder I had at the time was a big, fat man who used to wear tracksuit bottoms without any pants on. I didn't like Mr Dangley very much but he was a hard-looking man. At Coventry people were climbing up the scaffolding on the outside of the building to try to get in the windows. It was incredibly dangerous but they were just fanatical. During the show a side entrance door was broken down and people poured into the venue. A lot of people got on the stage and Mr Dangley, instead of just helping them off, launched into them with a microphone stand. Understandably, the crowd got upset. I saw what he was doing and shouted at him to stop and, to my amazement, he turned sulky and stormed off. Then fights broke out in the crowd and I went mad, screaming my head off at the audience, telling them to calm down. I was so angry. It reminded me of the big fight in the White Hart and I was going to have none of it this time. The next day Simon Bates said on Radio One that I'd run from the stage in tears. It was a complete lie. I remember listening to Capital Radio one day and I was amazed to hear Nicky Home giving me a hard time because I'd apparently gone to a nightclub and refused to sign autographs. He said that I should remember who put me on top and look after my fans better. I could have killed him. I hadn't been to a nightclub and I've never refused an autograph in my life.

The tour was stressful, though. My entire world had turned upside down in just a few months and, although it was an incredible experience, it was a very difficult one to come to terms with. It seems so bizarre to me that people are expected to take fame and success in their stride. No one is given any leeway, any time to adjust to what is a monumentally huge shift in life. We are all supposed to automatically know how to deal with a million and one things, most of them for the first time, automatically. There is no school, no college course, on how to handle fame. You just dive in and then you find out if you can swim. It's a very, very difficult thing to try and explain. People see the money and they just assume that everything is worth it. That nothing can be that bad. To be under pressure, to feel stress, to lose your temper is to be a whining, spoilt, pampered, ungrateful little pop star shit. It doesn't work that way. The adjustment required to go from a normal everyday person to a very famous person, especially if you are a performer, is a demanding transition. The quicker that success occurs, the more difficult and painful that transition is likely to be. So many celebrities have killed themselves, developed drink problems, turned to drugs, or just gone off the rails completely. Money does not compensate for all ills, money can bring problems as well as cure them. It can strip you of trust. Some people handle the onslaught of fame better than others. I thought I was doing quite well because I didn't get big-headed, but that wasn't really the thing to gauge it by. I actually handled it quite badly.

By the end of the tour I was beginning to lose it. I was walking to my hotel room after the final show on the tour when the girl-friend of one of the road crew came up to me. You're shit, she informed me. I'd had that sort of thing every day since 'Are "Friends" Electric?' got into the chart so it wasn't the words that bothered me, it was the reason. I don't walk up to people in the street and say 'I think your shoes are crap'. We all have our opinions but common decency and respect for others means that we keep our feelings to ourselves. Not so if you're famous. Everyone seems to feel completely justified in telling us the most offensive and hurtful things, straight to our face. Why? I don't really know. Because it's assumed that we are surrounded by yes men perhaps, and so they feel we need to be brought down a peg or two. Maybe they think that we are all ego heads and that we love ourselves desperately. Maybe it's because we have, so they think, a great deal of money and so we should put up with anything that the public has to say. They made us, after all, they even own us in a way.

The 'You're shit' woman had a bad effect on me. I had a tantrum, or I just lost my temper, it depended on whether you liked me or not as to how it was seen. I did some damage, not just to the hotel but to myself, too. I punched too many hard things and did my hands no good at all.

Despite the horrible ending to the tour, it had been one of life's more memorable experiences. When we arrived at Hammersmith Odeon, for example, I'd sat in the same seat that I'd been in years before when I'd gone to see Queen and Mott The Hoople. To realise that I was now the man on stage, that people were coming in their thousands to watch me play there was a magical feeling. I donated the money from one of the Odeon Nights to the Save The Whale campaign. I was also given a white Chevrolet Corvette by WEA the afternoon before the final London show, on 28 September, on the understanding I re-signed a new deal with them. At the time I was renegotiating my deal because the original one I had with Beggars Banquet was pretty awful – eight per cent of 90 per cent, and half of that for the rest of the world. You could walk away from a contract like that now. Our lawyer was talking to other companies, just checking out what the rivals were prepared to offer, although we didn't really have any intention of leaving WEA. They heard about his approaches to other labels and thought that I was going to leave. They'd sent Dave Dee from WEA along to see me while we were making the 'Cars' video to see what was up. I had no idea why he was asking me questions. He asked if anything was wrong. I thought of Dave as a friend and so I assumed he was just

Above: Unsafe on primitive three-wheeler requiring mum's help

Above: In the arms of Nan

Above: Uncle Gerald lurking behind me; later at the back for Tubeway Army on drums

Left: Camping out in childhood

Right: Five-year-old suedehead with a buttoned up shirt

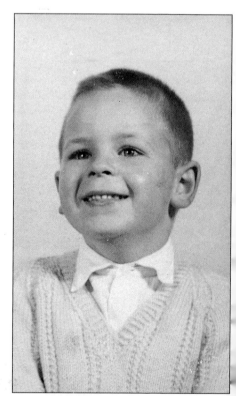

Above: Red hair hints at Bowie roots during a Tubeway Army rehearsal in late 1977

Left: Garry Robson, best mate and "guitarist" on the early TV appearances

Above: Tubeway Army take over *Top of The Pops* when we perform
Are "Friends" Electric?

Below: Applying the Max Factor 28

Above: White light, choreographed "shape" and the pyramid robots Huey & Duey

Left: Cars video, 1979

Above: Beggars Banquet celebrate Gold status for Replicas, as it shifts over 150,000 copies, half of its final UK total. Su Wathan and a bearded Martin Mills stand either side of me. Steve Webbon and disc-carrying Nick Austin are at the far right of the photo.

Below: The corvette, which later appears in video for I Die: You Die

Above: On stage with friend and bassist Paul Gardiner during the 1980 Teletour

Above: Silver lipstick & eyeshadow; tipped Bogart hat; Japanese brooch - Dance image, 1981

Above: Blonde with a Plan

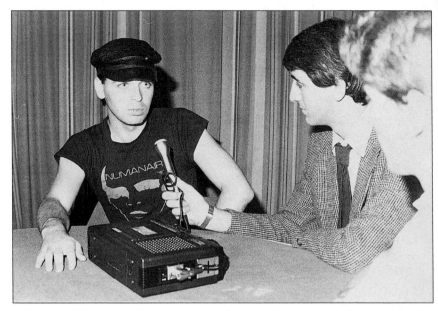

Above: Back at Heathrow airport after the first round-the-world trip ends when I am unofficially arrested for spying in India. The radio journalist asks if the arrest is a "publicity stunt"

Below: 1982 crash near Southampton. The wreckage is officially re-imported into the country by customs

making conversation. At that time no money had come in, so I was still driving around in my dad's old car. I said it felt a bit strange to be so successful, to be selling so many records but to still be poor. It was embarrassing to turn up to various functions in my dad's car. He asked what sort of car would I like and, still thinking it was a minor conversation, I said a Corvette, I'd always dreamed of owning a Corvette. The next day he came back and said 'What colour?' I realised then what it had all been about.

The night after that Hammersmith show Beggars put on a party at a club in Kensington. I wasn't really very interested, to be honest, I just wanted to get out and drive the car. After a while I snuck out, meeting Billy Idol who was coming in, uninvited as usual, but he was always a highly successful gatecrasher. As I went out the door I saw Steve Strange standing outside, unable to get in. He called to me as though he was my bloody friend. I told him to fuck off. A few minutes later I drove past the front of the club in the Corvette and Steve shouted out, 'You're just a fucking bitch.' He got the two-finger salute as I roared my way up Kensington High Street, laughing my head off. Life was good. I was 21, and the whole world had fallen in my lap.

The year ended well with a new single, 'Complex', which reached number six. I was a little disappointed that it didn't get to number one because I loved the song. When they reviewed it on Radio 1's *Roundtable* show they said it was the first ever electronic ballad in the history of pop music. I don't know whether that's true or not, but it was a nice thing to hear. I did feel that it was quite an innovative track, for a ballad, as was the accompanying video, one of the first to use video animation. One thing is for sure, we did release the first ever music video in the New Year, consisting of the 'Cars' promo clip and treated footage from the 'Touring Principle' UK tour. It's a small thing really, but I'm quite proud of the fact we beat Blondie's 'Eat To The Beat' video by a few weeks.

CHAPTER 5

Remind Me to Smile, 1980

My first North American tour started in Toronto Music Hall, Canada, on 18 February 1980. We air-freighted the whole set to America, even the robots came with us. Not only that but over the next few months we flew the entire custom-made structure to Europe, Japan, Australia and New Zealand. It was unbelievably expensive, but I'd just made it big in the charts and I was determined to make the most impressive entrance possible in front of a new, young audience. The American critics were a lot more positive, although they had their moments. One critic said it was the most spectacular show he'd ever seen, but what did it mean? He missed the entire point. You're supposed to leave the theatre, saying 'great show' not wondering what it meant! Big lights, spectacle, have fun, go home. I wasn't trying to educate anyone or change the world, there was no special meaning. At least the Americans were giving me some credit, though. I was losing a small fortune on every concert and yet I would pick up a British music paper and see these caricatures of me running off to the bank, with money falling out of my pocket. The UK music press were the worst in the world. I couldn't understand it because I was a British artist doing something new. I wasn't part of a parochial, little English scene, I was out there with fans all over the world. I would have thought the British press would be proud of me. Britain, through me, was once again at the leading edge of another musical revolution. And yet, after the anti-star sentiments of the punk scene, the stigma of success was still so powerful I was loathed from coast to coast by the music press in my own country.

One of the highlights of my visit to America was our performance on the TV show *Saturday Night Live*. The programme was one of the biggest shown on American TV and went out to an audience of 50 million people. It was not only a live show but you actually played for real, no miming. It was a very daunting prospect to be playing to 50 million people. We did two songs, 'Cars' and a track from the *Replicas* album called 'Praying To The Aliens'. My dressing room was opposite the actor Elliot Gould. The cast of *Saturday Night Live*, which is a sketch-orientated comedy show, read like a *Who's Who* of the decade's major stars; Bill Murray, Dan Akroyd, Gilda Radner. It was brilliant and gave us the biggest boost possible for a new band trying to break the States. After that programme 'Cars' became a big hit and reached number three in the US charts. The album, *The Pleasure Principle*, also did well and sat in the Top 20 for some time.

I turned 22 on 8 March. We played a show at San Francisco's Warfield Theatre that night and one of the crew announced my birthday on stage. The entire audience sang 'Happy Birthday', which brought a lump to the throat. The tour finished the following night at the Los Angeles Santa Monica Civic Center. I had a famous David Bowie bootleg album that had been recorded at the Santa Monica Civic, so just being there was rather epic to me. I loved America, it seemed to welcome success in a way that Britain has never really been able to do. I much preferred the American attitude, it was very refreshing.

The morning after that final show we were thrown out of the hotel. We were at the reception desk checking out so it all seemed a bit pointless to me. As Chris Payne walked past the swimming pool on his way to the exit he was pushed into the pool, which was empty. It bothered no one but the manager became very irate, called us 'English rowdies' and told us to leave. It reminded me of a time when we were banned from a hotel on the south coast of England. Billy Currie had ordered some refreshments after a show and, after waiting a ridiculously long time, walked downstairs, naked from top to bottom, through the busy restaurant and demanded to know 'Where's my fucking room service?'

After America we travelled to Europe for more dates, starting in

Brussels Auditorium Q on 21 March. One of the truck drivers fell from the main lighting truss before the show, landing on his back, and was rushed to hospital. It was a drop of some 30 feet but he eventually made a full recovery. We visited him in hospital the next morning before moving on to Germany, then France.

Shortly after the European Tour ended in France on 29 March, we demo'd some new material for the next album. One of the tracks, 'I Dream Of Wires', ended up on Robert Palmer's 1980 album, *Clues*, along with a co-written track called 'Found You Now'. I knew he was performing versions of 'Cars' and 'Me I Disconnect From You' at his gigs so I was very flattered when he invited Paul Gardiner and myself to drop by his home in the Bahamas, on our way to some promotional duties in Japan. He put us up in the house next to his, both of which were conveniently located only a few yards from the studio. The sea came right up to the back wall of the terrace, and the spot was very beautiful. Over the next three days I did all my writing for his album armed with an acoustic guitar and a cassette player and I found it surprisingly easy to work with him, probably because I didn't actually write *with* him. He played me a couple of songs that he had been working on and asked me to come up with ideas for them, and left me to it. I taped my ideas, he took them off to the studio and fiddled with them for a while, then we went over the songs together. One track, 'Style Kills', didn't make it onto the album but it still keeps popping up on his B-sides and compilations. It's a shame I didn't write with other people after that but, increasingly, I went back into my shell and abandoned contact with the music world. My lack of confidence, rather than improving after all the success, actually got worse. I found it hard to imagine working with other people. I assumed my music was only really suitable for me and that my contribution to any collaboration wouldn't be worthwhile.

My Far East tour got underway in Japan on 2 May 1980. We sold out three dates in Tokyo, one in Osaka and one in Nagoya. They were all in 2,000-3,000 seater theatres, so I'd achieved a very healthy position for a Western artist. Japanese fans are the most organised in the world. They know the room you're staying in before you even check in to the hotel. On several occasions they had the room key before I did. The Japanese women were very keen and not the shy, demure creatures I'd expected. I sampled my first threesome with a couple of Japanese girls on that trip – which was something of a sexual milestone at the time. Japan made a big impression on me and I happily strolled around Tokyo at night with full make-up on and no one bothered me. However, sometimes their manners were a little too formal for me and made me feel awkward and self-conscious. When I met the Japanese electronic band Yellow Magic Orchestra they were so solemn. They all bowed and didn't smile at all, which made it hard to break the ice. I couldn't think of a single word to say to them apart from a mumbled hello.

The Japanese audiences were different to anything else I'd experienced. Rules about not standing up in the venues were very strictly enforced and so everyone stayed seated. I wasn't used to that. Normally people went berserk as soon as the house lights went down. Also, at the end of each song, they clap very loudly but only for a few seconds. I was told that this is because they want to hear what you say clearly, so that they have a better chance of understanding it. I don't really talk between songs so all they got from me was an awkward silence. I enjoyed playing in Japan though, and came away from the country wanting to go back as soon as possible.

The next leg of the tour was to New Zealand where we played dates in Auckland, Christchurch and Wellington between May 12-15. As soon as we arrived in Auckland the atmosphere darkened. I was shocked when I spotted anti-Gary Numan graffiti painted on walls on the trip from the airport to the hotel. I'd travelled over 12,000 miles, to the other side of the world, and I was getting the same stick that I got at home. One spray-painted wall declared, 'Numan is not Bowie' and another one read, 'Numan Go Home'. When we arrived at the hotel Cedric Sharpley was hassled by locals, who thought he was black. We decided to go out to a club with the road crew as we had no show to play that night. We weren't in the club very long when the DJ started being offensive about me. A girl came up to me and asked if what she'd read in the NME was true, so I soon found out where this little seed of hostility had come from. I said no, you shouldn't believe everything you read but she said, 'We have to believe it, it's all we have.' As she moved away cans started to fly across the room at us. There were quite a few of us in there but the mood was so ugly the tour manager herded us outside as quickly as possible. As we made our way outside skinheads from the club followed us and chased us down the street. I couldn't believe it. We'd only been in the country for a couple of hours. Outside the venue of the first show there was a religious group handing out leaflets to people which said, 'You've heard Gary Numan's ideas on God. Now hear the truth.' They'd obviously taken great care over these little pamphlets, because they analysed my lyrics and quoted from British rock magazines. This group claimed I was a demon, which surprised me because I hadn't taken a particularly anti-stance on religion at that point. To be honest, I thought this fanatical reaction was quite cool, at least I was making an impression.

Naturally, after this reception, I was a little wary about the reaction I was going to get from the crowd. I was even more unsettled when I saw just how primitive some of the locally rented equipment was. At one point everything just went off. The PA, the lights, instruments, everything. The crew were running around like headless chickens trying to figure out what had happened. It turned out a fire alarm on the outside of the building had been set off, automatically cutting the power to the gig. It took about 20 minutes to fix and we were left in almost total darkness. To fill the time I brought on a roadie who had a talent for balancing things on his head. I went on stage and shone a torch on him for a while as a makeshift spotlight. That inevitably ran its time and then Cedric launched into a drum solo, which kept them quiet for a while longer. I then came back on and asked if anyone knew any jokes and people were beginning to shout things out when the lights came back on. The crowd warmed to us after that and the gig was a great success. Paul Gardiner continued to provide most of the offstage anecdotes. Paul always reversed the charges when he phoned his wife because he claimed he never had any money. He phoned her up from New Zealand and we all left him to it because they were forever arguing. About two hours later a group of us peered through the open door as we walked past his room and saw Paul slumped on the bed. There was this small, angry voice on the phone screaming his name. It was his wife. They'd argued, as usual, Paul had got fed up and instead putting the phone down, he'd just placed it to one side and fallen asleep. He did this three or four times on that first world tour, and when we got back his wife sent us the phone bill for hundreds of pounds.

After New Zealand we headed off to Australia where we played nine excellent shows. Australia was a more pleasant experience than New Zealand had been, but Paul still had his own unique way of approaching problems. He used to like a few drinks before a show to help him relax a bit. In Australia he drank an entire bottle of tequila before we went on. I don't know much about drink but I'm told that tequila doesn't affect you straight away. Paul just thought it was a crap drink and carried on swigging from the bottle until it was all gone. He stepped onto the stage feeling warm and relaxed and then the lights, and the heat, hit him. In the first song I swaggered down to the front, a sneer cutting across my face as I played the big rock star, when suddenly I heard this strange banging noise. I half turned, trying to be cool, and out of the corner of my eye I glimpsed this shape going past me. It was Paul, completely out of control. He was falling forward at a 45-degree angle and running blindly towards the front of the stage, all the time hitting notes randomly on his bass. I was sure he was going to drop right off the stage when his guitar lead suddenly reached its full stretch and jerked him backwards. Now he was unbalanced in the other direction and I just stood and watched as he hurtled backwards, arms flailing like a possessed windmill into his gear, which rocked back and forth with roadies desperately trying to grab it before the whole lot went over. Then the crew turned him off and I remember watching my dad's arm coming from behind the curtain, grabbing him by the neck and pulling him off stage so quickly that his feet hardly touched the ground. It was just like watching a cartoon. Another classic Paul Gardiner story also occurred a few days later. One night he decided his legs were sore from all the gigging so he completely smothered them in Deep Heat before we went on stage. The stage lights were really hot and within moments of him walking on he started hopping around screaming, 'My legs are on fire, my legs are on fire.' He was in absolute agony so he pulled his trouser waistband forward and poured a pint of beer down there to cool his legs. It immediately poured out of the bottom of his trousers and the crew was running around desperately trying to mop it up because of all the electrical gear. This went on in front of about 3,000 people. Paul's other strange quirk was to go

87

missing. You'd normally find him asleep in a flight case with the lid shut. He was so much in his own little world he would often wander off and get lost. We loved him.

My next single, 'We Are Glass', was released the week we came back from Australia. I'd written the song about how I felt in the wake of my success. Fragmented, transparent, hard, brittle, cold, sharp and just about ready to break apart into a thousand pieces. I re-introduced a heavy, choppy guitar riff to this new song, because I was interested in blending different sounds and instruments together. Synthesisers had become accepted very quickly, and within a year of 'Are "Friends" Electric?' it seemed as though every-one had one. After all the song and dance about them it was no longer valid to stand next to a keyboard and say, Look at me, I'm different because I use a synthesiser.

The BBC banned the video for 'We Are Glass' because they argued that I was promoting violence by destroying TV sets with a sledgehammer. I can't believe people are that easily led, that stupid. I just couldn't see how that video would encourage people to pick up a sledgehammer and smash their television to pieces. I'd like to credit the public with more intelligence than that. The video also had lasers and several very cool props. I liked it, it's probably one of the best videos I ever made. However, I was still extremely self-conscious when I made it. At one point I had to clear everybody out of the building, apart from the director and cameraman, because I just couldn't handle people watching. Again, it's a difficult thing to explain, I could go on stage in front of thousands and have no prob-lems, but I found it virtually impossible to film some simple miming in front of a small film crew. Often situations that appear to be simi-lar are actually very different and it's small things that can swing it one way or the other. The proximity of people, eye contact, expres-sions even. I find that the bigger the event, the more people there are, the less personal it becomes and the better I feel. 'We Are Glass' reached number five in the UK charts, which was okay with me. On the B-side was an electronic cover of Eric Satie's 'Trois Gymnopedies', a piece of music that I'd loved all of my life.

'I Die You Die', which came out on 30 August, was a straight-forward statement to the British press. The press had come at me so hard, so aggressively and without a single pause for breath that

I felt very hostile towards them. I didn't think, still don't, that I deserved a fraction of the scorn, ridicule and abuse they fired at me. 'Are "Friends" Electric?' sold a million copies in the UK alone, so what could I have done that was so terrible? How could the song be as horribly offensive as they claimed? It seemed to me, and this was the reason for writing 'I Die You Die', that they needed new stars as much as we needed them. We were the bread to their butter, for people as big as me sold papers, sold magazines. Every time they had a go at me they lost sales to people who liked me, and there were a lot of people who liked me. I thought that such severe hostility towards performers in general made the business bloody depressing. Everything you read, about virtually everybody, was bitching and sarcastic. I got it the worst but it was pretty much the same story across the board.

The single climbed to number six shortly before the release of a new album, *Telekon*, which went straight in to the album chart at number one in September. The word Telekon is taken from telekenisis and has nothing to do with British Telecom. BT, then named the GPO, changed their name to British Telecom just as the album came out. To this day people call it the Telecom album.

The lyrical content of the album has nothing to do with telekenisis, I just liked the sound of it. On the cover of 'I Die You Die' and *Telekon* I wore a leather jumpsuit that I'd found in a shop in Kensington called Reflections. I came up with the idea of the parallel red belts from a roadwork sign in Germany and I also incorporated the design into the cover artwork and tour T-shirts. The final touch was a streak of red dye in my hair. On the *Telekon* sleeve I'm holding a silver object which looks vaguely like a weapon of some kind. It's actually a tube from my mum's Hoover, the ends were airbrushed so you couldn't tell it was hollow.

I didn't include either 'We Are Glass' or 'I Die You Die' on the vinyl version of the album. I had a surplus of new songs and I wanted to give the fans the best possible value for their money. It probably wasn't the smartest thing to do as it made the album less attractive to people who weren't part of my hardcore fanbase and bought everything, people who hadn't bought the singles but went straight for the album, expecting them to be on it. However, I didn't give it that much thought at the time. Within a couple of weeks

Telekon was certified Gold in the UK, with sales of 150,000. This was outwardly very impressive, but in fact the album only sold, at best, about half as many as either of the previous two.

I recorded the bulk of the album at Rock City Studios, Shepperton. By this time I'd set up my own publishing company, Numan Music, and we had also started the Gary Numan Fan Club, which was run by my mother. I thought it was nice for the fans to have direct contact with my family but it was an enormous amount of work for my poor old mum to take on. Musically I felt *Telekon* was a big step forward from *The Pleasure Principle*, with the guitars back to add a rawness that had been missing on that album, and a new level of production and writing.

Telekon is extremely dark and introspective in places, and the whole album has a very doomy, almost oppressive, feel to it. This was my first new album after the success, so, rather than fantasising about life as a pop star, I now wrote about it from a position of real knowledge. The reality that I found myself in was a thousand times worse than I had ever imagined. I felt battered. Scarred inside and out, I was struggling to keep it all together. The album is a clear example of a young man, whose dream had turned swiftly into a nightmare, trying to make sense of it all, trying to reason out loud. It was not, despite having some punchy, driving tracks, easy listening. It was a much darker experience than anything I had written before.

I already wanted to stop the constant round of touring and promotion, just to be normal again. As I was writing the album I slowly began to make the decision that the *Telekon* tour would be the last of my career. In particular I was very hurt and offended by the press. I used to read the music papers religiously before I became famous, so I knew they could be savage. However I'd never come across anything quite as hostile as the reception I was getting. I couldn't see what I'd done to warrant it. One of the worst things a journalist wrote was that my mum and dad should have been doctored for giving birth to me. One paper portrayed me as a 'fat white grub', another as a skinny, spotty nerd. They said I couldn't sing, I couldn't write songs, I couldn't produce. Although it was hard for them to criticise the lightshows, they still twisted it so I was made out to be this lofty super-ego trying to elevate myself above 'the fans'. Either that or they trashed the concerts for being empty, old-fashioned 'showbusiness', which was still a dirty word in the wake of punk. I became successful without any real support from the press and reached number one before I was ever interviewed. Possibly that irritated a lot of music journalists. The other thing that the press did that I found unforgivable was to accuse the fans of being brain-dead for liking me.

Synthesisers too took a lot of stick. They were cold, a monkey could play them, people didn't make music any more because the machines did everything, etc, etc, etc. When the Musicians' Union tried to ban synths and claimed that I was putting musicians out of business I was baffled. I couldn't believe they honestly thought a young band with a limited budget on a tiny indie label who wanted a string part would call up the Royal Philharmonic Orchestra or a string quartet instead of plugging a synthesiser into a basement studio in Soho. We were producing similar effects but in a new way. I didn't put anyone out of work who was any good.

It didn't take long for the press to turn me into a laughing stock. I became the sort of artist people are embarrassed to ask for in a shop. When I was young I wouldn't have been seen dead buying a Bay City Rollers record, even if I'd loved them, because my mates would have given me a hard time. That's what the media did to me. You can't endure that much hostility for too long without it damaging you somewhere along the line. Being un-cred can really hurt careers, it takes away the fringe buyers, the casual browser – and they form a big part of any album's sales. Their attacks made the hard core harder but took away everybody else. It took away any chance of support or kind comment that might have come my way from other artists. I heard of one writer who wrote a reasonably good review of *Telekon* and was barracked so much by other writers he rewrote the review, before the magazine was printed, and slammed the album. People were actually pressured to write bad reviews and to constantly dig and snipe at me, even if they didn't fully agree with the point of view.

All this actually had an effect on my everyday life. I felt embarrassed when I was out and about because I thought people would have read so much rubbish about me. Becoming famous is the ultimate justification for my natural paranoia. Even a trip to the petrol garage was difficult. I felt extremely defensive and awkward when the petrol pump attendant looked at me. I expected everyone to have something to say. I withdrew almost completely from the business. I stopped giving interviews, I stopped sending records out for review and I definitely decided that I would quit touring once the *Telekon* tour was over. After little more than a year, I'd had enough. It wasn't just the press or the public, with all the death threats that seem to go hand in hand with success, it was the job itself. A year before I had been sitting at my battered old piano, trying to think of stuff, and now my hobby was big business. People talked about records as units, I was product. I found the phenomenal pace of touring with its wall to wall promotion, endless rounds of interviews and back to back gigging schedule to be counterproductive when it came to writing. I couldn't write on the road, I was getting behind in my recording commitment to the label, I didn't have time to write and record new songs at my previous rate. I wanted to step back, I wanted to make it a hobby again, I wanted it all to slow down and back off.

Since *Telekon* was put together with all this going on in my head, it's not surprising that it seems a little heavy lyrically. The first line of the opening song, 'This Wreckage', reads, 'So what if God's dead', which was part tongue-in-cheek about the way I was seen by some people. I was referred to as a demi-god by someone quite early on, so I was playing around with the idea of pop stars being seen as gods. I certainly didn't think *I* was one, a criticism levelled at me after its release. It was also a clear dig at God. 'The Wreckage' was as close to a self-portrait as I could get. The Japanese lyrics on the song said, 'I leave you'. A Japanese girl, who I went out with briefly, spelled out the characters for me. I was already sure that I was finished with touring so it was a disguised way of saying goodbye to the fans, long before I announced it for real.

The entire album is full of confusion, disappointment and paranoia. It makes repeated references to leaving, to being used. The title track is particularly dark. I remember being in a nightclub in Japan one time and they played *Telekon* because I was there. They'd obviously spotted me, run out and bought the album and stuck on the title track because they thought, Oh, that's got to be a good one. I was so embarrassed when this dirgey, world weary thing came on the PA and emptied the dancefloor in seconds. I scurried away as quickly as possible. 'Remind Me To Smile' is also about being famous and reflects my reaction to it. The line 'We could remind ourselves that we must laugh' summed up how false, how unnatural it had all become. 'Keep all your fantasies, that's all we are' was another. 'The Aircrash Bureau' is a supernatural horror story about a pilot who was killed during the D-Day invasion of World War Two. He comes back to warn people before they fly if their aeroplane is about to have an accident. 'Sleep By Windows' is about the fans. Right from the start they were quite extreme but it didn't seem strange to me when they started dressing in my images, because I used to do it. The lookalike fans have taken a lot of ridicule which I consider totally undeserved. If you go to a heavy metal concert or a rave, you will see people dressing the same because it's a way of being identified with something. The only difference is that my fans dress as a particular person, me, while others dress in a style or a genre. I really don't see any difference. It adds something to their evening. I find football fans who wear their team's strip on the terraces far more bizarre, although it's the same principle at work: it makes a statement, it says something about them, it says what they like, what they support. Also, it's often that they just happen to like the look. It might be partly why they're into me in the first place. I don't believe many soccer enthusiasts honestly like their team's strip as a fashion statement, but somehow wearing a lurid green shirt with a big advertiser's logo emblazoned across it is socially acceptable.

I do have my hardcore followers, who can be a little eccentric. There's one man who, for 15 years, always stood at the front of my gigs with his arms folded. He'd studied a picture where I'm stand-ing with folded arms looking moody, and he wouldn't move a muscle for the whole show. We went to Brussels to do a gig and there he was on the boat, walking about. I'd never seen him actu-ally move before. We've only recently got him out of the habit, but he's a perfectly normal person when you speak with him. That's a little extreme but not seriously weird. I remember going to a Gary Glitter concert when I was younger and there was a man there dressed in a silver jumpsuit, who imitated his hero's every single movement about half a second late. I thought then, that's a bit strange, but he was obviously enjoying himself. This form of adulation has been around pop music since the beginning and I enjoy it.

I have another fan who, if she's on form, will arrive at the gigs with a set of handcuffs, one handcuff on her wrist and the other one open. When I stroll down to the front of the stage she'll have her handcuffed hand out, inviting me to touch her fingers and, as soon as I do, she'll whip her other arm round and try to handcuff me. She never brings the key with her so if she succeeded that would be the end of the show. So far her only victims have been fellow fans. The police have had to be called on several occasions after she's handcuffed herself to some poor unsuspecting man that she's taken a fancy to.

There are some fans, though, who can't differentiate between fantasy and reality. I think all artists attract their fair share of people who are a little unstable. It doesn't matter whether you're Gary Numan or Jon Bon Jovi. One girl, who was actually kept in a mental home after throwing acid in someone's face, thought she was married to me. She would send me letters talking about how good our life would be together when she got out. She escaped once and the hospital phoned us to warn us. I was living with someone at the time, so God knows what she would have done if she'd found out that 'her husband' was living with someone else. Luckily she was recaptured fairly quickly, but it was a bit scary. However most fans are happy with a rummage through your dustbin or stealing flowers from the garden. It's an irritation at times, but harmless.

I thought of the track, 'I'm An Agent', when I woke up one morning in a flat that I had in Ealing. I was dreaming it and woke up singing the line, 'we are clean, don't ask, I'm an agent', ran to the telephone and sang it down the line to a friend, as I didn't have a tape recorder and I didn't want to forget it. The line in the song, 'send in dreams, lovers on corners, clean my sheets' refers to all the girls. There were lots of girls. When I first started touring I was quite shy about the whole sex thing. I would take girls down to breakfast in the morning and be almost apologetic for sleeping with them. After a while you get more used to it and you approach things a little differently. Very differently. I stopped feeling bad about it. Everything took some getting used to, even that. I was not a good man to go out with. I was up one minute, down the next, and horribly unfaithful. 'Secretaries, nothing more, you can be replaced you know' is a reference to Su Wathan, the girl who worked at Beggars. I was very unfair to Su and she did not deserve such childish comments. We'd had a casual relationship on and off for some time and we were good friends. She had been close to me long before success came along. As soon as I started touring I slept around a lot and made no secret of it. However, when we arrived in Canada in early 1980, she began seeing the tour manager, I threw a complete wobbly and got very upset. I was a hypocrite from top to bottom, double standards poured from my mouth, and it was truly pathetic. I had been through it all with Su. At the end of the Glasgow Apollo concert in 1979, she was the first person to come up to me from the side of the stage. She was with me when I signed my very first autograph. She was a brilliant friend and I very much regret the way it ended.

'I Dream Of Wires' is pure science fiction. Philip K. Dick's masterpiece *Do Androids Dream Of Electric Sheep* was the starting point for it. The song outlines the thoughts of the last electrician on earth, who is looking back nostalgically at better days, when he was known as 'The Sparkle'. 'Remember I Was Vapour' was written specifically for the fans, reminding them I am human and that all the things that hurt them, will hurt me. All the things they need, I need. I wrote 'Please Push No More' about quitting touring but it's written as though the final moment has just happened. I was trying to imagine how it would feel the moment after I'd played my last song.

The UK 'Teletour' ran from 4-29 September and included four nights at the Hammersmith Odeon in London. Every night was sold out but I still lost over £100,000. I used the light panel idea again, but this time they were redesigned into new square shapes. The stage set consisted of two hexagonal cages for the keyboard players at the front, both clad in the new panels, and raised platforms for the other band members with ramps at the front. Paul Gardiner used to find it a bit tricky getting up his ramp for some reason, during rehearsals he kept getting halfway up and then falling back down again. We put sticky bits on them to help him walk up but he usually stopped halfway, went down on his knees and crawled up. He hated it. We also fitted other panels together to form a giant T-shape at the back of the stage. On this tour I introduced a little spacey looking vehicle that I would drive around in which was actually built around the frame and motors of a wheelchair. I thought it would be cool to move around as if I was hovering in the dry ice, since I've always liked stage sets with different levels and moving objects coming out of the ground or from above. So, on the 'Teletour', we built up the atmosphere with a very pretty, delicate piano introduction for the song 'Down In The Park', then the bass synths kicked in and I emerged, in the car, from under the drum riser into a wall of dry ice and smoke with dazzling white lights behind it. It was all quite dramatic. People have made fun of the car since, and I can understand that but, at the time, the crowd went ballistic. I could steer it with this little joystick in the middle, a couple of switches on the side controlled a pair of lights at the front and I used a radio microphone for the vocals. I used to glide across the stage, then spin round and round in tight circles so the lights would scan across the set and the audience. The really awkward part was steering it back under the drum riser at the end of the song. I missed the entrance and crashed into the riser itself a couple of times.

I would come up with bigger and ever more elaborate ideas for the shows all the time and, because I had the money to do whatever I wanted, I was never really calmed down, not for quite a few years anyway. Some of the ideas were good, some weren't. The car was a big success but we hardly used the 'Teletour' radio-controlled robot, Big Al. Al was a monolithic, black perspex box with a light on the top and a full size mannequin inside him. He was over six feet tall and looked great but the problem was when you turned the motor on he would shoot off at a tremendous rate, rocking backwards and forwards. He was close to toppling over the whole time and we just couldn't risk using him. Several thousand pounds wasted there then. I also had two black radio-controlled cubes, each with a mannequin head inside which lit up. They'd glide down to the front of the stage and spin left and right; less ambitious than Al but they worked well. At the right moment the heads, unseen behind the dark perspex until the lights came on, would light up. It was meant to be moody but I don't think it ever had the desired effect. People used to giggle at them most of the time. We used 22 different synthesisers on the 'Teletour' – a couple of Poly-Moogs and an Arp Odyssey in each keyboard tower, plus other bits and pieces for me, for Rrussell, Paul and even Cedric had some keyboards to play. I was paranoid about them breaking down so I had extra synths as back-up, just in case. The old analogue synths were pretty unreliable, so we had a permanent crew member whose job was to fix the synths every night. That's all he did, fix them, and he was kept busy. The support act on the 'Teletour' was a Canadian artist, Nash The Slash. I had come across him when we played in Toronto earlier that year. Someone said, 'You've got to come to this club, there's this violinist who performs in bandages'. Sure enough, there were all these netty, camouflaged drapes around this small character in a white suit, top hat, dark glasses with his face wrapped in bandages. He would jam the keys down on his synthesiser with match packs to hold chords and then he'd start to play violin or mandolin over the top. He was brilliant, and I thought he was perfect for a support act. I took him on the road with me there and then, cancelled all the other support bands, which was a bit unprofessional, looking back, and took Nash instead. It was funny when we met him afterwards. Nash is quite small, a bit dumpy and he was losing his hair even back then. He's a very happy-faced bloke but he'd developed a manic onstage mystery persona. I asked Nash why he had put together that particular image and he said that he was never going to get anywhere on looks so this was the answer. I spoke to him recently for the first time in years. He's still going, still totally off the wall.

I was much happier with my own performances on the 'Teletour'. Although I still had much to learn I was a little more animated than on the first tour and less wooden. I used the stage better and, in general, looked a little bit more like I belonged there. Even so, I was still uncomfortable and it didn't change my mind about quitting live work at the end of the tour.

On 14 October I opened a 19-date North American tour at the Toronto Maple Leaf Gardens. The American record company, Atco, didn't want us over again so soon with another new album. They had advised us that *The Pleasure Principle* still had plenty of sales in it and it would make more sense to let them concentrate on that. However WEA in the UK were keen to squeeze in more sales before the end of 1980 and I didn't know any better, so I thought it would be best to push on and really go for it. I was keen to see the new stuff come out as quickly as possible. Career-wise these were suicidal decisions. *Telekon* crept in at number 64 on the US charts, killing *The Pleasure Principle* stone dead. Not only that but the American record company were upset with us, so they hardly made any promotional effort with the new album. My decision to quit touring, and to say so loudly at every opportunity, only alienated them further, and the tour promoters were furious with me. I not only killed the biggest market in the world for Gary Numan music, I was also going through money like water. We lost another £60,000 on the American shows, despite some limited tour support from the record company.

My slightly improved confidence on-stage helped to make it a smooth, largely enjoyable tour although it had its share of bizarre moments. I arrived at a soundcheck one day at about five o'clock and discovered nothing was ready. By this time the set should have been completely built and the sound and lights ready to go. It turned out we were caught in a dispute between two unions, representing the electricians and the props departments. These two men couldn't decide whether the car should be lifted on stage by the electrician, as it was electrically powered, or by the other man, because it was a prop, albeit motorised. They finally resolved this brain-numbing problem by one of them picking up the back end and the other holding the front, as they carefully lowered it onto the stage at the same time. Then another problem reared its union head. Who was going to drive it during the show? I was forbidden because it was a prop and, as it was electrically powered, the electrician also had to be involved. They eventually came up with a scheme, quite brilliant in a way providing being clinically brain-dead was a virtue, whereby the props man, for a suitable fee slipped into his back pocket, would stand at the side of the stage and not touch it while the electrician sat inside the vehicle with me in his lap. They were completely serious about this. Eventually, I had to bribe both men to stand at the side of the stage while I drove the car. I must admit that it didn't exactly endear me to union culture, even if this was in America.

I made some fairly stupid decisions myself while I was in the States. On one occasion I had been to a show on Broadway, to see Bowie in the *Elephant Man* and afterwards found it hard to get a cab. So I walked back to the hotel, in full make-up, through one of the hardest parts of New York. For someone so careful and alert at any other time it was an incredibly dumb thing to do. Nothing happened but people were horrified the next day when I mentioned it. Paul Gardiner created another top story the day he found that he was running low on headache pills. He was a very lovable man, but a bit of a hypochondriac who always carried a bag full of tablets for one ailment or another. So he phoned reception to say he needed more pills and they completely misunderstood him. I guess his slow, London accent was hard for them to decipher and they just heard the word, 'pills'. As he was in a band they assumed he was phoning for help after an overdose and instantly dialled 911 for the emergency services. Within minutes a Medivac helicopter landed in the hotel car park and an ambulance screeched to a halt in front of the lobby doors with its sirens blaring. A team of paramedics sprinted into the hotel with axes ready to break down the door of this OD'd musician. By now the commotion had got everybody outside. I watched in amazement as the axe-wielding medic went straight for Paul's door. Paul also heard the commotion, a bit later than everybody else as was his way in these things, opened the door in his Y-fronts and saw a man coming towards him with an axe. He was still holding the empty bottle in his hand and he waved it at them, saying, 'No man, you've got it wrong, I've run out and I want some more.' The emergency services really tore into him about wasting their time but it wasn't his fault at all.

Shortly after the US tour ended on 12 November, I decided to put out 'This Wreckage' as a single. It was a very poor choice for a single and did nowhere near as well as previous tracks, only just scraping into the Top 20. I think I was trying to make a statement. I was sowing the seeds of the big goodbye.

In addition to performing 'This Wreckage' on *Top Of The Pops* I was supposed to be doing 'I Die You Die' on the *Kenny Everett Christmas Show*. It was an excellent and very important show to be on as the ratings were massive. The programme's director was a man called David Mallet, who also directed many of David Bowie's videos at the time. After I'd recorded my bit for the show, Mallet told me that Bowie was going to be there the following Thursday and did I want to come along and watch? I turned up a week later, very excited and a little nervous, to watch the great man in action. There was a little side room which I stood at the back of, well out of the way, behind Bob Geldof and Paula Yates, and a reasonable group of other people whom I didn't recognise. I was very intimidated by the whole thing. I'd only been famous myself for a short time so I was still completely in awe of famous people. Bowie started performing his track and then suddenly everything stopped. A whispered discussion with Mallet followed and then Mallet came over, took me to one side, and said that Bowie had seen me and it would be better if I left. So I was thrown out which, apart from being extremely embarrassing, was really quite sad because I was a huge Bowie fan. Then, a few days after that, I was taken off the Christmas Special as well and I ended up on a normal Kenny Everett show a couple of months later. I was told at the time that Bowie's hold on Mallet had ensured that I was taken off the programme. I was stunned by the whole affair. That a man so huge in stature, practically a living legend, would be so insecure about a new pretender like me was very disappointing. I had expected him to be far above any of that. He seemed so much older than me, so much more at ease with things, firmly established. It surprised me to find out that he was just as racked with insecurities as I was, as anybody else.

I've now been around a long time and I don't get upset when I see people selling more records than I do – just as well really as most people are selling more than me at the moment. It's the nature of the business, we do well, we don't do well, we just do what we can. I've seen hundreds of people come and go since I first made it. You just have to fight for your own career. The success of other artists very rarely has any bearing on your own career, the success of others is nothing to be scared of. I had expected Bowie to be more mature but then again he was younger then than I am now, and I still have a way to go on the maturity front, so I don't really blame him any more. It was all part of growing up for both of us, I suppose. He also had a dig at me in the music press. He said something along the lines of, what I did, I did very well, but he'd already done it on his *Man Who Sold The World* album. I read also that the line 'Same old thing in brand new drag' on the *Scary Monsters* album is about me. Who knows? Who really cares? After

Kenny Everett, I didn't give a shit one way or the other. He was as scared as I was.

His friend, Mick Jagger, said that he hated me, which I thought was a bit strong. Another friend of Bowie's, Brian Eno, wasn't too kind either. He said that, for somebody, me, who had three albums in the album chart you would expect there to be a little bit more going on. It seemed as though the old guard were getting a little upset with me. At first I was very disappointed, not with Jagger – whom I had considered sad for years – but with the other two. After a while it helped to make me feel as though I was part of a new generation. They no more understood what I was doing than people had understood them when they were new, before they became part of the rock monarchy, the respected elder statesmen.

Happier memories. I finally got my pilot's licence on 1 December 1980. I'd actually started flying lessons in October '78 but had to abandon the course, with only two written exams to go, because of the success of 'Are "Friends" Electric?' and the workload that came with it. Apart from a few trips in October '79 I wasn't able to get back and finish the course until November 1980. I'd had no real problems with the course and had gone solo quickly. My biggest fright came during my spin training. With little warning as to what was coming the instructor put the aeroplane into a spin in the most dramatic fashion. Up went the nose, over and down, round and round we spun, dropping towards the earth like a stone. Everything blurred and I couldn't help myself as my arms and legs flew out in all directions. I cracked the instructor on the head, my shins on the control panel. It took several seconds to calm down. With the lessons now successfully completed I was qualified to fly single engine aircraft, and on 18 December I bought my first plane, a four-seater Cessna 182. I was so excited I would go down to the airfield at night and sit quietly in the cockpit. I couldn't believe it. This was actually my own aeroplane.

CHAPTER 6

I Leave You, 1981

For a while, I became a big fan of the band Japan. I loved their *Gentlemen Take Polaroids* album when it came out in 1980. A woman called Connie Fillapello, who was doing Japan's publicity, had started bringing them along to some of my 'Teletour' gigs. We had a lot of pictures taken together, which I think was done to get them noticed more than anything else, but that was cool with me because I liked their music and wished them well. I went out with them a lot. David Sylvian and I talked about writing together but it never happened. However, at the end of 1980 their bass player, Mick Karn, joined me for some of my next album sessions while Japan's ex-guitarist Rob Dean also guested on one of the new tracks.

While we were hanging out together they vaguely invited me to guest with them on their Japanese tour at the turn of 1980–81. it was an informal arrangement and they were supposed to call me when they arrived in the country, because I was already in Japan. I was surprised when I didn't hear anything, especially when I found out they were in Tokyo. I saw a poster advertising one of their shows for the following night. I managed to locate their hotel by ringing around and I met them there the following morning while they were having breakfast. They seemed surprised to see me and there wasn't much conversation so I felt a bit awkward. Then they said they were going to get ready, so off they went to their rooms, leaving me sitting in a breakfast room. Suddenly I noticed them running out of a side door of the hotel and climbing into some wait-ing cars. I was so naïve it pains me to think about it. Could I have been any more dense? I thought they must be stressed about the gigs and they'd *forgotten* me. I had a minder who used to look after me and so we followed them to the station. Once there we bought our own tickets and sat on the train with them, but there was no real conversation. They were fairly big stars in Japan and so there were a lot of fans waiting when we got off. We got in our own cab again and followed theirs to the gig where we were briefly shown into the backstage area before I was made to go out into the theatre. I thought, all right, they want some privacy. I watched them soundcheck from out front but no one invited me onstage to work out what we were going to perform together. Right up until the theatre doors opened I assumed it was all still going to happen. When the doors opened a roadie very kindly came out and said, 'You'd better come around the back because the audience is coming in.' I watched the show from the side of the stage, they came off, walked straight past me and away they went. Go figure.

Anyway, what to do next? I noticed that Queen were playing at the Bodokan in Tokyo so I bought some tickets and went to see them. I had been sitting in the audience for a while when a strange commotion started. People were standing up and looking around. I couldn't see what was going on so I stood up and started looking around as well. Then I realised that they were all looking at me. I was amazed. Brilliant as it was, I had to get out of there quickly as things were beginning to get out of hand. The concert security came over and took me backstage. Japan were doing small theatres and behaving as if they were the biggest thing in the world, yet Queen, who were playing to more people on one night than Japan's whole tour, were totally down to earth. I met up with Roger Taylor backstage and he was great. What a difference. When they found out what had happened with Japan they adopted me for the next few days until I went back to England. Wherever they went they took me with them. Freddie Mercury was one of the funniest people I've ever met in my life. Every inch of Freddie Mercury was made to be a rock star and he seemed to love every second of it. He was very entertaining, full of stories and everyone loved him. One night they went to a sushi bar. I did my best but I hated sushi so Freddie asked me what I wanted. I said, jokingly, a McDonald's.

Next thing I know a big limo turns up and out of it pops a man with a McDonald's burger and chips. Freddie pacifies the restaurant manager and so I find myself sitting with Queen in a sushi house eating McDonald's in Tokyo.

I told them I'd been to see them when they supported Mott The Hoople and when they first headlined at the Rainbow. I also mentioned having to use the fiver that they'd autographed to pay for my train fare home. I asked how come I'd never seen them guest on other people's records. They replied, 'No one's ever asked', so I asked. When we got back to England Roger Taylor came to the studio and played the drums on a few tracks on the next album, and John Deacon hung out at the studio for a while. One evening Roger was in the studio with me and I told him that my brother, John, also a drummer by now, was playing his first gig at a pub in Feltham, called The Airman – spookily enough, as John is now an airline captain. So Roger said, 'Why don't we have a break and go see him?' I was pretty big at the time, Queen were massive, so it caused quite a stir when we walked into the pub together. Roger had a good chat with John and gave him some drumming tips. John was over the moon. Queen gave me several important lessons, both before I was famous and afterwards. Look after your fans above all others and, no matter how successful you become, keep your feet on the ground.

I used to see Freddie Mercury once in a while at a club called Legends in London and he would always give me a big kiss on the cheek whenever he saw me. He was an excellent bloke and, although I never knew him well, he was one of those people who made you wish you did. Everyone was drawn to him. I would be very surprised if his passing hasn't left a large, unfillable gap in the lives of many, many people.

By 1981 I'd earned a fortune. I'm told I earned something like four and a half million pounds in the first couple of years. Too much to take in, too much to keep on top of. I couldn't even comprehend what that sort of money meant. You know it, but you can't relate to it at all, so I just kept spending it on bigger and bigger tours in those first couple of years. I bought a few things apart from the plane, a house for one, but most of the money was ploughed back into the career on equipment, stage sets and so on. The house was on

Wentworth Golf Course Estate, Virginia Water, Surrey. It was a fairly wealthy private estate and I remembered walking around it as a kid, looking for famous people's houses. For a long time I just lived in one room upstairs and for the first year my old friend Garry Robson had one of the end rooms.

I didn't have any furniture, no carpets at all, and I lived in one room rather like a bedsit. I had flattened cardboard boxes as a carpet, a bed, a deep fryer, a kettle, stereo, telly and a video, there was a built in wardrobe, a clock and a telephone. That was it. At the time I had no interest in making a home, everything I wanted to do I could do in one room. Garry Robson had a regular girlfriend so he was out a lot and I was on my own in the house quite a bit. I genuinely believed the house had a character to it and it didn't like me being around after 10 o'clock in the evening, so I used to scurry off to my room at 10 o'clock and not come out again until the morning. It wasn't a ghost, just a personality. I believe to this day that houses have personalities and that one seemed to be mischievous. It used to let me know when it didn't want me around. It used to feel like the house wanted the place to itself, so I'd go upstairs, lock the door, make my fish fingers and chips in the deep fryer and happily stay in there until morning. I did experience one or two unusual occurrences. Once I was upstairs talking to Garry when we heard a young girl's voice call our name. We went downstairs to see who it was, the front door had been left open, but no one was there. We searched around the grounds but couldn't find anyone. I thought that she must have got nervous and run away, but it did seem strange that she could run out of sight so quickly. We went back upstairs and immediately heard the voice again. Running this time, we reached the front door in seconds. No one was there. We searched the house, the grounds, up the street. Nothing. Garry also once saw the front door catch turn by itself once as he walked towards the door. My biggest ghostly experience had also been with Garry many years before. We had got off the underground train at Piccadilly Circus in London. We were going to look at a guitar shop in Shaftesbury Avenue. Without paying too much attention we simply followed the flow of passengers as we made our way to the station exit. A few people were behind us but not many, as we were one of the last to leave the train. In front was an elderly man in a grey coat and wearing a grey trilby. As we reached the top of the escalator the man turned to the left, we followed and walked straight into a wall. No man, no corridor, just a wall. We had both seen him. I've never run so fast from anywhere in all my life. The Wentworth house did get a bit strange for a while. So strange, in fact, I briefly moved out. It began to feel oppressive, brooding, and it made me very uncomfortable. I would make a point of leaving extra lights turned on before I went out and yet would come home, often at night, to find the house in darkness. The final straw came one night when I had turned my light off and was trying to sleep. The bedroom light turned itself on for a few seconds and then went off again. I was terrified, too terrified to move. I lay there awake until the dawn and then left. A few days later I went back and everything felt fine. It stayed that way for the next six years, until I moved out for good.

Eventually, after being moaned at by successive girlfriends, I did decorate the house, but it was never finished. I had an inflatable dinghy with an outboard engine that I'd pumped up in the front room for some reason. It stayed there for nearly a year before I thought to let it down and put it back in the garage. I did have a stuffed Alaskan timber wolf in the house, which I had come across on the second American tour and had crated and flown back to England. I used it as a burglar deterrent, placing it with its head poking around the corner at the top of the stairs, so anyone who broke in and started walking up the stairs would just see this wolf's head looking at them. Scared the life out of visitors if I forgot to tell them it was there. I have lots of regrets about the wolf. I'm so anti-hunting that it seems very strange I ended up owning a shot animal. My intentions were sound though. I saw it in an airport shop in Seattle and some kids were playing with it, sitting on it, hanging off its neck, which seemed a horribly undignified way for such an animal to end up. That's why I bought it, determined to do my best to give it a decent home. I had grand ideas about building it a tundra setting with a background that looked like Alaska but I never got round to it. I sold the house before I could do anything about his tundra setting. The house had a vast living room and it would have gone in the corner easily enough. Sadly it now lives under the stairs in my current home where there's no space to build him his own little set piece. It's an amazing-looking animal but every time someone sees it I go through the story and apologise for the way it's ended up under the stairs. Unfortunately some of my less considerate friends have hung their coats on it and broken its ears – they're a bit floppy now.

Overall I hadn't enjoyed the touring, I found the whole thing a massive strain. Being in the public eye was not coming easily to me and I tended to focus on touring as the main source of all my worries. Understandably in a way because, more than anything else, touring thrusts you into the spotlight in more ways than one. With hindsight, though, I was about to turn my back on the best and most exciting part of what success has to offer.

I had no regrets, no doubts at all that I was doing the right thing, as I planned my three farewell concerts. They were to take place at Wembley Arena on 26, 27 and 28 April.

I should have just quietly stepped back and taken some time off to catch my breath. But oh no, I had to go out with the biggest show ever seen, up to that point anyway. I had to be dramatic and tell everyone I was retiring from the stage. Knowing your own mind is at times a blessing and I've never been ashamed when people have pointed out that I have an incredible, single-minded drive to get things done my way. I quite like that about me, even though it has made me a lot of enemies and often has been badly misunderstood. But Christ it has its other side. If I was as smart tactically as I was determined, I would be scary. But I'm not, so I just keep on dropping myself in it from an enormous height. The 'I'm quitting' period was one of my largest plunges into the crap and one that, to this day, I still feel tugging at my heels like a bad dream.

We rehearsed on H stage at the Shepperton Film Centre because it was the only place in the country large enough to hold the show. It cost £250,000 to stage the three nights. The whole construction filled five 40ft trucks to get it from Shepperton to Wembley Arena and it took a team of about 30 men five days just to build it. The set consisted of five different levels, was 116ft wide and most of the various elements were motorised and moved about. Apparently, at the time, it was the largest moving structure ever built on a British stage. This freaked out the Wembley safety people because of the weight of the metalwork that would be supported by the roof, but the set had been well designed and there were no problems. A large segment of the structure was the *Telekon* stage set, with the 1979 tour panelling tipped on its side at the ends of long, raised walkways. Another massive additional set featuring a further 40 or 50 light panels was built on top. This was a motorised three-quarter circle of light, with two men placed in spotlight positions which were also motorised. These men were themselves incorporated into the styling of the show. They wore special helmets so they looked like Darth Vader-esque characters. We loaded CO_2 bottles on to the back of their spotlight cages which were made to look like something out of *Alien*. The operators pressed a keypad on the floor, the motor was activated and the CO_2 fired, so it looked as if they were being shot up into the air like a rocket. The entire upper structure was bolted to a 60ft by 60ft box truss – trussing is the metal girder grid that the lights hang off – which was also motorised. So this lighting grid moved up and down above the main 40 ft by 40ft lighting, which was itself truss above the main part of the stage where the *Telekon* set was erected. Underneath the stage at the front I had a hydraulic lift which would bring me up onto the stage from below. We also had a cage with tubular lighting on it which came down from the roof and I was raised into it as it descended. All the robots joined us, we used the radio-controlled car and we had the dance troupe, Shock, who were also the support band, perform with us on some songs. I wanted Shock to do the support because I liked what they did and I was extremely interested in one of the girls. Lust, eh! Still, as a chat up line, 'Do you want to support me at Wembley Arena?' was better than most. It was through Shock that I became friends with Tik and Tok. Nash The Slash also came on stage during the shows and added some maniac violin playing on a few songs.

The floor underneath Wembley used to be a swimming pool, so there was this big cavernous space into which we loaded bass cabinets. When we hit the low notes during the show the floor actually shook. One of our engineers also came up with the idea of bolting the framework of the PA stacks to the balcony, so it actually transmitted the vibrations of the speakers into the fabric of the building itself. It was awesome, the whole building shook, and you could feel the music as much as hear it. All this for just three shows. We played to eight thousand people a night and we lost £20,000 a show. When I walked on stage the roar from the audience was so loud I could hardly hear the music and we had the most enormous PA system. The place looked vast from the stage. Right to the back wall, every single seat was sold and when the special effects lit up on stage you could see the looks of wonder in their faces. People were pointing up at things and grinning. It was an incredible experience. And I was just about to turn my back on it.

Each night we played non-stop for two and a quarter hours. Even though we had just come off a tour and the band were very tight, the music alone had taken two months to rehearse. I must admit I was close to tears when I realised the true nature of what I was giving up. I was performing these songs, or so I thought, for the last time. 'Please Push No More', which had been written with just such a situation in mind, was especially difficult to get through. It was incredibly appropriate and very sad.

In terms of size and spectacle, it was the show I'd always dreamed of staging and those three nights were everything that was good about being a pop star; screaming fans, adulation, hysteria, emotion. I wondered, as I looked out at that vast sea of screaming faces, whether I was doing the right thing.

When the last song was over I certainly didn't think 'Thank God for that'. I kept saying to myself, Oh no, what have you done. I was very upset on the last night. When it was all finished and everyone had gone home I was still there. I went back out onto the stage for quite a long time, just sitting at the front, looking out. It felt like only seconds had passed from that first appearance on the *Old Grey Whistle Test* to this moment, when, in many ways, it was over. If I'd been hanging to the train by my fingertips before, now I'd just let go and hit the ground hard. I would have to pick myself up, see where I was, mend the damage and start walking.

In the back of my mind I thought that retiring at Wembley, virtually at the peak of my career, would make me a living legend. I was totally wrong. I've spent the rest of my career trying to get back to that level. Wembley was a massive full stop, it gained me nothing whatsoever, other than the time to come to terms with what I'd become. Having that time, that breathing space, was vital. I don't think I would be here now if I hadn't taken that decision but, after Wembley, I became far less than I was, so I had to deal with the horrible reality of that as well. Stopping touring killed my career dead in America. It didn't kill me in Britain, but I'd well and truly shot myself in the foot. I lost a huge amount of my support and, without it, I couldn't hope to fight the press. Only my massive success had been any kind of answer to their spite. After Wembley my sales dropped alarmingly.

In April we released a box-set of live material from the first two tours as a 'story so far' of my career. 'Living Ornaments' went straight in at number two and the individual albums, *79* and *80*, also charted. For the second time in my career I had three LPs in the Top 75. I'd also had about a dozen or so death threats within the first two years, which was definitely not what I expected when I sat at home and began to write 'Are "Friends" Electric?' People said they'd cut me up, kill my dog, beat up my girlfriend, shoot me, burn my house down. Both my brother and my parents were threatened. A few days after Wembley someone sent me a live 303 bullet in the post, a hard thing to come by, with a note that said 'I was going to kill you at Wembley Arena but I was enjoying myself so much I didn't bother'. My dad moved his car one day to find a petrol bomb underneath. My mum was put under police protection after they received a tip-off about a kidnap that was being planned.

I continued the sessions for the *Dance* album in the late spring. Mick Karn was back on board. I'd been quite taken aback when Karn and Sylvian rang me up at my hotel in London and asked if they could go on the guest list for Wembley. I think they blamed everybody else for what had happened in Japan, their management and so on. They said enough to smooth over our disagreement at the time. Nash The Slash also added some creepy, unearthly violin parts to *Dance* and I co-wrote two songs with Paul Gardiner, 'Stormtrooper In Drag' and 'Night Talk'. Paul was, by now, becoming increasingly addicted to heroin. Although we weren't sure exactly what it was at the time, we knew he had a drug problem of some kind. Paul was a very creative musician and he came up with some inspired bass lines at times, although on 'Stormtrooper in Drag' and 'Night Talk' I played the bass and Paul the guitar. I really enjoyed writing with Paul. We had been together for years and he hadn't shown any real desire to write songs before. It was an interesting off-shoot but, unfortunately, as his drug problem worsened the opportunity to do more work together faded away. He came

110

into the studio one day and started to play and then he just keeled over, cracking his head quite badly on the side of the console. I thought he was unconscious but he was asleep, and when we tried to wake him we couldn't. We couldn't move him either, so tightly had he wedged himself into the side of the console. He woke up hours later and thought the track was still running. I was very worried about him. He had always been a bit flaky but this was different. This was quite scary.

I think I saw a UFO once on my way home from one of those *Dance* sessions. It was a short time after the Wembley shows, about 2 o'clock in the morning. I was with my new girlfriend, Michelle Adams. It was very dark and a little damp as it had been raining and the cloud cover was quite low. We were driving alongside a major motorway junction when a light shone down out of the clouds. The strange thing about the beam was that it appeared to be in the shape of an upside down pyramid. The apex of the ray appeared to just touch the surface of the road. At the point where it came through the cloud it was perfectly square and very large. It didn't move and there was no discernible sound. I stopped the car, feeling frightened to be honest, and we watched this object for several seconds. I knew from what the cloud was covering, local hills, pylons that kind of thing, that the cloud base was only about 400 feet up at best, and the width of the beam as it came through the cloud was at least that, if not more. This ruled out helicopters or any other flying vehicle that I was aware of, as did the lack of noise. The light vanished as quickly as it came, like flicking off a switch.

On 25 June 1981, I went on a course for an aviation 'B' Rating. A 'B' Rating enables you to fly multi-engined aeroplanes and, on 3 July, I passed the test. I was really quite pleased with myself because I got the rating with the minimum amount of flying hours possible for the course. On 7 July I bought my own twin-engine aeroplane, a Piper Navajo. The Navajo was an 8-seater and I had it painted in *Telekon* colours. It was mainly black with two red cheat lines running from the nose to the tip of the tail. We also had the face logo put on the tail fin. It had a slightly nose-down stance on the ground and looked very menacing. It was registered G-NMAN and a company operated on our behalf as air taxi. We started a company called Numanair and had vague hopes of building it up as a small, air-char-

111

tered company but it never really made any money.

Under the guise of Numanair we also sponsored a Formula Ford 1600 racing for the a year, which was painted in the same *Telekon*-style colours as the aeroplane. The driver, Mike Machonochie, was a former workmate of my dad's. Mike was very quick and won several races, including the first with us as sponsor, but he also had a few accidents along the way. Mike wanted to progress to Formula 3, but we were unable to guarantee the amount of money he needed for racing at that level and after a few drives he pulled out.

1981 was definitely a year for treating myself. I bought a Ferrari Boxer. I ordered a brand new black Ferrari 308, but it was going to take a few months to deliver and I just couldn't wait. I went back to the dealer and looked at a BB512 Berlinetta Boxer, which was a bit more expensive, but a much faster car. It was metallic blue with a black underside, a beautiful looking thing. I went out for a test drive and it was savagely quick. When I put my foot to the floor it was like a rocket had gone off. That Ferrari is one of the most exhilarating machines I've ever been in. We used to put our hands in the air and the acceleration would push them back behind us. The handbook rpm limits meant that you had to change from first to second before it reached 60 mph. I bought a book written by the engine designer and he said that the engine was actually good for another 500 rpm. That meant 0–60 in first gear in just over four seconds. In the Ferrari you sit quite low and the sensation of speed was just stunning. I was stopped for speeding only once but I was lucky to keep my licence. They measured me at an average speed of 94 mph, but in fact at one point I'd been doing over 150 mph. The reason I had an average speed was because I had actually pulled over for a while, which was how they caught up with me.

At the Earls Court boat show I bought a two-man hovercraft. I took it to Littlehampton in the winter and tried it up and down the quiet beach, then out at sea, which wasn't so successful. The hovercraft stopped dead, throwing me over the front into the water. I didn't quite understand how it worked. I ran a dog over on the same day. I gave a little boy a ride and his dog went berserk. This big Alsatian must have thought the child was being hurt and he ran at the hovercraft, which went straight over him. He popped out the other side and then tore off into the distance, ears flat to his head.

I also bought a Fletcher speedboat. It was powered by a huge Ford V8 engine and could go over 50mph, which is pretty quick on the water. I didn't know how to drive a boat either. I thought you went as fast as you possibly could and then simply hung on for grim death. I hit one wave so hard the boat took off and rolled onto its side. I was floating in the air, both hands gripping the steering wheel but completely weightless. As soon as we landed back in the water the jolt threw me onto the side of my seat, which left me in absolute agony. My body had gone one way but my intimate parts were left on the seat – it sure felt like that anyway! Another time I let my guitarist Russell Bell drive it, while I went to the front and popped my head out of a hatchway to take photos. We hit a wave and the impact hurled me over the side, except for my ankles which some-how got caught on the hatch. The boat was still roasting along and I was desperately trying to climb back in, half drowning in the water. We cracked the hull on that trip, unfortunately, and it started sink-ing so we had to head back in. I didn't go out in it much after that, as my interest turned ever more towards aeroplanes and I began to get busy again musically.

I flew gliders a few times that summer as well but I didn't really take to it. It seemed far too tame. I do recognise the skills involved in flying gliders, but to me it's the aviation equivalent of stamp collecting. No power, no interest as far as I'm concerned.

On 24 July I started a helicopter pilot course. I took to it quite well and went solo after just a few hours. In fact, apart from one other person, I went solo quicker than any other student the flying school had ever had. I was very proud of that. It took me about three weeks to get the licence, a PPL (H), which enabled me to fly piston-engined helicopters only, so I immediately went on a Jetranger course and passed that two days later. The courses were not without their anxious moments, though. On one of the trips the instructor, as he climbed out and sent me off solo, didn't do up his seat belt straps properly. During my flight they came apart and, unseen from where I was, they jammed under the collective lever which made it difficult to descend properly. It was only when the passenger seat cushion that the straps were supposed to hold down came away and hit me in the face that I figured out what had happened.

In August I flew a Jetranger, which is quite a big, roasty machine, to Southam for the filming of the video for my next single 'She's Got Claws'. It was my first trip in the Jetranger since getting the licence. We were filming in a miniature safari park which, so the owner said, had a big field that we could use to land the helicopter. I arrived at the park and was setting the helicopter down in an adjacent field when a horse came galloping out of nowhere and started running wildly around. It was impossible to land in the field so I pulled away and went back to the safari park. I saw the owner running around pointing to this postage-stamp-sized lawn next to the tiger's cage, the famous Esso TV commercial tiger no less. This lawn was the big field he'd been talking about. Not only was it quite small but it wasn't even flat. The surface was very similar to a corrugated piece of roofing and I had to land the helicopter evenly between two turfed rises. It was a high skid version, which made it even worse. Due to the cost of the film crew I allowed myself to be pressured into that landing, which was a poor decision. Luckily I actually made a good job of it, but what I should have done was go home and come back in the car. It was a cool way to arrive, though and going home the next morning was fun. At one point I wanted to make sure that I was in the right place so I hovered the helicopter down beside a sleepy little railway station, checked the name, and flew on.

Julien Temple directed the 'She's Got Claws' promo. I think he was a bit disappointed with me because he was looking for a very actor-like performance and I was still rather inhibited. He wanted me to act out various scenes but I felt extremely self-conscious and really couldn't get it together. That's probably why the woman and the panther featured in it more than I did.

'She's Got Claws' was released on 29 August and went straight in at 15. The following week the song climbed to number six, so I was happy. On the sleeve I unveiled a new 1930s gangster style image. I'd decided to kill off the black image at Wembley. The new look was actually on the cover of the *Replicas* album back in 1979. There is a Grey Man outside the window, dressed in a trilby and long grey overcoat. I loved the ambience of the old Sinatra and Bogart films and I thought the 1930s were, visually, a really cool era. It was the last age when everyday men looked stylish just going to work.

However the atmosphere I was trying to create with the image and some of the music was mostly rooted in an imaginary 1930s.

For years I'd had these pictures in my mind. Newspapers rustling through wet, empty streets, everything slightly vague and ghostlike, mostly grey, little colour. The style of the architecture was American, with fire escapes and old street lamps, but it wasn't necessarily in the past, more timeless. There were no cars and the buildings were always empty and derelict, apart from a few half-guessed at perversions in upstairs apartments. The *Dance* image, unbeknown to me at the time, had a strange connection with a recurring nightmare my mother had had since she was very young, which involved grey men. A man dressed in a long grey overcoat and trilby was always lurking underneath a lamppost, half-lit in the darkness. She was shocked when she saw the *Replicas* cover, because it was her childhood bogeyman and she'd never mentioned it to me. The *Dance* image was that dream made flesh, so it made her quite uncomfortable for a while. It also reminded me of the ghost I'd seen in Piccadilly Circus.

Dance charted at number three in September '81. It sold just over 60,000, a far far cry from *Telekon* and light years away from *Replicas* and *The Pleasure Principle*. Although experimental and atmospheric, commercially speaking, *Dance* was the wrong album at a time when I badly needed to pick up momentum. However I had things to sort out in my head. Where *Telekon* had been dark and oppressively inward looking, angry and lashing out, *Dance* was haunting and full of sadness. It had much of how I felt in the aftermath of Wembley running through it. I thought I was taking a brave, more personal direction after the oppressiveness of *Telekon*. The subject matter of the new songs was full of reflections on the previous two years, but one or two in particular were inspired by a relationship which turned very bitter.

In 1980 I had gone out with a particular girl for a few months. She gave me three different names while I was with her, so to this day I'm still not sure what her real name was, but the one she ended up with was Debbie Doran. She was older than me, extremely worldly and stunningly good looking. Everyone told me she was bad news and to keep well away from her but I didn't listen. As far as I was concerned it was all sweet and wonderful. I used to tuck her kid into bed at night, everything seemed cool to me. Not only that, she was teaching me stuff in bed that I couldn't believe. On the other hand, she used to wind me up very badly. She knew how to press all the right buttons to spark off my temper, and while I screamed and ranted and broke things she wrote it all down. Then she tried to blackmail me. She said she'd sell her story to the papers unless I paid her more than they were offering. I was angry but I was also heartbroken since I thought the world of her. It turned out that everything about the relationship had been set up. It had been arranged that she and her sister would be sitting near me in a club one night. It was a safe bet that I would fancy one of them. Whoever it was would make it easy for me, start a relationship if possible, get some gory details and sell it. I have to admit it was a good, if rather cold, plan. Fortunately the record company got wind of this and it turned out someone at the label, whom I began to see in a new light, had something on Debbie's brother, a small-time villain. Whatever it was, she withdrew her threat and I never heard from her again. She certainly hung out with some shady people. Her friends looked like modern day gangsters. We'd go to a club and these heavy-looking people in sharp suits all knew her. They were scary people and I wasn't thinking straight at all. It was a learning experience, to say the least. For the first time I realised I'd become a ticket to money for some people. They will use you, lie to you, sleep with you, just to get money out of you. It took me a long time to get over the experience.

I had one further release in 1981. On 5 December, Beggars Banquet released 'Love Needs No Disguise' which was written by my old backing band, Cedric Sharpley, Rrussell Bell, Chris Payne and Denis Haines who were now known as Dramatis. They were keen to keep together as Dramatis from the moment I told them of my intention to retire from the stage. 'Love Needs No Disguise' was a song about our time together, which just happened to be playing in the studio they were working in when I popped by for a visit. They played me the track, which I loved, and so, while I was there, I sang the vocal. We made a video for it and the single reached 33 when it came out, which was quite respectable. It also featured on their album, *For Future Reference*, released the same year. I wasn't able to get involved in a full promotional push for the track as my dream of flying round the world was already coming together.

CHAPTER 7

Round The World: East and West, 1981

I had several reasons for wanting to fly around the world in a light aeroplane. I wanted my dad to respect me as a man. I had never been a drinker, didn't smoke, didn't fight. I didn't do many of the things associated with young men, didn't want to, but, deep down, I felt guilty. I was now famous and wealthy, but I didn't think that counted. I was running around wearing make-up and being pampered most of the time – not exactly manly stuff. I wanted to do something that would make my dad proud and I didn't think my success would do it. These thoughts were nothing to do with my father, they were built up by my own insecurities. I saw him as a man's man and I felt that I had let him down somehow by becoming a musician. I thought the Round-The-World flight would be the answer.

Not only that, I thought it would make people in general see me in a different light. Up until then I'd been viewed as a pouting youth, strutting around looking vaguely confused, sulky and alienated. I hoped people would consider the trip at least worthy of some respect, if not popularity. I also wanted a plain old adventure of my own. I wanted to know how I would react when trouble came. You hear stories of great courage and skill, of sacrifice and daring, and you wonder what you would have done in those same situations. I think everyone would like to believe that they would rush into a burning building to save a child, but would we? The Round-The-World flight was my burning building. It would force me to face things that I was terrified of. Deep water, for one...

117

It's one thing to talk about adventure when you're sitting warm and cosy by your English fireplace. It's another thing entirely when you come face to face with the awful reality of what makes an adventure worthy of the name. In those moments you would rather be anywhere else on earth. It's one of the reasons why I like Richard Branson so much. His critics say that he's got all the money in the world so it's easy for him, but money doesn't make you invincible. The man is out there doing it for real, facing real dangers, and all the time he's waving the Union Jack and winning things for Britain. We've always had people like Branson but, where in the past we idolised individuals like Donald and Malcolm Campbell, now we ridicule them.

In my own small way I also flew the flag. I made sure my aeroplane had a Union Jack painted on the side for the Round-The-World trip. I was intending to be the first pop star ever to try such a trip and I wanted it known that I was British. Members of the public have said to me, 'You're okay at flying aeroplanes but that's because you've got loads of money.' Does that mean as soon as I've got a big cheque I suddenly receive all these skills and my brain clicks over onto a new level? No! I may have more opportunity to practise because I can afford to, but my skills are earned, just as much as anyone else's.

I'd already learned to fly when I decided to do the trip. After getting my licence in December 1980 I flew a few hours in January 81; three days in February; five in March; three in April, two in May, then I did my twin-engine course where I put a week aside; three more days in July, two in August, two in September and then the trip itself. So I wasn't a very experienced aviator at all. I was just squeezing in days here and there.

After making the decision to attempt the trip, there was a bit of a cock-up with the plans. I'd seen a TV programme about an Englishwoman who'd flown solo to Australia. The man who planned her journey was a famous balloonist, Julian Knott. We got in touch with him to plan our trip, met him a few times to discuss things and then left the organising problems with him. I was planning to co-pilot the trip with my first instructor, Tim Steggles, although it soon became obvious that he would probably be unable to spare the time for such a journey. One day I was in the restau-

118

rant at Blackbushe airport and I started talking to Bob Thompson, a highly skilled display pilot and owner of an air freight company. I mentioned our plans to fly around the world and he told me in no uncertain terms that it wasn't going to happen. He said 'You're never going to be ready in time if all the visas and clearances aren't in place.' I assured him that Julian Knott was experienced in this kind of thing and that he'd been involved in similar trips before. Bob turned out to be absolutely right; Julian Knott hadn't done a thing. He thought I was all talk and that I wouldn't actually go through with it, so there was no aeroplane waiting, no airspace clearances, no maintenance booked, no hotels arranged. He'd done absolutely nothing. I told Bob the horrible truth and he said, 'Well, I'll do it. I've got a company that can organise everything for you and I can also fly the aeroplane.' Bob was ex-RAF, a jet pilot, he could fly helicopters, he had years of experience. So he came to a quite lucrative deal with my dad and took on the trip. Because the planning was now being done in a mad rush, so that we could still leave before winter set in, we were unable to secure much in the way of sponsorship. I was undeterred. If we couldn't get sponsorship I'd pay for it all myself. In the event it was to cost me in excess of £180,000.

Bob Thompson found an aeroplane. He selected a Cessna 210 Centurion, a high-wing, six-seater, single-engine machine. It was turbocharged, had de-icing, an oxygen system and a good range of navigation and radio equipment. We would need far more specialist gear, though, for a trip such as ours. It was also reasonably big, allowing us plenty of room for extra essential equipment but not much else. We took out the four back seats and had extra fuel tanks fitted just behind the two remaining crew seats. We also had extra long-range tanks installed in the wings. We did what we could to keep the weight down, because we had to carry a lot of extra fuel. Any extra weight would have to be accommodated by removing fuel and that was unacceptable. Even the carpets were taken out because it would free up about six pounds, nearly a gallon's worth of fuel. We would travel light, when it came to clothes and personal items, because we had to find room for extra kit such as parachutes and a life raft.

All the red tape was sorted out. Corrupt officials in various

119

embassies were bought off and handed over the necessary visas. We also bought a set of gold epaulets and white flying crew shirts. Bob said it would pay dividends in certain countries. Doors that said Staff Only opened for you. Air crew were treated with great respect in many of the more far flung places where, if you didn't look the part, people would point a gun at you. It was a good idea and made things happen on more than one occasion.

We set off from Heathrow on 18 September, 1981. The Radio One DJs, Peter Powell and Kid Jensen, came along to see us off and Radio One were intending to transmit regular bulletins as the trip progressed. The aeroplane was late arriving because we had a last-minute problem with the undercarriage. The doors kept closing before the nose wheel had retracted, which obviously bent them. This was a portent of things to come.

Our circumnavigation was planned in an easterly direction so our first stop was in Paris. In Europe we were doing reasonably long legs and after a while it became cramped and uncomfortable. You could barely move, couldn't even stretch your legs. We also wore parachutes the whole time. The heavier than normal weight for the first part of each flight, meant it was safer to jump out of the plane rather than try to force land it should the engine stop for any reason. Up to a point, an overweight aeroplane can take off, but it can't land until you've used up the fuel and the weight is back to acceptable limits. As we flew into Switzerland's airspace I had my first close look at the Alps. It's a bit daunting when you're sitting in a little motor and there are jagged mountain peaks as far as you can see.

We started to get into the longer sea crossings as we headed towards the Greek islands. We were in a high-wing aeroplane, which has poor ditching characteristics. In the event of a crash you have to wait for the plane to sink and water to fill up the cabin before you're able to open the doors, due to water pressure. You start worrying about such things because you haven't got much else to think about. Once you're up in the air the autopilot locks onto the navigation system and all you do is monitor the plane, occasionally checking the fuel consumption and so on. There's not much to do and you run out of things to talk about after the first couple of days. There were continents of silence between us.

Flying on oxygen was unpleasant. We had little face masks and a bag which inflated and deflated beneath them. I was told I was going to feel quite good on oxygen but I actually felt sick most of the time. As an aeroplane climbs the air becomes thinner and at 10,000 ft you normally revert to oxygen. We were flying high for long periods and so we were often sitting there with our masks clipped to our faces. They would fill with moisture and make your skin quite sore after a while. I hated it, but we had to fly high to keep our fuel consumption down to a reasonable level. The higher you fly, the less fuel you burn.

We flew to Athens, and from there we were looking to cross the Mediterranean into Syria. The Syrian authorities wanted us to arrive at their border at 12.31 pm, at a height of 21,000 ft. They were very clear and we were left in no doubt that anything else was seriously unacceptable. We crossed the border on time and at the correct height but, as we proceeded over the Syrian desert landscape, it became increasingly obvious that we would not be able to maintain our height. It was just too hot, and we were too heavy. The aeroplane slowed down and began to sink below its assigned height. We lowered the nose to try and regain the airspeed and only lost more height. Painfully slowly we climbed back up to 21,000 ft, only for it happen all over again. We tried but eventually we stalled and fluttered down. We could just about manage 19,000 ft with the nose up, struggling to stay in the air.

We weren't able to talk to Syrian air traffic controllers on the radio but we could hear them. They were getting more and more angry and our fear was, if a military jet came up to examine us, we didn't look like your average light aeroplane. We had parachutes on and we had a big silver lump in the back, which was our extra fuel tank but could have been anything to a suspicious mind. In addition, we had oxygen masks on. It was difficult to get the clearance to be there in the first place because Syria was such a troubled area at the time. We were concerned that they would mistake us for something hostile and shoot us down. Eventually we managed to communicate with an airliner we spotted flying above us, and they relayed our message to the Syrian authorities. We continued across the desert to the United Arab Emirates. By the time we arrived it was dark and I saw something that was surprisingly scary. Scary for me anyway.

I have a terrible phobia about deep water, especially at night. One look at it sends shivers down my spine. The first time I remember feeling like this was as a child when we drove over the Walton Bridge on the Thames. I used to hide under the seat so that I couldn't see the black water of the river way below. I could never swim in the sea at night, I hate the thought of so much depth beneath me and all the slimy things that might be looking up at my lily white legs. As we approached the Emirates I could see oil platforms out in the Gulf, burning gases in big flames from the top of tall gantries. The fire reflected in the water, illuminating the big pillars of the oil rig as they disappeared into the sea, giving the impression of great depth and blackness. My stomach lurched as we flew by, heading for land.

We decided to take off from the Emirates at midnight, as that was when the air would be coolest and we'd already had some problems with the aeroplane vaporising fuel. It had an engine-driven fuel pump, a booster pump and an emergency pump and for long periods of the flight we had them all on to keep enough fuel flowing to the engine. It's not meant to be like that. As we began our take off down the runway it was very humid and the plane didn't want to fly. After using an enormous amount of a very long runway we got airborne. We had barely climbed to 400 ft when the engine started spluttering and we began to lose height. We were outside of the airfield boundary and had no idea what was below us in the darkness. We knew a reasonable sized mountain wasn't too far away to the north-east, because our planned route took us over it. It was pointless going back to the airport because we were much too heavy to land. If we'd attempted it the undercarriage would have collapsed, and the plane almost certainly blown up, full of fuel as it was. The situation looked a bit grim. If we could climb to the cooler air, the engine would run better, but even with all the pumps on the fuel was vaporising and starving the engine of petrol. So we step climbed. Bob knew the technique, where you descend very slightly, let the plane accelerate and then you climb gently for as long as you can, until the speed falls, pushing it over the top to level flight again. We did this for half an hour or more with the engine coughing and spluttering the whole time. Eventually we gained a few thousand feet where the air was cooler. The engine started to run better and we were able to make bigger steps until the problem cleared and we could set course. For me it had been a very frightening experience.

Our next stop was Madras, India. There didn't seem to be anyone there. We parked outside what appeared to be an abandoned old hangar and shuffled around for a while. Then along came this big old fuel bowser, people hanging off its sides. It looked as if it had been left behind by the Germans in World War II. It was completely rusted from top to bottom, leaking fuel all over the place. Whole bits of metal weren't joined any more and were just flapping on the outside. This vehicle was going to re-fuel the plane. I was scared about what was going in because the liquid was such a strange colour. This was also the vehicle which took us to Customs. You just hung on the side with everybody else and hoped for the best. We sat in Customs for quite some time until a friendly man sidled over to us and explained that we would not leave the airport until we had given the official on duty a financial consideration. The locals were very welcoming, although you got the impression that having a photograph taken of yourself was the equivalent to being on *This Is Your Life*. Everybody wanted their picture taken and I was weighed down by the number of names and addresses that were handed to me by smiling youngsters after they'd bobbed up and down in front of my camera.

The next morning we took off and headed up the east coast of India to a point where an airway crossed the Indian Ocean towards Thailand. At this point we hit a monsoon. I'd never seen anything like it. It was the middle of the afternoon and I couldn't see the front of the aeroplane, so heavy was the rainfall. We emerged out the other side and, soon after, turned right to follow the airliner path to Bangkok, staying well below the airway. I'd dreaded this particular leg because I'd been told the Indian Ocean was one of the most shark-infested places on earth. Unease sat quietly on my shoulder until, about 70 miles out from land, the engine gave a small cough. Unease almost became a loud scream of horror but I managed to hide my panic behind a commendably calm 'What was that?' to Bob. I'm not sure where my mouth got the words from because all my brain was saying was 'Fuck. Fuck, oh shit. FUCK!!'' Then the engine began to run quite badly, a delayed reaction to the monsoon drenching. Water had worked its way inexorably back and semi-drowned the motor and so we turned back towards India. Moments later I had got the dinghy on my lap and clipped to my RAF life jacket, with emergency beacons and flares checked and ready for use. My parachute straps were triple checked. I was thinking, 'If I'm going into the water, by crash or by parachute, I've got the dinghy.' I had yet to bond with Bob sufficiently well to even consider courageous gestures of support, especially if the emergency involved sharks! By way of easing my conscience I reasoned that, when I was safely in the dinghy, I'd have a very good look around for him. I'm sure that would have come as a relief to him as Great White things nibbled away at his toes. I also had some shark repellent in my hand. That little blue sachet was like a gift from heaven and I could barely take my eyes off of it. There were no guarantees that it would actually work, though. According to the manufacturer some sharks find it unpleasant but some of them actually like it. I think the idea is if one of these toothy monsters comes along and doesn't like it, great, if it does, at least the end will be quick.

We declared an emergency and slowly made our way back to the Indian coast. With strong head winds against us it took the best part of half an hour, the engine coughing and spluttering all the way. The closest airfield was a semi military base called Visakhapatnam. When we arrived overhead we still had too much fuel on for a safe landing, but the motor was running so badly we decided to risk it. Flying aeroplanes, especially on these kind of journeys and in the air display world, means that you take major decisions regularly. Choose wrong and you can die. It has always amazed me how, as a display pilot, you can suddenly find yourself in a life-threatening situation, sort it out and then carry on as though nothing had happened. I was once in an old World War Two aeroplane that caught fire during a flight test. I sorted it out, got it down, told the engineers, drove home and went shopping with my girlfriend. That would be considered perfectly normal behaviour by any display pilot. To have made a fuss about what was, after all, a fairly major moment, would not be the done thing.

The Vishak' landing could have been better but it was good enough. Somewhat relieved we climbed from the aeroplane and started to look at the motor for obvious signs of distress but could see none. We'd been there for quite some time with no sign of

Customs or Immigration officials turning up so the airport manager said we could leave. It turned out he didn't have the authority to release us and so the problems began.

We slipped away in a cab, unaware of the impending trouble. Bob christened the local taxis 'Flame out cabs' because, as soon as you got in, they drove to the nearest fuel station and tried to make you pay for it. The petrol tank was actually an oil can chopped in half, with a tube coming out of the open top which led to the engine. This dubious contraption was sliding about between the driver's feet. The petrol station itself was a rusty old pump of considerable vintage in the middle of a square of mud. Eventually, after much bartering, he took us to a hotel. The word hotel actually does the place a considerable favour but, to be fair, it could have been worse. The lizards on the wall were cute.

I discovered that eating was going to be a problem. I didn't like a single thing of the three things offered on the menu. Trying to contact anyone to help us out was very difficult and we decided to get an early night and make an early start the next day. We needed to rearrange clearances and, of course, get the aeroplane fixed. Customs and Immigration eventually turned up and were most upset. They seemed particularly peeved that we'd left the airport before they got there. We explained that the airport manager had given us permission but they said they were going to prosecute him for allowing us to do just that. The manager got his rule book out, which said something along the lines of: the airport manager, in the absence of Customs and Immigration, has the authority to allow people into the country. Then the Customs men leafed through their rule book which had a slightly more recent date, 1949 I think, compared to his 1947, and theirs stated that he didn't. That's how the law seemed to run. If you had the most recent rule book you were in the right. They were arguing face to face with these books between them. I couldn't believe my eyes, it was like going back in time. I was informed by one of the Customs officers that this was all our own fault as we were English and we had given them the rules in the first place.

Later that night they returned, announcing their arrival by banging on the door and kicking it open at about 2 o'clock in the morning. There was a great deal of gun waving. Two men had rifles and some others handguns. At first I was somewhat cocky, full of typical self-righteous English indignation, but that soon evaporated and I became more than a little scared. They took our passports and generally behaved in a highly aggressive and threatening manner. I had visions of being dragged away into the night, never to be seen again, and so I was grateful for Bob's calm and authoritative approach. It didn't do much good though, they still took our passports away.

We both had on two watches, which seemed inconceivable to these local officials, who assumed we had to be smuggling. Two watches were necessary as one was set at local time and the other at Greenwich Mean Time, which is a world constant and used for international flights. I also had a big 35mm stills camera, a small stills camera and a 16mm movie camera. That proved, apparently, that we were spies. It was an unbelievable scenario. A few hours ago we had breathed a sigh of relief as we touched down on Indian soil, having survived a potentially grisly end, and now here we were being 'unofficially' arrested on suspicion of smuggling and spying. They started asking us if we were taking pictures of the Russian submarine base and then, incredibly, told us where it was. I felt like gagging the man, he was telling us far more than we knew and certainly more than we wanted to know. We did find out that all the other people in the 'hotel' were Russian families. The officials exposed all our film, so no pictures for the children of Madras. We were allowed downstairs but we couldn't leave the 'hotel'. We were held there for three nights and each night they would wake us up between 2 am and 4 am and say, 'Unless you co-operate you will be taken to Customs House.' They made it sound like Alcatraz. We were under armed guard at all times. I didn't have the right temperament for this at all, so I leaned heavily on Bob and let him do all the talking.

In order to communicate with the outside world we were allowed to send telexes from an airline office in the town. It was all very dramatic whenever we went there, which was once a day. We were put in a jeep with several armed soldiers, while two more packed jeeps escorted us. This convoy weaved through town at high speed with people throwing themselves out of the way as we passed. We delivered our telex message and then the same convoy would take us back.

126

Our only phone call out of the country had been on day one and, somehow, it had been overheard by the telephone operators at St Paul's in London. Over the next few days they would ring the 'hotel', pretend to be from the British Embassy, get me on the line and then say, 'Hello, it's us again, who do you want to speak to?' and then connect me with whoever. They were excellent. I felt like Steve McQueen in *The Great Escape*.

I also rang the British Consulate in Delhi. I explained to the official there, a lady by the name of Mrs Fitzgerald if memory serves, that we were being held at gunpoint. She said, 'You're too far away, Delhi's on the other side of India, I can't help you,' and put the phone down. I sat there for some time with the phone in my hand. I was stunned. Luckily, back in England my dad rang up the press and the *Daily Star* got involved. They made big noises with the Foreign Office and the situation was resolved almost immediately.

The Indian officials made a great fuss of the fact that we had landed at an airfield with military connections. They behaved as though we'd stumbled across some top secret base. The only aeroplane there, apart from mine, was a Britten Norman Islander, built at Bembridge on the Isle of Wight. I told them that I'd toured the factory where the aeroplane was made and, not only that, Bob Thompson had worked as a test pilot for this particular model. He had almost certainly flown the actual aeroplane that we were arguing about. It made the charge of spying seem weak, to say the least. On our fourth day they let us leave, but not with my aeroplane, which was still broken. As we left the officials handed us back our passports and asked if we would send a letter to their superiors saying what a good job they'd done. 'Of course,' we replied, 'delighted to.' 'In your dreams', we thought quietly to ourselves as we walked out to the aeroplane.

Indian Airlines took us out on an F-27. Bound ultimately for Calcutta it was first scheduled to stop at a place called Hyderabad. It was, quite possibly, the worst landing I've ever been able to walk away from. It was so heavy the wings flexed down at the end and I thought they would break for sure. I was badly winded and it took me a minute or two to get my breath back. Afterwards the captain came strutting over from the cockpit, gold braid aplenty, and introduced himself. We had by now slipped back on our own gold bars so he thought he was amongst his own kind. I secretly filmed the take off from Visakhapatnam and caught a classic shot of our little Cessna parked forlornly on the tarmac, a soldier standing guard nearby.

From Hyderabad we flew on to Calcutta where we met the *Daily Star* journalist and photographer. In Calcutta the level of poverty was really horrible to see. Visak had been bad: I'd seen people defecating in the street and living under shelters that had no sides with roofs made of leaves. I had never seen poverty like it and it was deeply disturbing. Calcutta was worse. Lepers begging in the street, old ladies with tiny babies that were clearly not their own. I was told that younger women actually rented out their babies to older people so they could beg more effectively from tourists. Everything was old and worn out, even the babies. Apart from the officials, the Indian people themselves were excellent and I had nothing but admiration for them. I couldn't imagine living the way they were forced to and yet, with a few exceptions, they were polite, friendly and helpful.

We met Mother Teresa during our stay in Calcutta. The *Daily Star* men knew where her building was in the city and so we went to find out if we could see her. When we arrived at what was a very unassuming little wooden door we just walked in. It didn't even have a lock. A nun came out to greet us and we asked if it was all right to say hello to Mother Teresa. Off she went and, a few minutes later, Mother Teresa herself came out to see us. She shook us all by the hand and then went about her business. I was very impressed that she had time for people. She had no idea who we were, we were of no special importance and yet she had time for us. It made pop stars with all their security and special access passes seem a bit poncy. Another lesson to be stored away.

I also got talking to a boy who stood outside the hotel, opening the doors for us. He was 19 and, for all his lack of formal education, very sharp. It was he who explained the 'renting babies' situation to me, along with lots of other things about India's poverty trap. He said if he had his own rickshaw then he would be able to earn a reasonable income for himself and his family. I was impressed and so I gave him the money to buy his own rickshaw. I've often wondered what happened to him. It's quite possible I was the victim of an extremely eloquent scam and that he may have simply got drunk and spent all the cash on the best prostitute in town. I like to think he was genuine, though.

I had a curious mixture of feelings as I stepped onto the British Airways jet that was to take me home. I sat down in the first-class compartment and looked out the small window. Outside people would watch this aeroplane fly overhead knowing that they would never be able to leave, would never know the life that I took for granted. I felt very guilty. On the other hand I was glad to be leaving. The flight back was like waking up from a horrible dream.

It seemed our Indian disaster had been big news back in Britain and I was interviewed by various media people when we got back to Heathrow. The first man I spoke to asked me if the entire Indian episode had been an elaborate publicity stunt. I was very disappointed with that. It seemed as though, because I was a public figure, everything I did had to be for publicity, that I had no other desires, no other reason for living. I had wanted publicity from the trip, that much was true, but I had no need to fake incidents to make it seem more interesting. We had been facing dangers that I felt deserved some respect. I told him we were going to have another go.

After some hurried reorganisation we prepared for take off at Blackbushe airport, Camberley on Sunday 25 October. This time we took my black twin-engine Piper Navajo. Bob had returned to India with an engineer to fix the Cessna and had brought it back to the UK, while I oversaw the preparation of the twin. We eventually decided that we would have to fly the second trip westwards around the world. The Indian delay had set us back quite badly, and crossing the North Atlantic in winter was too great a risk. Going west would get that crossing over at the start of the trip, before winter set in. A number of people questioned our choice of aeroplane. Some thought that not using a single took away much of the risk, others said that it increased it. Both arguments were correct in a way. With a single, if the engine stopped, you were going down. On shorter legs, with a low fuel load, if an engine had stopped on the twin we could have landed safely on the remaining one. On longer legs however, with the unusually heavy fuel loads required on such a flight, the aeroplane could not fly on just one engine. In this condition, with two engines, and therefore twice as many things able to go wrong, the twin was far more dangerous. Something like 85 per cent of our flights were in this heavy fuel load condition and so our exposure to risk throughout the journey was actually higher with the twin, overall, than with the single. I found the take-offs particularly stressful. Filled to the brim with fuel, in special tanks tucked into every nook and cranny on the aeroplane, even a slight loss of power on one of the engines and we would have gone down. It felt to me like we were sitting on a massive bomb every time we left the ground.

One of our first stops was in Reykjavik, Iceland. I was amazed at how far I could see as we flew towards Iceland. The air was so clear, the lights from the cities glistened like crystal from hundreds of miles away. In Reykjavik we were taken out to a nightclub where a man said to me, 'What are your politics?' I said, 'I don't pay much attention to politics, I'm too busy getting on with life.' Wrong answer, apparently. I'd already given him an autograph but he pulled it out of his pocket, spat on it, screwed it up and threw it on the floor. That was the first time politics got me into trouble. A man from the Icelandic record company drove us out the next morning to see some hot springs. We never made it. With nothing to see but foggy gloom, snow and the distant outline of savage-looking mountains, we went off the road and became buried up to the axles. I'd assumed that, being an Icelander, his 4-wheel-drive vehicle would be full of winter equipment: shovels, blankets, that kind of thing. He had nothing. I ended up trying to dig his car out of the snow with a car jack. It would have worked eventually, if we'd lived that long. Luckily, after a few hours of frustrating jack-digging, another car came along and towed us out. He said we were lucky, people hardly ever used that road any more and we could have been there for days.

After Iceland we flew to Sondrestrom fjord in Greenland. On the way we passed an American tracking station, called Cry Baby I think. Again, the quality of the air was such that we could see the small silver dome of the station when it was still a long way away. In fact we flew with it in full sight for well over half an hour before we came overhead. It was hard to imagine what life was like for the handful of men based there. After seeing things on the very edges of civilisation, you realise there are still bits of the planet which are largely untouched, and what that actually means. To read about it is one thing, to see it on TV is impressive, but to see it for real is awe-inspiring. It was terrifying in its scale and its capacity to make you feel so absolutely insignificant. So much of the planet has a raw edge which is just waiting to kill you. Near the Arctic, we were able to see icebergs quite clearly, even at night, because they seemed to glow in the dark. The light would fade out as they disappeared beneath the surface of the sea. That terrified me, since it made the darkness and the depth all too apparent. It made me long for home and the safety and comfort that I was used to.

The approach to Sondrestrom fjord was impressive to say the least. It was only permissible in daylight and good weather for non-military aeroplanes. Initially we approached along a valley, between two mountains, whose jagged rocks seemed very close. At the end of the valley we turned to the right, almost 180 degrees, and then back between another two mountains. We were descending all the time and the mountains began to feel not only incredibly close but also seriously hostile. The runway came into view and, at the far end, another mountain reared its sinister shape up into the sky. This was not a place where you could afford to mess up the landing. We night-stopped on the military base and left the next day. Our departure was delayed slightly when we discovered a small oil leak on the right engine. An engineer came out, tightened up this and that and sent us on our way. An hour later the leak was back, and much worse. We turned around and headed back to Sondrestrom with oil flowing along the cowlings like black treacle. Greenland is a fearsome place and to be flying over its savage landscape with a sick engine was not enjoyable. The approach through the mountains was even less so but, eventually, we touched down safely back at the base. Out came the jolly engineer, tightened a few more things, changed a few more and, seemingly happy once again, waved us goodbye. We had lost a lot of time by now. For the first few hours things seemed fine. After about two and a half, roughly the halfway point, the leak came back with a vengeance. Oil flooded out of the engine, which was on my side of the aeroplane. I could see flashes of fire as the hot liquid touched the turbocharger shroud, itself glowing red hot, and ignited. It was as far to go back as to go on, and the terrain behind us was slightly more dangerous than the icy sea below, so we elected to press on. We didn't know how much oil the engine was losing but it looked bad. If the oil level got too low the engine would seize and we would be unable to feather the propeller. Feathering is turning the propeller into the airflow to minimise the aerodynamic drag if an engine fails in flight. Unless the prop was feathered we would not be able to maintain height on the one remaining engine and we would go down. Unfortunately we were also heavy with fuel and could not shut the engine down as a precaution for we were too heavy to fly on one, at least for a while. Eventually we decided to divert to a place called Frobisher Bay on Baffin Island, just outside the Arctic Circle.

On the way to Frobisher we had another mechanical problem. The cabin heater broke down and the temperature inside the plane fell to minus 58 degrees Centigrade. The autopilot made it possible for us to bury ourselves in clothing. We were fully thermalled up in our underwear, we had winter flying suits on, heavy duty clothes and thick gloves. We were also wearing North Sea survival suits which could keep you alive in zero degrees water temperature for four hours. On top of all that we were inside sleeping bags and yet we were still so cold we could barely do anything. The aeroplane just kept on going even though most of the dials were freezing with our breath. We landed at Frobisher in a ferocious crosswind that swirled up the falling snow into something similar to fog. Bob handled it with great aplomb and considerable skill. I just sat there and froze my arse off.

Frobisher was an amazing place. I was told many things about it by the locals during the time I was there. The sea freezes solid in the winter, leaving them completely cut off except by aeroplane for about six months of the year. They have constant snow patrols going up and down the runway to keep the runways clear. They also rely on special ships that drive up onto the ice as it starts to melt in late winter. At the time we were there the VD rate in Frobisher Bay was 80 per cent. Although the landscape is beautiful, quite stunning actually, it's extremely hostile, minus 28 degrees Centigrade was by far the warmest day we had there. Many people seemed to be constantly drunk, mainly the local Inuit or Eskimos. On the perimeter they organised wolf patrols because the animals came into the town in search of scraps of food in the rubbish.

The Navajo was in a bad way. One of the right-hand engine's six cylinders had sheared some of its bolts and twisted the others. You could move it up and down with ease. We were lucky it had kept running. I sneaked away to Los Angeles to get some parts for the repairs and take a break in the sunshine. Even getting out on the jet was an experience, for although the aeroplanes that service Frobisher Bay are airliners they're a bit different too. They have various additions to protect them from the harsh Arctic environment and the cabin is a mixture of freight and passengers. A lot of them have a section for injured people, so you might have to walk past six people in stretchers, then through a section with a few tractors, and into a passenger area at the back which is half full of drunken Eskimos. I felt very English and totally out of my depth, surrounded by all these really hard people in lumberjack shirts. I really did feel part of the old pioneering spirit. A spare part. These people are magic though, drunk or not.

We got out of Frobisher itself okay but then we had to make a stop in a place which seemed even more basic. A few more stretchers were loaded on, along with what looked like a wolf and three more of the largest men I'd ever seen. The plane started to throttle up the engines way before we got to the runway. After that it was like a scene from the Keystone Kops, it actually skidded onto the runway and there was snow being blasted all over the place. As it got airborne the end of the runway suddenly flashed past and I realised that we had had little more than yards to spare. Apparently this is quite normal. The runway isn't long enough for the plane to take off when it's above a certain weight so they start the take off on the taxiway to get a bit of a run up. Can you imagine doing that at Heathrow?

With the necessary parts in hand, brought out to us by my father, I left Los Angeles a day or two later and flew back to Frobisher. My dad came with me and, surprisingly, flew with us on the next few legs. I did an interview with the town radio station who were a little surprised to see me there. The Navajo had been put into the hangar at no cost to us, which was a major concession, for things were expensive there. To supply such a remote community, and to pay wages high enough for people to consider working there, made some services very expensive. To even open the hangar doors to move an aeroplane in or out normally cost 200 dollars. Our trip aroused their sympathy, however, and the aeroplane was fixed with great speed and at a very reasonable charge.

After Frobisher we carried on further south, stopping at a number of places including Toronto, Ottawa and Montreal. Eventually we flew to New York where we landed ten minutes before President Reagan's Air Force One. When the security people saw our black aeroplane they were all over us. The fact that it was black seemed to arouse people's suspicions on more than one occasion, not just with the President's men. After a lengthy wait, and many questions, we were allowed to leave – only to find, however, that Reagan was staying in the same hotel, so we had to go through it all again. They wouldn't let us in at all for about an hour.

We zig-zagged our way across America. It was not the quickest way to travel from east to west but I was trying to generate as much interest in the flight as possible. The *Dance* album was out and I wanted to use the flight to attract attention to me, and therefore to it, as much as possible. The plane was serviced in Houston and I took time out to go to Harlingen, the home of the Confederate Air Force. I bought a uniform and became, as does everyone who joins, a CAF Colonel. We then flew into a place called Ozark Inter-Mountain Regional Airport, actually a tiny concrete strip with huge mountains either side. While we were there an old man turned up in a motor-glider. If there weren't any good thermals to help him glide he pulled a rope and an engine popped out of the top. We thought we were intrepid but he said he was going around the world in that. I don't know if he ever made it or not.

At times, to be honest, Bob and I grated on each other. I think he resented the act that I got the lion's share of the media attention wherever we went, even though he was doing the bulk of the planning and the larger share of the flying. It had always been made clear that the trip was as much a promotional trip as anything else and media attention would be sought wherever we went around the world. I never once gave Bob anything less than full credit for his flying abilities. On the other hand, I also wanted people to know that I wasn't just a passenger. I was also doing a great deal of the flying and I faced the same dangers. I was a very new and inexperienced pilot and I felt, for a while, that Bob rammed his vastly superior ability down my throat. With hindsight much of our brief, but unpleasant, period of bad feeling was understandable. Flying day in day out in the same tiny little space would be difficult enough for any two people. Tot up the stress that danger added to some of the trips, plus our different ages, temperaments and backgrounds and it was a wonder we ever got on at all. It was to be a near fatal disaster that made us both, I think, reevaluate the other and from then on, things were much better. A mutual respect grew that overcame and minimised our other differences. Before that happened though, we had a few other hurdles to get over.

As we flew from Seattle, along the Rockies down to Las Vegas, we encountered a phenomenon known as mountain waves – massive waves of moving air that made it impossible to hold a steady height. At one point for example, even with the throttles fully closed and with the aeroplane pointing down, our three tons of metal was still going up at a rate of 2,000 feet a minute, much faster than it could climb on its own power. Then the opposite would happen. With full power and the nose pointing upwards it would descend at a frightening 2,000 feet a minute towards the mountains. On the way to Los Angeles we had to divert around a sandstorm which we could see clearly from the cockpit. From LA we flew up the coast to San Francisco with my brother John on board. John had flown out to LA with my parents to see me before the big Pacific sea crossing. It began to feel a bit like the last good-bye and this was the stage of the trip I'd been dreading the most.

In San Francisco we put in the big extra fuel tanks. We had 165 gallons in the main tank, another 27 in the nose, 120 in three large drums in the cabin and another 150 in big silver tanks that were fitted on top of the drums. Yet another 30 gallons were in cans which were squeezed in by the drums. It was a lot of fuel and, at over seven pounds per gallon, a lot of weight. We were running the aeroplane at least 27 per cent over its normal maximum load. From a legal point of view not entirely acceptable to the British CAA but absolutely necessary, as they well knew, to get across the Pacific.

Effectively we were in a flying bomb. For me to get to the back of the aeroplane I had to collapse my seat and then pull myself along the right-hand floor of the aeroplane, along the tiny space we'd left to crawl through. It was like a pointed arch but with one flat side, about 12 inches wide at the bottom going to a point about 18 inches above the floor. It was incredibly claustrophobic and I barely fitted. God knows how Bob ever made it. That was the only way to the door and it was at least ten feet long. It took several minutes to crawl through this when the aeroplane was parked on the ground, so trying to do it in an emergency was virtually unthinkable.

So off we went to Honolulu, Hawaii. We took off at night to make best use of the cooler night air to try and ensure that we arrived in daylight. My family watched us go and my mum has often told me how much she hated the sound of the plane as it faded slowly into the darkness. She said it sounded so lonely and small, and the ocean looked so menacing and vast. The build-up to that flight had been hard work and we were both very tired. At one point we both fell asleep. When we woke we were horrified to discover that the aeroplane had flown well over a hundred miles without anyone watching over it. It was still dead on course though. It's things like that make you love flying. Call me weird, but after that moment I loved that aeroplane with a passion that was almost obscene. It had looked after us when we should have been looking after it.

The flight to Hawaii was expected to take about fifteen and a half hours. The best height for fuel consumption and wind currents was 12,000 ft. This meant we had to fly with oxygen but so be it. We were flying just above thick cloud. It had been cloudy for hours but the stars were out and looked very pretty. They made you feel, as so many things did on that trip, small and fragile, meaningless and insignificant in the great scheme of things. We'd flown about 1,200 miles, about halfway, when both engines quit. The phrase 'I bet that got your attention' doesn't come close. This was a nightmare come to life. Different tanks were selected, pumps were put on, everything that had even the vaguest connection to the problem was flicked, pulled and twisted. Nothing worked. We were going down. We descended through the cloud. The aeroplane was strangely quiet except for the whistling of air passing the airframe and the whirring of gyros that continued to tell us the awful truth. Heavy as we were, and without power, we were going down at about 800 feet per minute. We had 15 minutes at best until we died.

We were over the middle of the Pacific, there was no one around for a thousand miles in any direction and, under the clouds, it was absolutely black. There was no vague horizon, no hazy outline of clouds or the surface of sea. It was like being inside a black vault. You could look up, down, sideways and see nothing. There was no ambient light at all. No distant street lights reflecting from the clouds, no star light breaking through the cloud. Nothing. Just the most impenetrable dark you could ever know. We didn't know what had happened but we had plenty of time to think about it as we made our long fall towards the unseen sea. All the time in the world to think about how you might die. We would never see the ocean unless we put the landing lights on. But, to put the lights on, we had to lower the undercarriage because the lights were fixed to the nose wheel. Landing on the sea with undercarriage lowered was not what you wanted. What a horrible dilemma. No lights, crash, lights on, crash.

If we survived the crash, unlikely as that seemed, what then? We would never drag ourselves along that tight little space to the back door before it sank. It would be a miracle for one and surely impossible for two. Would we fight in a desperate struggle to get out first? What if we did survive the crash, and we did get out, what then? The idea of surviving the crash and getting out into the water without a small cut of some kind was unthinkable and then? Sharks. The darkest night, the deepest water, and the sure knowledge that, sooner or later, the sharks would come for us. It was a nightmare scene that was beyond belief and yet it was happening. We passed 10,000 ft quickly, down we went and passed 5,000 ft. The eerie whistling of air seemed like the siren call of death itself and I began to hate it.

We didn't say much to each other. Bob whistled a little tune and I was humming quietly to myself. Bob said later that at any moment he expected me to start screaming and become a problem. I was quite calm. The moment had an inevitability about it that made any show of emotion pointless. What would be would be. There was nothing we could do but wait. I had no thoughts of home or family, no flashback of life, just an emptiness inside, a quiet cold fear that had nowhere to go. I would have welcomed a task or two, something to keep me occupied until we hit the water, but there was nothing for me to do. We passed 2,000 ft. We had about two and a half minutes left before we would hit the sea when, without a single splutter or hiccup, the engines burst back into life. On went the power, up came the nose and we soared skywards once again. I was almost more scared now than before. I would rather have been dead than go through that long wait again. But the engines continued their song and we climbed purposefully back to our cruising height. As we broke cloud and saw the stars again it was almost a religious experience.

Thirty minutes later it happened again. Down we went for a second time. If I had died and come face to face with God I would have punched him fucking hard. Why the torture? This time though there was hope. They had sorted themselves out before, why not now? This was far worse. With hope came a deeper fear. No sense of quiet acceptance now, I just wanted to live. My nerves were frazzled but I wanted this thing to go away. Once again, as we got close to the sea the engines fired back into life. And then Bob figured it out. We had a tube on the nose of the aeroplane that took in ram air and put a small amount of pressure into the nose tanks. The moisture of the clouds had frozen over the tube and caused an air lock. The fuel was unable to flow until, as we descended into warmer air, the ice melted. For the remainder of the flight we flew at a lower altitude, keeping well away from the cloud. The fuel consumption went up but it was acceptable. Seven hours later we landed in Hawaii.

In Hawaii the aeroplane was due for a major overhaul and so we had a free day or two to enjoy the sights. This turned out to be less than I'd hoped for. Most of the first day was spent in and out of banks, trying to sort out money arrangements. We took a drive round some of the island but it rained for much of the time. We went to Pearl Harbor, site of the infamous Japanese attack that brought America into the last great war, but it was a fleeting visit as we had more things to sort out with the aeroplane. High winds roared in from the west Pacific and our departure looked as though it might have to be put back. The islands were catching the tail end of a distant hurricane but we decided that, with other storm fronts forecast for the region, it was either leave now or stay for a while. We felt the need to push on, winter was drawing ever closer. As we taxied out the winds were extraordinarily vicious and the Navajo was bucking and writhing around in its thin undercarriage legs. We were slightly out of Centre of Gravity limits which is not something to be recommended, since it affects the controllability of the aeroplane, but with fuel burn we would be back inside limits within an hour. A small risk but, again, necessary for the distance we now had to fly. The take-off was interesting but went smoothly enough and the big black machine clawed its way once again into a turbulent night sky. Control wise it was 'sloppy' for a while but, as the weight came down, it began to feel better and so the second long Pacific leg got underway.

From Hawaii we travelled to Majuro in the Marshall Islands, a tiny group of islands in the middle of the Pacific. We flew for another 15 hours in that cramped cockpit with nothing to look at but darkness and then, as the sun came up, endless sea. After thousands of miles of vast ocean we saw a tiny strip of land: Majuro. It looked as big as my drive and if we had been one degree off course we would never have known we'd missed it. The runway was as wide as the island, with the edge actually bordering the sea. It was a beautiful place, one of those old Hollywood paradise islands. We landed and filled the aeroplane with fuel, hand pumped from drums that had been taken to the island just for us. We took some rest in small, round huts on the beach. I would have loved to have stayed there a while, so idyllic was the setting, but we had to move on. The storms were moving across our path and we had to leave quickly. The decision to leave became a little easier after a local explained that, every few years, freak waves rolled in and washed everything away. He talked about it as we talk about the occasional spring shower. I didn't like to ask what happened to all the people when these waves came.

We flew on to Guam, another long trip of about 1,800 miles, all of over the sea. The Pacific Ocean was vast beyond anything I had ever imagined. I was so used to travelling by airliners, high above the world and at tremendous speeds, that I'd lost my sense of proportion. Even though we were travelling at around 200 miles an hour, we were now on our third day and still the ocean spread from horizon to horizon. We set out from Majuro, once again at night, and soon we were high above the watery depths and surrounded by stars, twinkling with that remarkable clarity rarely seen where man lives. On the High Frequency Radio we heard an emergency as a plane crashed on the other side of the world. That was chilling. I hated the HF radio. As Bob turned the dial it would put out constantly changing tones and squeaks and squeals, or small clips of garbled speech, heavily distorted like the voice of an alien. Suddenly it would come clear and you would pick up the voice of someone maybe 12,000 miles away, having his own problems. Listening to this when we were flying over the darkest ocean made me decidedly uncomfortable. Bob liked it however, and fiddled with the HF all the time. We ended up skirting a cumulonimbus storm over the Pacific, massive clouds that could tear us apart; the tremendous air currents that roar through them are so powerful even big airliners avoid them. We didn't have radar but, even in the dark, we knew they were across our path. They were much higher than we could fly so we couldn't go over them, and we could only make out their shape by the fact that they blacked out the stars. To me they looked like black lumps of evil, towering up for miles and miles above us. The only way we could avoid them was to head for the areas where we could still see starlight. We zig-zagged our way carefully across the Pacific, through these most dangerous clouds until, inevitably, there came a point where there were no stars at all. All we could do was aim for the point where he had last seen some and hope for the best. We flew into the black at our best speed for turbulent air. It was scary, a very oppressive feeling to be encased in absolute darkness like that. We were thrown around like a toy and we were still quite heavy which only added to the stress that the aeroplane was suffering. I had visions of the aeroplane clapping hands, I was listening for the sound of popping rivets. It didn't last long and soon we blasted out of the last of the menacing clouds to a clear star-lit sky once again.

Our times on the ground had, for the last few days, been unfortunate in that nothing had been available to eat. Not for me anyway. I eat very simply, burgers, chips, that kind of thing. By the time we got to Guam I hadn't eaten a thing for about 48 hours. Much to my annoyance we arrived at Guam late at night, shops were shut, and left before anything opened up again in the morning. Without food I became very irritable. Still, next stop Tokyo.

Japan was better, at least I could eat. Our only problem was that the main airport didn't have fuel suitable for our aeroplane and so we had to fly to a small local airfield to refuel. No major problem there, except for the fact that the only place with suitable fuel had a short runway. With our tanks full for yet another long ocean trip we didn't have enough room to take off again. Before we even got there, though, we ran into another problem. As we taxied out from Tokyo's main international airport we were asked to hold near the end of the runway. There was a problem with our clearance and so we were then asked to taxi back to the parking area. Irritating though this was, it saved our lives. We parked the plane and got out only to find that the right-hand engine had dumped its entire contents of oil onto the ground. If we had taken off we would have lost the engine, without being able to feather, and down we would have gone. On examination it turned out that the oil filter had been wire-locked incorrectly and that it could have come off at any time. We had flown over thousands of miles of ocean with it like that. I had to sit down for a minute or two. We arrived at the local airfield eventually and got around the short runway problem by adopting the Frobisher technique of using the taxiway as the starting point for the take-off. We had about 30 mph before we even got to the runway. Worked a treat.

We had planned to fly south towards Australia via the Philippines but our clearances had expired and they were awkward, to say the least, about authorising new ones. Rather than waste more days arguing we flew back to Guam and from there to Papua New Guinea. A pleasant night stop, with food, in PNG and then it was on to Brisbane, Australia. There we really got into trouble. First of all we had somehow managed to leave our passports in PNG. Secondly, and more importantly to the Australians, we accidentally contravened one of their laws that says all arriving aeroplanes must be sprayed before the passengers can get off. I should have known, really. On previous airliner trips to Australia we had always been made to stay in our seats until men in shorts had walked up and down the plane spraying aerosol cans into the air, thereby presumably, ridding all the filthy passengers of bugs and diseases before stepping off into the clean air of Oz. When we arrived in the Navajo I was almost deliriously happy, for the Pacific was behind us. As we taxied in I opened the back door and leaned out to get a lovely 16mm movie shot of the airport name as we pulled up in front of the terminal. I got another good shot of two men in shorts walking purposefully towards us and waved them a cheery hello. They waved back but it seemed strangely hostile through the camera lens. 'Shut that door,' they shouted, in what I assumed, by quoting from one of our finest TV comic moments, was a friendly acknowledgement of our British status. But no, we were in big trouble. They ripped into us rather forcefully, I thought. It was as though people flew little aeroplanes from England to Australia every day of the week. I had expected TV reporters, cheering fans, media representatives of all kinds to witness this epic moment. I was the first pop star to fly a light aeroplane around the world, albeit with Uncle Bob in charge. Instead we were taken in to an office and made to write a formal letter of apology to the Australian Government for breaking the rules. They kept us there, like naughty children, for several hours. After that we returned to the aeroplane only to find that Customs wanted a thorough investigation. They took it apart almost down to the last nut. Everything was laid out on the airport tarmac. They crawled upside down behind the control panel and pulled wire looms aside in their desperate search for whatever it was they thought we had on board. I was furious. They were heavyhanded, to say the least, and that equipment, which they were happily wrenching about, still had another half of the world to take us around. They found nothing, said nothing and walked away. It took Bob and me another couple of hours to put everything back again. By the time we left the airport what media had come along to meet us had long since gone home.

We flew to Sydney and took out the big silver fuel tanks which, although the cabin was still cluttered with the three 40-gallon drums and spare fuel cans, made it possible to get in and out more easily. Our journey took us down the east coast, along the south and then across part of the outback to Perth. I made the huge mistake of reading a magazine article about shark attacks as we flew over the Great Australian Bight. Towards the end of the article I discovered that the very sea that we were now rushing over was the breeding ground of the Great White shark, the most deadly and ferocious of them all. That flight had been very exciting for other reasons, too. For much of it we flew barely above the ground, our shadow formatting on us as we twisted and turned around rocks and hills. It was great fun. A few hours out of Perth, though, I began to feel ill. I lay down in the back across the top of the fuel drums as best I could. A peculiar tingling in my tummy gave way to a pins and needles that spread from my fingers and toes all over my body. My muscles contracted so badly my blood couldn't flow properly to my hands and feet and they turned blue. I felt muscles in my neck pull and damage themselves under their own power. It was incredibly painful. I tried to be sick but tipped head-first into the portable toilet and stayed there, with vomit pouring down my face, for quite some time. I was paralysed, I couldn't get out. I fell out of it eventually when the aeroplane hit a particularly turbulent bit of air and I just lay there in a scrunched up little ball. When we arrived in Perth the doctor gave me some Valium. His diagnosis was classic: an anxiety attack brought on by a childhood memory. Okay then, that'll be right. I took one Valium, calmed down, and threw the rest in the bin. It turned out that I had hyperventilated due to not eating and overheating.

After Perth we travelled up the west coast to Port Headland where we refuelled and continued on our way. At Port Headland one of the engines cut out as we lined up on the runway to take off, which added a degree of tension that I could have done without. Our next leg took us over the Timor Sea, one of the most shark-infested seas in the world, en route to Djakarta, Indonesia. The city had two airports, only one of which appeared to be in use. They were lining us up for the one that was shut. The runway was supposed to be ahead of us and it was black. Bob knew something wasn't quite right. I kept hearing him mumble 'This isn't the right place.' I was too busy watching the lightning leaping from cloud to cloud on the far side of the city. I wanted to keep well clear of that, no matter what. You could see the clouds lighting up inside, like Chinese lanterns. It was one of the most amazing things I'd ever seen but I certainly didn't want to be amongst it. We were anxious to get down because this storm was moving towards us. Bob eventually sorted them out and we landed safely onto the wet runway.

143

We parked the plane and then got into another argument with the local officials. Their monetary 'requirements' were demanded far more aggressively. I took an instant dislike to the place; to me it felt corrupt, violent and dangerous. For some reason, I was convinced that the taxi driver was going to take us to a place where we were going to be ambushed. My imagination was running riot, over-tiredness probably, but I was absolutely sure of it. There was something in the way he kept looking at us in his rear-view mirror. Djakarta itself felt quite heavy, it had a brooding, aggressive atmosphere and it looked like every street corner had a gang on the prowl. I had my trusty Swiss Army knife in my bag so I took out one of the more ferocious blades. I sat behind the taxi driver, who couldn't see what I was doing luckily, with the blade behind his neck the whole journey until we got to the hotel. If we'd stopped in a dark street I was going to stab him. I had it all planned. I was going to stab him, pull him out of the seat, jump in the front and drive off so we didn't get shot. Bob was just giggling. He thought I was a twat and quite rightly so. I now put it down to too much life-threatening stress.

From Djakarta we journeyed to Singapore, which was excellent. A local club had a Gary Numan lookalike contest which I had to judge. No one looked like me at all. I don't even think they were fans, I think they'd been dragged in and paid to do it. We went out shopping and I went into a place selling panda toys. They had a huge panda as a display model, about 6 feet tall, so I bought it and had it air freighted home in a crate. For a long time I kept the panda underneath the staircase in my other house, but it got ripped and ended up in the shed. The rats got it eventually and so I had to burn it. I wish I'd looked after him better.

Then we arrived in Bangkok, Thailand. This was where we had been heading for when the engine coughed and forced us back towards India – it seemed like a lifetime ago. In Bangkok I gave a press conference in full gangster suit and make-up image. I spent some time chatting to the Thai liaison woman afterwards. She explained that the men sitting at the end of each corridor in the hotel were there to make sure the moral standards were maintained. I thought that was the most extreme case of double standards I'd ever come across. This was the same Thailand of child-prostitution infamy, wasn't it? While we sat talking on the hotel veranda, looking out over the river at the most beautiful sunset, I saw a dead donkey float past. It was not romantic.

Next stop, Calcutta. I had not been looking forward to getting back to India at all. This time, though, things were much better, although we did have one near disaster. Another old rusty bone-shaker fuel bowser brought the Avgas fuel out to us. Avgas isn't always easy to get at airports that deal mainly with jets. Airliners use a different fuel. Our Avgas bowser might have had its fuel slushing around inside it for years, who knew? As before in India, I was a little uncertain as to what they were giving us. They almost didn't give us anything but a fireball. Soon after they started to pump the fuel into our wing tanks the nozzle flew off the end of the hose, which began snaking around like a mad thing. Fuel was spraying everywhere, over the aeroplane, the hot engines and, most painfully, over me. I was amazed we didn't all ignite in the most spectacular fashion. They brought the hose under control eventually, replaced the nozzle and finished the job. My body was in trouble. Already hot and sweaty, the fuel had soaked into my open pores, the vapour was in my eyes and I was in a lot of pain. It took a while to clean up and sort myself out. We stayed in Calcutta that night and left early the next morning for Karachi, Pakistan.

As we approached Karachi the right engine problem returned. Oil began to pour back along the cowling. We were only minutes away from touchdown but, even so, it was a tense few minutes. The oil was gushing out. The engineers had a quick look over it and told us that we had exactly the same problem – the same cylinder had sheared and twisted the bolts that secured it to the main engine block. I had to fly back home to pick up more spare parts. I wasn't in England for more than a few hours: I got off the jet, drove to the hangar to get the spares, drove back to the airport and got on the same jet back to Pakistan. My dad came with me again, as he had a few business details to sort out with Bob. We spent a couple of days in Karachi while the plane was fixed. The hotel also had corridor guards so that the 'shameful Western flight crews behaved themselves'. Food was a problem again so I was glad when the repairs were finished and we set off for Dubai. Dad went back via British Airways but, strangely enough, we both landed in Dubai within minutes of each other. His aeroplane was just making a brief stop to pick up more passengers, while we had run into another problem. The starter motor on the left engine had failed.

Partially fixed, we left Dubai, stopped in Bahrain for fuel and then flew on to Rhodes in the Greek Islands. Rhodes airport had a limit on the amount of crosswind they could accept before they were required to close the airport. We approached with a howling crosswind making the aeroplane appear to be pointing virtually sideways to the direction we were actually travelling in. The controllers kept saying, 'The airfield is now closed', then, a few minutes later, 'The airfield is now open', right up to the moment of landing. Bob and I had already agreed that, whatever they said, the airfield was open to us. We were too tired to even think about going somewhere else, and he, I and the aeroplane were all starting to show signs of wear and tear. Because of air turbulence throwing us up and down so violently, I had friction burns on my skin from the seatbelts – it looked like a giant love bite – from the shoulder down. After we landed safely at Rhodes, with it being declared open less than 20 seconds before our wheels touched the ground, the aeroplane's left starter motor failed completely. My dad had been home less than three hours before he got the phone call. He drove back down to the airfield, picked up a starter motor and flew off again to meet us in Rhodes. By the time he got to us he hadn't shaved. He'd spent the last three days on aeroplanes so we all decided that he should come back to England with us. Compared to where we'd been it didn't seem that far.

The replacement starter motor was fitted, it worked, and so we took off the next day in a heavy rain shower and made our way to Rome. We stopped for no longer than the time it took to refuel and then we were on our way again. The French air traffic controllers were on strike as usual so we decided to fly around France rather than over it. This extended our journey time considerably, but it was better than being messed around and diverted here and there and everywhere by the French. We arrived back at Heathrow at 9 pm on a snowy Christmas Eve. There was no big fanfare, just my family. The press had completely lost interest by now. To this day they often claim that we 'crashed' in India on the first attempt and gave up.

The homecoming was a bit of a non-event, to be honest. When we got back I put about 40 rolls of film in to be developed and Kodak lost them, so I never got a single photograph of the entire trip. My brother took some photographs of us arriving back at the airport, the only photos we had of us actually completing the trip, and Kodak lost those as well. I have hardly any record of our achievement save for some 16mm film that we took very sporadically throughout the journey. Not only that, but UK Customs gave us a thorough going over as well. By the time we left Heathrow it was Christmas morning.

Traditionally we always have a family get-together of uncles and grandparents on Christmas Day. That evening I was round my Aunt Maureen's house. I found myself sitting by a cosy fireplace in England and yet the day before we'd been fighting with a sick engine. For the previous two months I had led a bizarre life, facing real danger on a daily basis and making hugely important decisions. Now I was back home again and people were asking if I wanted some cake. I was almost dazed by it all. It took me a while to adjust to ordinary life again.

For a short time I felt like a different person but then I drifted back to normality. You don't get wolf patrols in Essex after all. When I first got back I had intended to become active in all sorts of fund-raising ventures to help out some of the people I'd seen on my travels. Unfortunately my own problems came back to the forefront all too easily. Nevertheless, I did finally realise courage comes in all shapes and forms and I put the self-doubt about my own character to sleep once and for all. I felt more at ease with myself after the trip. I could have quit at anytime, the press already thought I had, so no one would have been any the wiser, but I hadn't. I was scared virtually every day, so I'm no hero, but I stayed with it. Without Bob things could have been very different and the credit for that trip sits fairly and squarely on his shoulders. I was just glad to be a part of it and as a writer, it was a dream come true. A new range of extreme experiences and emotions now inspired my songs. The hostile, isolated environments that had dwarfed us for much of the journey also influenced my music and lyrics. I felt that I'd grown up a lot and I'm more proud of that trip than anything else I've ever done.

147

CHAPTER 8

My Dying Machine, 1982

I was in a plane crash once, on 29 January 1982 to be precise and the press had a field day with it. To this day I still have to put up with 'witty' remarks and insults about my flying ability. The truth was somewhat different to what you may have read.

Our problems started on the day before the accident. I set off from Southampton en route to Cannes in France, for the Midem Music Conference, with my ex-instructor, also a friend, who was in charge of the flight because of my relative inexperience. I would always take someone experienced along whenever I was doing something new or reasonably lengthy, because it gave me a feeling of extra security and it meant that I could relax and learn from an expert. Building up your own experience as pilot in charge is useful and good for your early confidence but on some trips, such as this one, I felt it more sensible to take an experienced man along with me. Shortly after take-off the warning light for the alternator flashed on. The alternator supplies the electrical power to the plane and charges up the battery, just like in a car. I had always been taught that this was a no-go fault and so had actually started to turn back to the airfield when my friend said that it wasn't a big problem and that it was okay to carry on. Okay, I thought, this is obviously clever stuff so on we went. It all went very well, to be honest. We flew with most of the electrics turned off to save battery power, navigating by map mainly, and only occasionally turning on the radio navigation aids to check on our position. Several hours later the French airfield loomed up, right on the nose, and I sat back highly impressed.

The festival went well and that night we talked about the return trip to Southampton. My father was to come back with us in the aeroplane, as was Bill Fowler, then head of radio promotion at WEA. Bill was not a good flyer and agreed to come back with us more as a show of faith in me than anything else, I think, as the press had already started to give me a hard time about my flying after the round the world flight problems. My friend was also keen to take back Michael Appleton, a BBC TV producer we knew, who was also a friend of Bill's, and that, for the first time, started to make me slightly unsure about some of the decisions being made. I was far from being an expert, and lacked aviation experience in every area but, according to the flight manual as I understood it, to get five people onto the plane meant taking off some of the fuel. From what I could make out we could not afford to take off the amount of fuel required to take another fairly large man, who weighed about the same as the fuel required for two hours' flying. I was very worried about all this and talked it over at length with my father before going to bed. I decided that we could not carry the extra man but, not wishing to offend my friend, I made it seem as though he had other business and couldn't come with us after all. Meanwhile, my dad had told this lucky man the truth – we didn't have the capacity due to fuel weight.

The alternator was supposed to have been fixed in France but my friend said that, on investigation, it was ridiculously expensive to have it done there, and that it would be better to fly it back to England in the same way that we flew to France and fix it there. Again, little alarm bells were beginning to ring in my head but I lacked the confidence to argue. The aeroplane was filled with fuel, checked by the fueller, my friend and myself. Without doubt it was full to the brim because as we turned onto the runway a small amount came out of the overflow. She was full and heavy.

On the return trip the weather took a turn for the worse and I began to feel in my bones that something wasn't quite right. I have since built up absolute faith in these feelings of unease and if ever I get them I land. Better to have the engineers find nothing back on the ground than an accident investigator find something in the wreckage. There came a point when we'd already flown for a full hour longer than our entire outward trip to Cannes but we still hadn't arrived at the French coast. This extra time couldn't be attributed to the weather alone. My friend insisted there wasn't a problem but his increasingly frequent use of the radio navigation equipment signalled otherwise. I could sense his growing unease and was about to say, Look, this is my aeroplane and we're going to land it, when the Channel suddenly appeared. My friend's confidence shot back up and that silenced me for a while, but I was still far from happy.

The communication radios were getting weak and crackly, which meant the navigation radios were also struggling. The battery was obviously on its last legs and here we were heading out across the sea. We took a course direct to Southampton. I noticed the right fuel tank was showing empty and that the left had fallen to a quarter. This didn't make sense. We'd left France with the tanks full, enough fuel for seven and a half hours' flying time, and yet at this stage we'd flown for less than five. We should have been showing a lot more fuel than that. My friend seemed unconcerned by this saying we couldn't trust the flight gauges because of the electric fault. By sheer coincidence as he said the words the left gauge fell from one quarter to nought, which graphically backed up his argument. I was feeling really edgy: we were unable to make radio contact with any of the airfields on either coast, the battery was gone, the aeroplane felt as though it was dying. I swear you could feel it was trouble. I looked him in the eye and told him I wasn't happy. We were flying across the Channel at an angle, good for the distance to Southampton but bad in that it increased our over-water time. Making a forced landing into a rough sea in a high wing aeroplane is no light undertaking. I wanted to be over land as quickly as possible and to fly in a straight line to the nearest part of the English coast. Our overall flying time to Southampton would be extended slightly, but more of the return route would be over land. If there was a fault I didn't want to crash this particular aircraft, which had to sink before you could open the doors because of the pressure differential, into a choppy sea with four people struggling to get out. We started arguing. He was against a course change for the bizarre reason that if the engine stopped we wouldn't land at a Customs airfield and they would be upset. I replied, 'Fuck Customs' but he wouldn't listen. I still didn't quite have enough willpower to say, 'I'm doing what I want'. It was my aeroplane but he was in charge of the flight. However I did make a slight course adjustment. His vision of my gauges was obscured slightly by our relative seating positions, allowing me to quietly cheat a few degrees and split the difference between his intended flight plan to Southampton and mine to the nearest coastline.

When we came over land I turned slightly left and we headed towards Southampton. I was relieved to be over solid ground again but by now I was convinced that we were in big trouble. About 60 seconds after crossing the coast the engine spluttered briefly and stopped. We changed tanks, put on both the emergency fuel pumps and breathed a sigh of relief as the engine fired back into life. The weather over the south coast was poor and we were quite low, about 800 ft, to stay under the dark and menacing clouds. We flew along for about another minute, so we could now see Southampton and the wet glistening runway in the distance. We had quickly talked over what we would do if it stopped again. Without electrical power the flaps would not operate. Flaps, in effect, adjust the wing shape and make it possible to land at slower speeds. Without them we were going to land much faster than normal. Not a big problem on a long runway but a hell of a problem if you ended up in a field. The main problem though was the undercarriage which worked on a hydraulic system, but the pump was electric, and without the electrics the undercarriage would not be pumped down. My job, should the engine stop again, was to lower the undercarriage manually with a hand pump located in the floor. I'd never done it before, and I couldn't remember for the life of me what the manual had said about it, so I had no idea how long it would take to get the wheels down by that method. My dad, who was sitting in the back, had noticed the arguing and sensed that things weren't right. Then the engine stopped for the second and final time. I ripped off the access panel to the emergency hydraulic pump and began to whizz that little lever up and down like a madman. My friend did a quite brilliant job. We were actually going past the only field we could land in, everywhere else was either full of trees or the fields were too small. Because we were so low our options were virtually nil. This was the one and only field that could take the plane but it was already slightly behind and, strangely enough, too close. He pulled the aeroplane up and over and aimed for the field. Without flaps, and with the wheels extending painfully slowly, the aeroplane had no way of slowing down. We were, if anything, accelerating in the dive towards the field. No choice.

I knew that unless the wheels were down and locked we were in bad shape and I pumped like a man possessed. I called out to my dad, 'Can you see the wheels, can you see the wheels!' but he couldn't. I didn't think I was going to make it as I felt my friend lift the nose of the aeroplane as the ground came up to meet it. Suddenly I felt the lever jump in my hand and it would move no more. I looked over my shoulder, still trying to exert more force on the lever, and I saw trees going past. I sat bolt upright and pulled my shoulder strap tight just as we hit the ground.

The first impact was hard, very hard, and we took off again. I think at that point we lost the nose wheel, which was never found. The plane soared up again in a huge bounce. This was not good, we needed the wheels on the ground if we were to have any real chance of stopping before we ran out of field. With no flaps the aerodynamic braking was virtually nil. Bang, another touch down and another bounce. The third time it stayed down but we were already halfway across the field. It was an L shaped field and we were going down the long part; at the end there was a small embankment about three or four feet high, with what appeared to be a small road going by it and, on the other side of the road, was a house. We must have thought the same thing at the same time because, simultaneously, we pushed on the right rudder to try and turn it up the short leg of the L-shaped part of the field, since it was obvious we weren't going to stop before the embankment. It didn't make any difference. The grass was wet, the nose was on the floor, and we were still moving fast.

The nose started to come round but then the left undercarriage leg collapsed and tucked itself up underneath. The aircraft was now on its belly, leaning to the left, one leg out and one leg collapsed. It wasn't really controllable any more, but it was still heading towards the house. Even though all this was happening at tremendous speed, I was aware of every noise. Everything was loud and crystal clear. I could see individual blades of grass and particles of dust, I was aware of everything. It was as if the whole world had slowed down to a crawl. I had, without thinking about it, accepted the inevitability of pain. I was strangely distanced from it and not at all concerned. I was almost fascinated by how and where it would hurt. I remember thinking, 'It will probably be my legs first', and so I pulled them back, as if it was going to make any difference. I wondered how it would feel as the bits of metal started cutting into me. It was the most bizarre series of thoughts I think I've ever had. I was curious, almost as if it wasn't actually happening to me at all, as though my mind had left my body and become just an interested bystander. One thing was bothering me though, and it was a terrifying thought. It looked as though we were going to hurt those poor people in the house, which was getting closer and closer. I clearly remember thinking how unjust it would be to be doing nothing more dangerous than playing in your back garden when an aeroplane comes hurtling through the hedge and kills everybody. I don't think I've ever felt so helpless or desperate. I didn't think about my dad at all which amazed me afterwards. My dad said that he didn't think about me either, he was more concerned about Bill Fowler. My dad said he felt terribly guilty because Bill had shown good faith and the plane had crashed. For his part Bill was completely unaware of what was going on; he genuinely thought it was a normal landing.

As the embankment came upon us we both pulled back on the control column in an attempt to lift the nose and minimise the impact. A slightly glancing blow would be more survivable than a head-on, nose-down smash. We still hit hard, but it worked. The poor old aeroplane took off once again, for just a second. The right wing sliced into a telegraph pole, which went halfway through the wing. We were pulled sharply round to the right, the pole still buried deep in the wing, and then the nose dropped. For what felt like an eternity, we seemed to just hang there, pointing down at the road. It was as though time had stood still for a moment. I remember noticing the white stones, cracks in the tarmac, a whole mass of trivia, and then we hit the road and stopped dead. We were almost perfectly placed on the central white line.

Everything was strangely silent for a few seconds. There was a noticeable moment of reflection as we realised that we were completely still and that no one was hurt. It was deathly quiet except for the ticking of the cooling metal, that strange pinging sound. I can remember thinking how bizarre it was that nothing hurt, almost as if it was an anti-climax. I wasn't exactly disappointed but it felt like something more should have happened. It was all too simple, there hadn't been an explosion, no bits of metal coming towards us. Then my senses came back and I, brave as always, was the first one to shout for us to run for it. My friend got out and ran, I was already out. I looked back and my dad was also out and running, but Bill hadn't made a move at all. He was so shaken, he'd completely frozen. We didn't know why the plane had crashed at this point so we thought there might still be a lot of fuel in it. Luckily I was still clearly in shock at this time or else I would probably not have done it, but I went back into the cabin to get Bill. My dad and Tim were long gone up the road but I felt responsible for Bill. I climbed back into the plane and he was just staring ahead, looking like he'd just woken up, so I had to undo his straps. He's a big heavily built man and I'm only little so it was quite hard to get him over my shoulder and pull him out. He was staggering along, more dragging his feet with me supporting him than actually walking. It took him a while to get it all together.

My dad hurt his right eye when we crashed into the embankment. He'd hit it on Bill's head, having decided to lie over Bill in an attempt to protect him. The veins ruptured and created a U-shaped blood bubble. Although the doctors said it would go away within a month or two it never has. If he shuts his left eye and just uses the right he has an opaque horseshoe shape in his vision. The impact of the collision stove the front of the aeroplane up, twisted the fuselage and tore off various bits and pieces. My friend had a lump come up on his knee, Bill cut his lip and I just got bad press. I call that a result, personally.

Two rows of traffic had now stopped. There was a little old lady at one end in an orange Austin 1100. She was edging forward to get past and so I ran over to her and said, 'You'd better stay clear because the aeroplane might blow up any minute.' She was more worried about her husband's dinner and I could not believe her reaction. Here she was, driving along this quiet leafy back road when an aeroplane crashes down in front of her, and all she was concerned about was her husband's dinner. Not so much as an 'Are you all right?' She turned round, very grumpy, and drove off. In fact no one tried to help. People got out of their cars, some of them anyway, and just looked. One group of people got out of a car and started taking photographs, within seconds of us running from the wreckage. The first thing that somebody said to me, and I swear this is true, was not words of comfort or concern, it was, 'Can I have your autograph?' I ran up to a girl with a camera and asked if I could borrow it, pumped up with adrenalin as I was, I also wanted to get a few photos. I wasn't thinking straight, who would be in that situation? I was laughing and giggling and we were slapping each other on the back. It felt like a big adventure for a few hours afterwards. It's only later you realise what you've been through and then your body reacts. I borrowed her camera, took the film with me and she gave me her address so that I could send her pictures on to her. It was all so polite and proper, with the plane broken and creaking away behind us. When I had the film developed it became clear that she'd been to a very 'interesting' party before we landed in front of her. She was all over the place with different men, doing a variety of things.

The police and fire service arrived fairly quickly. A local pub landlord had made us all a cup of tea and allowed us into his pub to sit down. I stayed outside to keep an eye on the aeroplane. The police said that even though we'd had an accident and we were in the middle of the road, we weren't allowed to leave the scene until HM Customs turned up. Because you have to temporarily export an aeroplane when it flies abroad, when you come back you have to officially re-import it again. That was how things were then anyway. Eventually a man from Customs arrived and we went through this rather formal procedure of signing a form to officially re-import the wreck back into the country. Paperwork has no sympathy. A while later a truck came to move the aeroplane. The man with it went to work but he was really butchering the thing. He then started talking loudly to anyone around that it had no fuel in the wings and how it was the pilot's responsibility and what idiot runs out of fuel etc etc. For someone with his arse hanging out of his trousers, who was so thick he could hardly put a sentence together, I thought he was talking slightly beyond his station and said words to that effect. That nearly ended in a fight, stopped by my friend and the police, luckily for me, because he was as large as he was stupid and he would have no doubt slaughtered me.

Then the TV people turned up and within an hour of actually crashing I was live on the local TV news. I have no idea what I said, I think I was still bubbling, still wound up and excited so I probably came across a tad cavalier.

One good thing about it was I actually had the aeroplane up for sale and because of the crash I got all the insurance money. Because nobody was injured in our accident there wasn't a full investigation, so the exact cause wasn't determined at the time. The aeroplane had clearly developed a problem and dumped, or used somehow, two hours' worth of fuel more than it should have, and we didn't know because of the electrical problem. Many years later, after a number of similar accidents occurred, the aeroplane manufacturer was taken to court in the States. It was said that a design flaw in the fuel system and its placement had been the cause of these accidents, one of which resulted in the death of a pilot. I had always said that the fuel problem had to be at the heart of our accident, it had already behaved strangely during the first round the world flight attempt. The press was relentless in their attacks on me after the accident, but none of them was the slightest bit interested when the facts about the design flaw came out. We should not have flown on with the faulty alternator and that did make the other problem difficult to detect. The cause of the crash, however, was due to poor design. As I wasn't even the pilot in command I never quite understood why the press consistently, to this very day really, have never acknowledged that important truth. It was much more fun to make me a laughing-stock and so why let the truth get in the way of a good lie? They said that I shouldn't get upset, that it was only done in fun, but it wasn't funny from where I was sitting.

The press came up with some great variations on what happened. They said we landed on a busy motorway in rush hour, narrowly avoiding two petrol tankers. That we'd missed a school by inches, that people dived for cover, that I'd done it on purpose to get publicity. Then they started saying that I shouldn't have my licence because I was dangerous. One paper said that it was scandalous that Laker Airways should be going bust while I was still allowed to fly. What the fuck did Laker have to do with me? After saying things like that how could they say it was only said in fun? It was vicious, spiteful, untrue and pathetic, and it hurt me very much.

One argument appeared to be that you're automatically an idiot if you're a pop star so therefore it must have been my fault. If I said I wasn't the pilot once I said it a thousand times. Nobody cared, it just didn't read as well.

Sadly, it also had an impact on the flying community. I took a lot of stick whenever I went to an airfield. It used to upset me quite a bit. For the next two or three years of ordinary flying, I would fly somewhere and people would say, 'Landed it on the roof have we?' Ha bloody ha. I felt particularly annoyed that other pilots, who really should have known better, were also saying snidey things about me, to my face and behind my back. I can't really blame people who read the newspapers, but the accident report eventually came out in various aviation mags and so pilots had access to the truth. Even when I got into display flying a year or so later I still got shit from people who could barely fly Cessnas let alone the big World War Two stuff that I was roaring around in. Everyone was just waiting for me to make a mistake. I have to say it took a lot of determination to get through that. I knew if I bounced even slightly on the landing people would say, Oh, look at that idiot. The pressure was enormous. Every single flight, every touch-down felt like I was being closely watched, you could almost feel the knowing sneers if I was even one step below perfect. When a pop star tries to do anything you have to be twice as good as everyone else to be given half the credit; it's hard and it seems very unfair.

On one occasion my girlfriend had driven to Blackbushe airport and was sitting outside the flying club waiting for me to arrive. As I came in to land a group of men sitting nearby, and not knowing that she was with me, made some comment about landing in the car park. I was surprised and hugely disappointed, when I went over to them to have a word, that one of them was none other than Richard Noble, the land speed record holder. I had expected more from a man like that. I had intended to donate some cash for his Thrust 2 project, but after that I thought he could stick it as far up his sniggering backside as it would reach. Pointy bit first, preferably.

My dad and I both went through the same kind of reaction after the accident. I slept for nearly a week, 15 to 16 hours a day. Apart from feeling tired and listless I didn't have any psychological or physical ill-effects from the experience at all and went straight back into flying. The way I looked at it, I was statistically one of the safer pilots in the country at that point because I'd just been in a crash. I was very unlikely to be in another one soon, so for a while I felt almost indestructible. I flew again the following week for a *Daily Mirror* feature. They wanted me to fly the Navajo towards their cameras at high speed and low level. They actually wrote a very complimentary piece but it was one of very few.

January '82 was a month for doing unusual things. A week or so after the plane crash I had my first hair transplant. Part of the reason for my trilby, gangster image was because I knew the operation was coming and I wanted to have that image, with the hat, already fixed in people's minds. I did not intend to make a secret of my transplant but I didn't want to make it a big issue either. Covering up the scars, while things healed, seemed as good a use of image as anything. As soon as I had that first operation I went public. Elton John, who was more coy about his, took so much stick in the press after trying to keep his a secret I thought it would be better to just admit it. I wasn't the slightest bit embarrassed about having it done and if anyone joked about the hair, I just went along with them. As soon as you react to something like that people know they can get to you, so I've never let it bother me. I even let the clinic that did the first two operations use me in their advertising. Although I've taken some digs about it over the years it's not been that bad really. People have said that I've had a weave, that I wear a wig, some other things that I can't even remember now. It's as though they find it hard to believe I would own up to something they feel I should rightfully be embarrassed about. They seem to assume therefore that the truth must be a carefully hidden secret. I've had four transplants now, two of the old punch-graft technique and two of the newer microsurgery technique. It works, I'm happy, I'm not embarrassed and I would recommend it to anyone. The first, and second, punch-graft operations were pretty gory. They took me to a room and cut short the bits at the back where they were going to remove the hair that would be implanted into the front. Then they marked out where they were going to put the hair in with a series of dots, all done with marker pen. After they had worked on the hairline, they took me into the operating room and laid me face-down on the bed. I put my head against a V-shaped

158

pillow and was given swabs, which I was told to put against each ear. They didn't tell me what they were for but it was to soak up some of the blood. When I was in position they started injecting my head with anaesthetic. If you've ever stuck your finger into polystyrene you'll have an idea of how it sounded in my head when the needle went through the skin. I could hear the needle crack the skin and there would be pain. I was thinking, 'this is meant to be an anaesthetic to deaden the pain and it's killing me'. It just went on and on and on. I had 20 injections around my head, maybe more, I stopped counting after a while and just waited for it to end. They then got a machine which sounds exactly like a dentist's drill but is actually a little circular saw which cuts a circle into your head. They pushed it down into my head and cut out a very small tube of skin like the end of a straw. I had 96 bits of skin taken out eventually, with about 15 hairs in each one. They put those into a tray filled with some solution, stitched up the back of my head, one stitch for each circle they'd taken out, and then rolled me over onto my back. This was when I saw what the swabs were for. 96 holes in your head makes you bleed a little. It was gruesome.

Next they did a similar thing on the front, except that instead of the electric saw the gadget was more like a screwdriver. As they pressed it, it turned and a little cutter on the end drilled out a small hole, the skin from which they threw away. The surgeon then put the bits of skin with the hair follicles that had been taken from the back of my head, into these holes in the front. They were carefully arranged so that the hair was growing the right way and matched what I already had. They bandaged me up, took me into a little room with a bed in it where I mellowed out for an hour, and I was allowed home.

I was given a woolly hat to cover the bandages, since I was bandaged up quite heavily and it looked like I was wearing a turban. The hat was really oversized, so that it fitted over the bandages, and I looked deformed as I walked back to the car. They gave me a choice. I could either vomit up the anaesthetic, which sounded a bit grim but was apparently quick, or I could let it drain though my face, which is what I chose to do. It was pretty horrible actually. As the anaesthetic drained out of my head my face swelled up so badly I was unrecognisable. The only part of my face that wasn't changed was my left eye and a very small amount of skin underneath it. Everything else had inflated, my eyebrows had actually turned over and were facing down. My right eye was shut completely, my mouth was pulled off to one side and my nose on one side was flattened. I looked horrific. Pino Palladino, the new bass player, went out to my mum, having spoken to me for some time, and asked who I was and what had happened to me. I'd been working with him for a few weeks but he had no idea who I was. Because my mouth was so twisted I couldn't talk properly. The swelling was horrible for another reason: it was pulling open all 96 stitches on the back of my head. It hurt so much I didn't know what to do with myself. I had been given this stuff which made me slightly zombied out, but it didn't really help that much. It took four days for the swelling to go down and in that time I didn't sleep at all. I couldn't lie down properly because there was a big ridge sticking out of the back of my head, so I was lying down as best I could by hanging my head off the side of the bed.

After the operation the first thing to happen was that tubular scabs came out where the transplants had been placed at the front. I looked like one of those suckers you put soap on in the bath. Then, as the scabs fell off, all the hair in the transplants went with them. I had been told it would happen but it still freaked me out. Suddenly I had no hair at the front whatsoever, just these weird, angry-looking scars. Slowly the new hair started to grow but it was very fine, like baby hair. It took about two years for the hair to grow fully. I didn't mind the fact the hairline had a slightly odd, dotty look to it. I was just glad that it had worked.

I was told that they can only put so many transplants in each time. This was to do with blood being able to circulate around each graft so that they could heal properly and so that the new hair could grow. If you needed more after that you could go back and have the gaps filled in. I had a second operation about eighteen months later – for free, because the clinic used me in their adverts. On the first occasion they had told me that I would feel a mild discomfort, so I went in there expecting mild discomfort, an act which took no courage whatsoever. The second one took some courage, believe me, for now I knew exactly what pain was coming to say hello, and it did. I had 110 grafts on that second visit and swelled up just the same. The drugs after the second operation were much better though; it still hurt but I had a pretty good time nonetheless. I couldn't remember anything, however. I would start a sentence and forget what I was talking about before I'd got to the end of it. The hair wasn't perfect, I still had to fiddle about with sprays and other little tricks, but it was much better than nothing, which was the way I was going. If I had known the damage it would do I might have thought again, and if I had known that micro-surgery was only a few years away I definitely would have waited. If I was to shave my hair off now you would see hundreds of scars, almost as though I'd been through a broken windscreen. I've got that for life, which is a shame because I would have shaved it all off for at least one image in recent years. The two micro-surgery operations I've had since are so much less aggressive and so much more effective. Still, can't grumble, it looks okay now.

In that January I also started the recording sessions for my next album, *I, Assassin*, which we finished a couple of months later. I enjoyed working and the ideas came quickly and easily. I had Chris Slade from Uriah Heap, now with AC/DC I think, on drums, Roger Mason on keyboards and Pino Palladino, who was a friend of Chris's and playing in Jools Hollands' band The Millionaires at the time, on fretless bass. I paid Pino £50 a track which, for him at the time, was good money but a fraction of what he was worth. He was brilliant. I had never heard playing like it and I was convinced that he was a major talent just waiting to be discovered. He came up with stunning bass lines, song after song. I leaned on him heavily during the making of that album. I pushed his playing to the forefront of the tracks and, inadvertently, created a new style. It was one of the first times that the fretless bass had been used as the lead melody instrument, allowing the album to be atmospheric, dreamy and funky.

When I wrote *I, Assassin* I had already decided to play live again and the decision greatly influenced the style of music. I wanted it to be much more up-beat than things I'd done previously. I wanted to see people dancing in the aisles. The decision to start touring again seemed like a quick change of heart to some people. I can't really argue with that, but it wasn't quite as quick as people thought. Although the Wembley shows had only been about nine months

161

earlier, I'd actually decided to stop touring in the middle of 1980. It was getting on for two years later now, and I had done a huge amount of rethinking in that period. I was becoming much harder, more resilient. I was beginning to dig my heels in and fight back.

Lyrically the album was quite different to *Dance*. It even had a flicker of humour here and there. 'White Boys And Heroes' a Top Twenty hit later in the year, had references to how some rock stars are also actors in a way, playing a part that's not really them, people like me. 'War Songs' was a fairly light-hearted look at being famous for a change. I'd gone through the paranoid, bitter, intro-spective period by now and I was beginning to get used to the job. I was more prepared for what might come my way, good or bad. The round the world flight, the plane crash, these were big things, major experiences that helped me shape a new opinion of myself. Those experiences gave me a self-confidence, a genuine strength that I hadn't had before. I was finally beginning that difficult transi-tion from boy to man, a few years too late of course, but better late than never.

In 'Music For Chameleons' I sing 'gowns for another show, maybe no one will come', which was inspired by the old classic 'Send In The Clowns', one of my all-time favourite songs. It had always touched a nerve in me – you've had your career, your best days are gone and there comes the time when you walk out on stage and no one has come. I had a certain empathy for that fear. 'We Take Mystery To Bed' was about not quite knowing who you're sleeping with when you take someone back. It's another Debbie Doran song really. A line in the track that reads 'no natural course of things for her to expect' was about me, or the way I'd become for a while after the initial success. I had been a little strange. I was like one of those toys you can wind up and then let run around a table without ever falling off. When they get to the edge they turn, but you don't know which way they're going to go. I was wound up and running every which way, but unlike the toys I did fall off the edge.

I thought *I, Assassin* was the best thing I'd ever done. It was a lot more accessible than *Dance* and I was sure that it would turn things around.

We did all the sleeves for the album and the next couple of singles in a room just off Oxford Street, in Geoff Howes' photographic studio. I said that I wanted it to look as though I was standing in a street and when I walked into his studio and it was as though he'd brought a street into his room. We did the cover shots to *Replicas, The Pleasure Principle, Telekon, Dance, I, Assassin* and a future album *Warriors* in the same 30 foot by 30 foot room. On the *Assassin* shoot the just-rained-on look was achieved with Geoff's little plastic spray can.

On 9 March I appeared in Uxbridge Magistrates Court charged with carrying an offensive weapon. This was particularly worrying because I was due to move to America a month later and really couldn't afford to have any kind of criminal record hanging over my head. Quite literally couldn't afford, actually, because I'd received a tax bill for about £200,000. It wasn't a case of running to the States because I didn't want to pay up, I just didn't have that kind of money to hand after the round the world trip. I was well on my way to being broke.

The court case should never have happened and the whole incident took away much of my faith in the police. It had all started the previous summer. I was having a really horrible day. A man tried to run my Ferrari off the road with his little orange Volkswagen Beetle, and forced me up onto the kerb, just pathetic stuff. I went to the aeroplane and some skinheads gave me a really hard time as I was going out to it. I thought I was going to get knocked about a bit but they got bored and eventually left. Then I was driving back home and some idiots in cars with CB radios were actually trying to pen me in, but I got away from them because I was in a fairly fast car. None of it in itself was that big a deal, but all in one day was a bit much to take. I was fed up so I thought I'd just get a burger and go home. We went to a takeaway van that we often visited whose owners we knew very well. While my girlfriend was ordering the food, I sat waiting on the ground outside with a little rounders bat. It was a nice summer evening and I was in a short sleeved T-shirt, just tapping my toes with it. I had no reason to have it really, but nor did I have a reason not to have it. It wasn't something I'd thought about, I just got out of the car and took it with me. It was no more contrived than sitting down on the grass and fiddling with a dandelion.

There were some gypsies walking along and one of them had a log stick. A passing police car pulled up and stopped them, had a brief chat and drove off. The police car went round the front of the burger van, which was on the verge and pulled up in front of my Ferrari. Then the policewoman came over, pointed at me and beckoned me with her finger. I thought that was a bit rude but assumed she wanted an autograph so I strolled over with the bat still in my hand, not thinking much of it. Then she started giving me all this shit about offensive weapons and asking why I had it. It hadn't occurred to me for an instant that it was an offensive weapon, but I claimed that I'd been playing bat and ball with it while I was waiting for my burger. It was quite believable, I'd seen people doing just that on many occasions. She asked, in what I can only describe as a highly offensive and arrogant manner, where the ball was so I said I'd lost it. I told her that was why I was sitting down when she passed and not playing bat and ball any more. I had always been courteous to the police. It seemed to me that they hold all the cards in these situations and, much as it may rankle, the best thing you can ever do is say yes sir, no sir, three bags full sir, until they go away and leave you alone. This was that one unfortunate exception. I just couldn't stomach the fact that I'd been hassled all day, with not a policeman in sight, and now, as I was trying to call it quits on a shit day and go home with my burger, the police were giving me grief. I got agitated and told her that, under no circumstances, was I going looking for the ball. She started getting heavy and said she didn't like my attitude. Then I really got fed up. I started saying how stupid all this was and what did she think I was going to do, mug the van for a fiver and then drive off discreetly in a Ferrari Boxer with a private GN 4 number plate? Then she said, 'If you don't calm down I'm going to arrest you.' This was it, I was a bit pissed off but I was hardly ranting so I said, 'Well bloody well do it then.' And she *did*. The official reason she gave for arresting me was that she was frightened for the safety of the burger van owner, because I was so angry she feared I might do something. Bollocks. I wasn't fucking angry until she started on me.

They wouldn't let me drive my car to the police station, about two miles away in West Drayton, near Heathrow Airport, so I had to wait for another police car to drive us there. I told them not to touch the Ferrari because it had a special gearbox and clutch and it required some knowledge to drive without damaging it. This was true. I'd burnt out the clutch within the first two hours of owning it before I was shown how to drive it properly. The policeman who drove us to the police station in his panda car was quite cool and helped the situation a lot. He said, 'Whatever you do stay calm. Don't get angry because they'll use it against you.' Actually, getting arrested had calmed me down pretty quickly anyway. I had my fingerprints taken and then they took mug shots, with the board underneath, a number, the whole works. While I was there I must have signed autographs for everyone in the building. They'd kept us there for hours and at one point I asked Michelle, my girlfriend, to call my parents. The police wouldn't let her use the phone in the police station. She had her summer clothes on, little short skirt, and they made her go out, in the dark, on her own, into a town she didn't know in order to find a public phone box. I found that unbelievable. Meanwhile they did take my car. The man at the burger van made a note of when they drove off, and by the time they arrived at the police station they'd been out in it for 30 minutes or more. It was a three-minute drive at best.

After that part of it was all over I was allowed to leave and, eventually, a date was set for my court appearance. For some reason my lawyer applied for a postponement and told me not to go. So I didn't. Bit of a mistake that, because the postponement wasn't granted. I didn't know that of course and my lawyer couldn't reach me to let me know otherwise. My lawyer stood up in court and explained that it was his fault entirely but, despite that, the prosecution claimed that I was demonstrating a cavalier attitude towards the British justice system and asked that I be arrested again. A warrant was subsequently issued for my arrest so, to save time, I went down to the same police station and was officially arrested again for absconding from bail.

When I did eventually go to court, I was really stressed out. I'd just had my first hair transplant and it looked less than ideal, to say the least, but I wasn't allowed to wear a hat. Then the policewoman stood up in court and read from her notebook. I couldn't believe what I was hearing. It was a work of pure fiction. According to her, I said, 'Go on copper, nick me if you dare' when she said that she was considering arresting me. She said I was hiding the bat up my sleeve in a suspicious manner which, considering I was wearing a short sleeved T-shirt, would have been a good trick. She got the colour of my car wrong and so many other little things, that I began to wonder if I was in the right court. Another policeman said he'd had no idea who I was and that I hadn't signed any autographs in the police station. Bloody liar. I'd done about three for his kids alone. They absolutely denied not letting Michelle make a phone call, but she was still walking back to the police station when my parents arrived. They claimed the Ferrari had been driven straight there. The thing that surprised me was that the three police officers who gave evidence all contradicted each other. One said that I couldn't have been playing rounders there because it was covered in broken glass, which it wasn't. Another said that I couldn't have been playing rounders because he'd been there the week before at about 5pm to buy his son a hot dog and it had been waist-high with stinging nettles. How could the other one have seen all the broken glass then? It wasn't covered with nettles either. not only that, but the van didn't open until 7pm and it had never served hot dogs, so he made himself look a complete idiot. You would expect, wouldn't you, that if they were going to stand up in court and tell lies, for whatever reason, to get me convicted, they would have got their stories together? Luckily they didn't, or I might not have got away with it.

The case against me was dismissed. I was advised by my lawyers to pay the costs as a gesture of goodwill towards the police 'misunderstanding' of what had happened, otherwise they would just pick on me from then on. Funnily enough I was driving in the Corvette a little while afterwards and I got pulled up on a random police check. As I got out a big baseball bat fell out onto the road. It was there quite innocently but I thought it was all going to start again. It was only about 100 yards away from where she'd arrested me, but this time they didn't say anything at all.

On 6 March, the same week as the court appearance, I put out the single 'Music For Chameleons'. I'd thought up the main melody line of the song somewhere between Kansas and Houston while I was on the round the world trip. I remember being fascinated by the ground, which looked like a checker board that went on for hundreds of miles. I started humming this tune to myself, which irritated Bob a bit, he cancelled the intercom and switched me off. Thereza Bazaar from Dollar sang on the B-side, 'Noise Noise', which is still one of my favourite songs. In fact one of the Radio One DJs said that I should have made the single a double A side and promoted 'Noise Noise' as soon as 'Chameleons' had peaked. Anyway, I performed 'Music For Chameleons' on *Top Of The Pops* a couple of times, which helped the song into the Top 20. A pleasant little incident occurred on one of the shows. Japan were there performing their 'Ghosts' single and no one at the programme liked it, and the technicians were taking the piss out of them for being so pompous and full of it. Halfway through their performance I had to walk on to another stage to prepare for my bit and half the people, at least, left Japan to come and stand by me. The *Top Of The Pops* crew had to round people up and push them back towards Japan again, otherwise it was going to look a bit empty.

I left for America in April. The police had to hide me in a storeroom at the airport because I was mobbed by fans when I arrived at the terminal. It was pandemonium and all the more exciting because I hadn't expected such a send-off. So off I went to live in Los Angeles, California, for the next seven months. I rented quite a big house with plenty of rooms and a heated swimming pool. The house was in Beverly Hills, right at the top of one of them. You could stand on the veranda, with this sheer drop underneath you, and look out across the city. At the lights from the Hollywood premières, at the police helicopters chasing someone, it was a magical spot. The pool lit up at night, so you could have late night swims and life felt very good there. The band still comprised Chris Slade, Pino Paladino and Roger Mason, but they were now joined by Rob Dean, the former Japan guitarist who had been sacked by the band. My brother John also joined the line up for the first time on keyboards. When my band came over they moved into the house and I rented an apartment on Horn Avenue, just off Sunset Boulevard, for me and Michelle. Pretty small but very nice. I also bought a car for them to drive around in. Then, apart from my John of course, they complained about having to buy their own petrol, which was less than a dollar a gallon at the time. They said

I was treating them very badly and I really lost it when I heard that.

I felt at home straight away in Los Angeles. I'd always enjoyed being there when I'd toured, always felt at ease. I bought a Jeep while I was there, a black CJ-7 with lots of chrome extras, and passed my American driving test. I also did a bit of aerobatic training but I didn't really enjoy it and stopped after about three trips. The smog was so bad it would burn your eyes as you climbed for height. It was also such a busy area we would fly one simple manoeuvre, a loop or something similar, and then have to wait ten minutes to get a clear piece of sky before trying again. It was a waste of time and money. I've always been a big fan of amusement parks so I also bought a season pass to Magic Mountain. Magic Mountain was a two-hour drive north of Los Angeles, but it was a huge place, full of excellent rides. We'd sometimes go three or four times a week. I love roller coasters.

I had always been interested in guns. I'd never had a real one, air rifles as a boy yes, but nothing too serious. In America I was able to go out and buy guns. I was amazed at how easy it was to do. I walked into a gun shop and bought two combat rifles. One was an AR15, which is the civilian version of the M16 military assault rifles. It's a semi-automatic version so you have to pull the trigger every time you want to fire, unlike a full auto version which keeps firing as long as you hold the trigger back. Nonetheless, it automatically loads the next bullet a micro-second later, so it was a lethal bit of kit. I also bought a Carbine version of the same gun, which was similar looking but smaller. I couldn't quite get used to the ease of it, or what I had in the back of the Jeep. I thought, I'm driving up the street with two assault rifles in the back of my car and 250 rounds of ammunition. In England I was arrested for possession of a baseball bat.

The novelty of having guns soon wore off though. I became a regular at the local gun club, which was out in the desert, and took it all very seriously. A bit later I bought a Berretta automatic pistol and a pump action shotgun. I went back to the same shop and asked for 'the gun that Steve McQueen used in *The Getaway*.'

I learnt how to fire them properly. I would practise how to take them apart at home but I saw that as part of having a responsible attitude to something that was potentially very dangerous. I wanted to know about them, how they worked, how to look after them properly. A few years later, my girlfriend sold a story to the papers saying that I was a gun fanatic. She had a picture of me holding a gun to her head but it was one of those jokey pictures that just happen. You put that picture into a family album and it was the family having a silly joke, put it into a story about a gun fanatic and it becomes sinister. It was taken by my mum, who was laughing at what had led up to the picture being taken and was completely innocent.

I would go to the desert firing range about once a fortnight to practise. The range was a far cry from the militia-like gung-ho type mountain hideaway that people sometimes assume such places are like. People weren't running around in combat trousers blazing away at cut-outs of Russian soldiers shouting 'Yee hah, I got me a commie'. It was very tightly run, very strict. No automatic weapons allowed, no firing of semi automatic rifles at a rate faster than one round per second. Break that rule and you were warned just once before being sent away. There was a lot of expertise there, people who would show you how to handle a gun properly. At each cease fire, before you went to examine your targets down range, each gun was examined carefully by the range supervisor and his staff to make sure that it was empty. Nobody was allowed near the benches, where each gun was placed, until the cease fire was over. Break that rule and you were out immediately. It was very impressive. Not at all macho.

The scariest part about being there was nothing to do with guns, but the fact you could hear rattle-snakes on the firing range. That freaked me out a bit. There were strict instructions about not shooting the snakes. I had no intention of doing anything of the sort. If I'd seen one I would have been a cartoon vapour trail in the opposite direction. I took a snake-bite kit with me for what it was worth, which I bought in a camping shop. Camping over there had a slightly different feel to camping in England. I'd never taken a snake-bite kit to Weymouth. A snake escaped from one of the Horn Avenue apartments one day, a Boa Constrictor of several yards' length, and I don't think I slept at all until they found it a few days later, in one of the air-conditioning shafts.

I went to live in Los Angeles fully believing that most people carried guns. Although I'd been there a few times before, working, I still had acquired most of my opinions about the place from TV and the movies. I thought that it was normal to carry a gun and, until I got one of my own, I actually felt quite vulnerable. I often carried my gun with me when I was living in LA, just for self-protection, especially if I thought I would be coming home late. The shop owner from whom I bought my guns was an ex-policeman and he told me some interesting, if a touch unnerving, facts about home defence. He said that the most likely time to be attacked was when you were going from your car to your front door. You're fumbling with keys, carrying bags of shopping, thinking of other things. He gave me hints such as, when you walk around a corner walk on the outside of the turn you're making. If someone is there, waiting to grab you, it gives you that vital extra second or two to do something about it. So he said anyway. After spending an hour in his shop listening to this stuff I was ready to believe that being attacked was not a rare occurrence but an inevitability. He told me that, if I did ever have to shoot an intruder, to make sure that he fell inside the flat and not outside, even if it meant dragging the body inside, as it would look better in the subsequent court case. He said if you have to shoot someone in self-defence, kill them. Don't leave them injured. This was because I could be sued afterwards. Apparently, again this is what I was told, even if a man is pointing a gun at your head saying 'I'm going to kill you', the court could claim that he didn't really mean it and I would therefore have had no right to shoot him in self-defence. It was probably all said just to make me paranoid and buy more bullets, but it did make me feel that a gun was an absolute necessity. I've learned better since, and wouldn't dream of carrying a gun ever again.

What would have happened if someone had actually tried to mug me at gunpoint? I had a gun but I bet the robber would have been far more prepared to use his than I was mine. What was I doing? I was lucky nothing happened. In fact I was very lucky because a few days after I moved out of the flat my neighbour, who parked beside me in the parking lot, was held up at gunpoint as he climbed out of his car. It was about 2am, the time I normally got home. It could so easily have been me, waving my weapon about vaguely as they shot me down. I probably would have shot myself.

One potentially horrific incident shocked me so deeply, it completely calmed me down. My parents had come over to Los Angeles to visit and were staying in the spare room. I heard someone walking around in the early hours and so I grabbed the Berretta and waited behind the bedroom door. I was terrified, naked, breathing hard with a gun in my shaky hand. As the footsteps drew closer I leapt out, pointed the gun down the corridor, only to see my mum standing there shouting out 'Don't shoot, don't shoot, it's me, it's me.' She was going to the kitchen to get a drink. I was horrified. I own nothing, absolutely nothing, that I would risk my life to protect. A TV is not worth dying for. A car is not worth a cut on my finger. If I hear a bump in the night I WILL NOT venture down the stairs to investigate. But self and family, that's very different. I would protect that with, I think the phrase is, 'extreme prejudice'.

Before the American tour started I had to leave the States for a while so I didn't get into trouble with their tax laws. I flew up to Vancouver and spent a fairly quiet six weeks hanging out at local airfields and walking up and down mountains. After Los Angeles life in Vancouver seemed incredibly slow.

In the build up to the tour many things happened. I flew to New York to film a clip for *Top Of The Pops* and, while we were driving around in the back of a Chevrolet, we witnessed a mugging. I had never seen anything like it, broad daylight and this man grabs a lady's chain and runs away up the street like an Olympic sprinter. I kicked myself later when I thought more about it. If I'd been quicker on the uptake we could have chased him and got the chain back, there were enough of us.

For me, the tour was a test of sorts. If it went well and, more importantly, if I enjoyed it, I would relaunch my touring career in England. The tour was good fun and I did enjoy it. The attendance wasn't as good as the previous two US tours but even that I found encouraging in a way. I was able to go out and get on with it no matter how many people were there. Big crowd, small crowd, didn't matter to me, I was enjoying myself. Lots of things happened. On one of the nights we shared a hotel with Iggy Pop. I spent the night in fear of an Iggy raid. When I woke up in the morning I found a very nice, hand-written note slipped under my door which said simply, 'Love what you do. Iggy.' I thought that was cool.

In Texas I was cautioned by the police for inciting a disturbance. I'd announced where we were staying during the gig and invited the entire audience back to the hotel. I thought maybe a few would come along and we could have a bit of a party. Hundreds turned up and the hotel staff were very upset. Another night a fire alarm was set off by some passing Hallowe'en revellers. We were on a high floor and as I ran down the corridor I saw my mum, sleepy eyed and worried looking, just ahead of me. I didn't think she was running near fast enough and so I picked her up and carried her down the fire escape as fast as I could.

The tour had actually gone a bit wrong at the start. We had decided to rent campers instead of tour buses but the crew camper broke down almost immediately. The band camper caught fire somewhere near Wyoming. I had been laughed at loud and long when I took a fire extinguisher on board when we first loaded our gear on. No one was laughing now. The fire was caused by a leaking fuel line in the engine bay and it was fierce. My dad had climbed into the bay and was tackling the blaze with my extinguisher but the flames were too much for it. I was terrified that the fuel tank would blow up and kill him, so I ran for all I was worth to a nearby petrol station. I couldn't believe it when they said they didn't have a fire extinguisher that they could lend me. A tanker driver said that he had one, but he fumbled around in his cab for several minutes until he found his smaller spare since he didn't want to lend me his bigger one. All this time my dad was inside my burning van. We got the fire out eventually, but the camper idea was finished. It was back to proper tour buses.

The only other hiccup was when Chris Slade hit me. I had asked him not to go on stage drunk, for whenever he drank too much he would forget what we were playing and just revert to heavy metal mode. I had a word with him about it and *thump*, he pushed me all the way down the bus, into my dad who pushed him all the way back again.

The tour finished in Chicago. We woke up in the morning after the final show to find that the tour manager had run off with all the money. His girlfriend had turned up in the night, with the limo that was supposed to be taking us to the airport, and they'd disappeared. We had no money, no plane tickets but, luckily, one credit card between us. It was a tour to remember but, despite all the turbulence, I'd had a really good time. I was beginning to see touring as an unmissable experience, an ongoing adventure.

After the tour I briefly flew back to New York then to Jersey, in the Channel Islands, which was to be my home for the next few months until I could go back to England. On the flight I met the Reverend Jesse Jackson who, much to my surprise, was sitting at the back with me in economy. He was with a group of people who I assumed were his staff. One of them asked me if I had seen the light, which was an incredibly corny opening, but he was nice enough. I eventually managed to convince him that I was a lost cause and as far as I was concerned, if God is real he shouldn't be allowed to get away with it.

The aeroplane was diverted to a small French airfield because of fog at Paris. It didn't have a Customs or Immigration facility so we couldn't get off. Eventually though we flew into Paris and I was delighted to see my own Navajo parked up on the next stand. I walked off the jumbo, across the tarmac, picked up my case, which had already been unloaded for me, got into my Numanair aeroplane and took off, feeling slightly flash! Michelle was waiting in the Navajo, which was being flown by a hired pilot. She had gone back to England when the tour started so I hadn't seen her for a while.

Jersey seemed unbelievably dull following, as it did, several months in Los Angeles and a big tour. After a while I settled in okay and found it a very restful place. To fill the time I became very active at the flying club. I took courses on night flying, instrument flying and basic aerobatics. All of my flying up to then had been on more modern nosewheel machines, and so I also took a course on an old tailwheel Chipmunk aircraft. I was keen to learn the skills required for the trickier tailwheel types.

For a while I had the Ferrari in Jersey, but given a maximum speed limit of 40 mph across the whole island it was a bit pointless. I could drive around all day and not get out of first gear if I wanted to. The car was vandalised as well, so I had someone take it home for me. I kept the Navajo there, though, and would often fill it with friends and fly around the islands.

CHAPTER 9

Survival, 1983-4

I wrote most of the next album, *Warriors*, while I was living in Jersey. I had about five months of my year out of the UK still to do. At first I stayed in a hotel but, after an interview on a local radio programme where I mentioned that I was looking for somewhere to live, a woman rang up and said we could live at her house. She had a two-room extension that she usually rented out in the summer. For a while it was quite a good arrangement, but then our landlady started to show her true colours. There was a door between her part of the house and where we lived which was supposed to stay locked to ensure our mutual privacy. But she would quietly unlock it and let her children come in with their friends to look at me. You'd be setting there, watching TV, in the bath, even on the toilet, and all of a sudden these giggling kids would come in and then run back out again. She came to the door once as we were leaving and complained because we hadn't stepped outside the house before putting on our outdoor shoes. Another day she noticed I had some of my synthesisers set up and so she said I had to leave because I was using too much electricity. Luckily, by then I'd written the bulk of the songs for the album using three synths and a set of headphones. I was glad to leave. It made me laugh at times, though, to think that here I was, a pop star, with my own fan club and famous all over the world, being thrown out of a house extension for using too much electricity.

The day after my 25th birthday Michelle left and went back to England, which came as something of a surprise. She said she was bored. Although we carried on as a couple for a while after that it wasn't the same. I thought it was a shitty thing to do and it dulled my affection for her considerably. Soon after she left I moved into a hotel near the airport. The hotel had the most dedicated room cleaner that I've ever come across working for it. The room didn't have a security chain on the door and so, for privacy, you relied upon a Do Not Disturb sign and the main door lock. Such things meant nothing to my cleaner. Every morning, without fail, she would use her pass key to open the door, come in and clean the room. I was often still fast asleep, occasionally in the bath, but rarely up and dressed. Eventually I tried barricading the door. I piled all of my trunks and cases against it, along with the set of drawers that served as room furniture. All to no avail. I sat up in bed, amazed, as she threw her shoulder against the long suffering door again and again. Each time my barricade would slide backwards an inch or two. Eventually she was able to squeeze her ample Mediterranean body through the gap and come into the room. Without batting an eyelid she cleaned as usual, moved my barricade back to its rightful place and then left. She never so much as said hello in all the time I stayed there.

While I was out in Jersey the record company, WEA, suggested I use a producer on the next album. I wasn't keen. I didn't like having to compromise, to be tactful, to accommodate other people's thoughts and suggestions, to be diplomatic about things when it was my album we were talking about. I definitely say what I think. I don't mean to offend but I can't stand around discussing things all day either. I'm trying very hard to change these days, but I'm still fiercely possessive about what I do. Not fiercely confident about it, just possessive. It may be shit, but it's my shit.

In May I flew back to England in the Navajo. It was an amazing experience. As we flew overhead the airfield at Blackbushe I looked down and saw thousands of people lining the fence and even more making their way towards the airfield gates. I couldn't figure out what was going on. For a moment I thought there was an event taking place that I was unaware of, maybe I'd blundered over the field when I shouldn't have. The radio crackled into life and the controller said, 'You've got quite a welcoming committee down here.' They were all fans come to welcome me back. I could hardly believe it. I'd been gone for over a year and yet here they were, and so many of them. It was a very touching moment, but it was almost a disastrous moment as well. As I brought the aeroplane to a halt by the fence they broke through and made a wild dash towards me. The engines were still running as they began swarming around the aircraft so I hurriedly shut the motors down, ignoring the proper procedures. I couldn't have wished for a warmer homecoming and it did wonders for my confidence.

However, I also realised on my return how I was getting into trouble with my so called 'right wing politics.' I have never expressed a political opinion through my songs and I never will. I have always seen music as escapist, both as a writer and a listener. However, as Gary Webb, almost from birth I've recognised how hard my dad worked for his family to lift us out of fairly humble beginnings. My own early success possibly hardened my attitude towards people who weren't prepared to take risks or work hard for their futures, but slagged me off for trying to do something different with my life. They seemed to be their own worst enemies and yet years later they were jealous of my success. I found it difficult to forget those comments. I want everyone in Britain to make a successful life for themselves, so it's important the individual's own drive and enthusiasm is allowed to flourish. To me, the Conservatives seemed to be thinking along the same lines at the start of the 1980s while the Labour Party was so blighted by the union strikes and in-fighting of the previous decade they didn't appear to offer people real incentives.

I wasn't the only person in the country to believe this and in these areas I think the Conservatives did improve things. It was also my honest, if unfashionable, opinion that nuclear weapons acted as a deterrent in the Cold War and that we had to defend the Falklands because the islanders themselves asked for our help. I believe in defending our citizens, even if certain politicians manipulated the situation to their own ends. For me, it was a matter of principle only.

I've got into trouble so many times whenever politics and music have been mentioned in the same breath. This is partly my own fault. I don't regret my opinions but I do feel uncomfortable about the way I expressed them. The fact that you're young and have

Above: Forty date UK comeback tour in Mad Max leathers, autumn 1983

Left: The "difficult" Berserker image which took several hours to apply every night on the 1984 tour

Right: Mid-80s with girlfriend Tracey Adam when The Fury's music and High Street-meets-Monte Carlo image went badly out of sync.

Above: Gary, Beryl & Tony Webb in formation with grounded Japanese-styled Harvard

Below: Aerobatics in the Harvard

Above: The Harvard formation team; (L-R) John Conlon, John Webb, and on my right Norman Lees

Below: Cloud scraping in the Yak-11

Above: Upright on the wing shortly before the plane enters a stall turn. You really don't want to know....

Below: Nan and Pop enjoy the Essex countryside near my home

Left: Gemma O'Neill, wife, fashion guru and lifelong fan

Above: The 1996 band (left to right): Ade Orange (keyboards), me, Rob Harris (guitar), Richard Beasley (drums), David Brooks (keyboards)

Above: 1994's Sacrifice was the start of big cathedral-sized sounds and Goth-noire styling to match

Above: (Left to right) Beck, Marilyn Manson and I backstage after Beck's 1996 gig at Brixton Academy

Left: 1997, part of session for Exile album

stared death in the face on several occasions tends to make you reckless and full of bravado. I've never been very good at playing safe. I set myself up and the press exploited the situation. I was once asked to appear on a British TV documentary that was designed to look at the increasing amount of political views being expressed by the Red Wedge left wing supporters, such as Billy Bragg and Paul Weller. I was told I was the neutral figure with Miles Copeland being the voice on the right. That was the strict understanding upon which I agreed to take part. The final programme was edited in such a way as my opinions were often given back to back with Paul Weller's, although unknown to the viewer, they were answers to completely different questions. That programme did more to cement my position as a supporter of the right than anything else.

In more recent times Labour has evolved into a modern party in touch with the people again, while the Tories have slipped ever deeper into sleaze, arrogance and inconsistency and all feelings of support drained from me. I have no faith in the Conservatives but although Tony Blair is impressive I have yet to give my absolute trust to New Labour. Now, more than ever, I'm a completely a-political animal who believes that whoever is in power should focus on improving the health service and the education system and making sure everyone in this country has an equal chance of making the most of their lives.

I'd actually had quite a hard time from WEA in the year or so building up to *Warriors*. Although *I, Assassin* had reached number eight in the UK Charts and spawned a top ten single 'We Take Mystery (To Bed)', it had sold very badly. They felt, quite rightly when I look back on it now, that a producer could give me the missing ingredients. I thought I knew exactly what I was doing at the time and blamed them for the poor sales because of their weak promotional campaign on the album. In some respects we were both right. They had said to me after *Dance* that they were content with the sales I was achieving and that they were only going to promote me enough to maintain those sales. I was being written off as an ongoing act and would, by their own admission and clear intention, not get any bigger. They would not risk any money promoting me to a larger audience. I had peaked, as they put it.

WEA were going through some turbulent times themselves. In

the space of a few months they had gone through several managing directors and numerous other personnel changes down through the company. Nobody would make a decision, everybody was scared of losing their jobs. It was not a good time to be on the label. Then along came Mike Heap. Mike had been at WEA when I first went there, via Beggars, and now he was back as the new managing director. He said things would be put right, that he was aware of how badly I had been treated, and now he was in charge I would be a priority act at the label. He promised a virtually unlimited promotional budget on the *Warriors* album and, if I got in a producer, WEA would cover all the costs. This was everything I could ever have wanted to hear. I agreed to a producer and chose an old hero of mine, Bill Nelson, for the job. A few weeks after that meeting with Mike Heap, though, *he* was out as well. When the new people came in, I was as far from a priority act as it was possibly to be. I felt as though they'd cut me down at the knees and it was the last time I ever got excited about a promise in the music business. These days, until the moment I have the reality in my hand, or before my eyes, I don't believe a word that anyone says. I am not a miserable cynic and I have not lost my enthusiasm, but your heart wouldn't stand up to the constant disappointments of broken promises if you allowed yourself to believe even a fraction of what is said to you. It's a form of emotional self-defence and it's why I'm still here.

I still thought Bill Nelson was the right man for the album, though. I'd loved his early band Be Bob Deluxe. I'd gone to see them years before, without knowing a single song, and had enjoyed every second. I had never, have never, been so impressed by a completely new band as I was at their Drury Lane show. Bill was my favourite guitar player, bar none. Bill flew over to Jersey to meet me and to talk about the album. He seemed nice enough and I thought that we would get along okay. When I came back to Britain we started to work on the album but the sessions didn't go quite as I expected, for we are very different people. It seemed as though our reasons for even breathing were completely opposed to one another. At one point we were talking about why we were in the business. I was pretty shallow at the time and I said, not entirely truthfully, that I got into it to sleep with as many women and make as much money as possible. In truth I do have a strong loyalty to the art of what I do, but I actually get slightly embarrassed if I'm asked to talk about the inspiration behind songs, my feelings about music as an art form. It all sounds a bit pretentious, so I tend to brush such feelings aside and hide them under a pile of brash statements, like those I gave to Bill Nelson. He was really offended by what I said. I may not remember the exact words of his argument but the gist was pretty much this: he told me that all creative people pick up beams of inspiration from across the cosmos and we channel it into creative art and we do what we do for the people. I said, 'That's complete bollocks', and it all went downhill from then on really, as we began to grate on each other quite badly. Sometimes I would come up with an idea and he would say. 'No you can't have that, it's incongruous.' I didn't even know what the word meant, I had to look it up. It got to the stage where I would go out and play pool while he was doing his thing and go back in later when he was finished. When he mixed the album I didn't like it at all, since I found the mixes very tinny. With hindsight it's quite possible that he was ahead of his time because mixes have become a lot brighter and more cutting. However I remixed it, put more bottom end into it and because of that he asked for his producer credit to be taken off. I haven't spoken to him since. Shame though. I still like a lot of the *Warriors* stuff and Bill Nelson really did a lot of very inventive things on it which, because of our other differences, I failed to appreciate fully at the time. To be with him in a room when he was playing guitar was an honour. I would just sit back and listen and all my antagonism would just float away.

Pino Palladino was supposed to play on *Warriors*. I'd paid him a retainer wage for about a year after the end of the *I, Assassin* tour so he would be available for the album. Then, just before we started, he said he couldn't do it – he had another gig with Nick Heyward or Paul Young, can't remember who for sure. Pino recommended his bass tutor, an American called Joe Hubbard. Joe turned out to be another player of formidable quality so things could have been worse. He was a lot of trouble, though.

Throughout my career I have always been of the opinion that I am not a particularly good player. I can play guitar a bit, keyboards a bit, a few other things, but I'm not really good at any of them. My voice has a sound of its own but I could never claim to be a 'singer', I don't have the range or the power. I've learnt now, and accept, that what I do have is a style of my own so I'm content. In many ways that is arguably a better thing to have but, in the eighties, I was desperate to improve what I saw as my weak musicianship and vocal talents. I had sold millions of records, won awards at the highest level, but I was more embarrassed about not deserving such things, than pleased to get them. I rarely went to awards ceremonies. I thought that by getting in some of the best players, and singers around I could make the albums more 'musical', and that my own limitations would be less of a problem. What I actually did was progressively bury the very style that my fans had enjoyed. For a while I still sang, of course, but I swamped my own performance in huge layers of backing vocals. Musically I became much more of an arranger of noises than a musician, at least that was how I felt. I didn't realise what I was doing but, starting with *Warriors*, I was lighting the fire of what came close to being my own funeral.

At the time I was massively into the saxophone, which is a very beautiful and atmospheric instrument. Somebody told me about a player called Dick Morrissey who was in a jazz band called Morrissey Mullen and, more importantly,to me, was the sax player on the *Blade Runner* movie soundtrack. That was all I needed to know, he was the man for me then. Dick Morrissey was brilliant, a musical genius. First take, perfect, not a single note wrong. He was very much from a jazz background and mainly hired to play jazzy sax and I was getting him to play a very different style of music. I hate jazz, to be honest, but it was the flavour I was looking for, not the full blown experience. Dick said that he was keen to do something different and so it was easy. He played on my albums, on and off, for nearly ten years after that. On *Warriors* I also had Tessa Niles on backing vocals, and she is one of the very best singers around. If burying myself under the impressive performances of these players was, ultimately, the wrong direction in which to be moving, it did give the albums some stunning musical moments. *Warriors* had as fine a bunch of players as it was possible to get.

The new image was based on the *Mad Max II* film which I'd seen in America in 1982. I owned an old ripped-up bomber jacket, a pair of leather trousers and lots of straps and belts from a sex shop in

Soho, London. I had a few special bits and pieces made up, added some American football lower leg protectors and tried to look hard. It was not entirely successful but it did have a certain appeal. To this day it remains the favourite image of some of the fans, who still turn out to concerts in full *Warriors* kit. The image worked much better on stage than it did on artwork or TV. With the full stage set around it all the pieces seemed to fall into place.

For the video to the first single from the album, the title track 'Warriors', I hired a T33 Shooting Star Korean War jet fighter. The *Daily Mirror* newspaper came along to the shoot and did a full page on it under the headline, 'You don't have to be mad to launch a new record but in Numan's case it helps'. I didn't realise quite how mad it was either until much later. I hadn't been told that it was the jet's first flight after being hastily rebuilt, that my parachute had not been packed, that my seat straps were twisted and would have done more harm than good if we had had to force land anywhere. I sat in the back, happy in my ignorance, and just had an excellent time. We roared over the Cambridgeshire countryside at some ridiculous speed, tight up behind the camera ship. It was only when a little red light came on over the gauge which said fuel that I began to wonder. We broke off and put down at Stanstead airport, refuelled and then hurtled off again. Apparently it's not that unusual to fly jets down to minimum fuel.

The man who flew the jet, with a flair that is hard to find amongst most modern display pilots, was called Dizzy Addicott. Dizzy was a World War Two fighter pilot and then a test pilot for many years after that. He took me under his wing so to speak and, for the next year or two, guided me to a level of flying that I hadn't believed possible, not for me anyway. I used to learn more about flying in a single conversation with Dizzy than I could from a year's worth of flying around on my own. I went from being an everyday club pilot to a warbird aerobatic display pilot in no time at all. In the process I learnt stuff that was to save my life on more than one occasion. A big bang, a puff of smoke, near panic, and then I would hear Dizzy's jolly voice float back into my head, reminding me of 'when this happened to me in Burma old lad'. And how to survive.

I began to fly with Dizzy more often, normally as co-pilot on a big World War Two transport plane called a DC-3, and so I was intro-

181

duced to the exciting world of air display flying. I had gone to air shows all my life and I was a huge fan of the display pilots. Their skills were extraordinary and I marvelled at the way they could make these impressive machines twist and turn the way they did. Now I was seeing it from the other side of the fence and it was even more impressive, since I knew for myself just how difficult it was to do what they did with an aeroplane. I felt totally intimidated, completely out of my depth. My flying reputation was in tatters thanks to the press and I was very aware of the guarded way in which I was greeted by many of the pilots. Thanks to Dizzy though, and Peter Hoare, a good friend of Dizzy's, I was able to build up some time and a little experience in this most demanding of aviation activities. I flew several displays in the DC-3 and, by the end of the year, began to look for an aeroplane of my own. I had a new dream, perhaps even more unlikely than my dream to be a pop star. I now wanted to be a display pilot. Towards the end of the year I got involved as sponsor for a big Warbird air show. It was called The Great Warbirds Air Display. Things didn't quite go as we'd been led to believe they would and the event cost us a lot of money. We did make a video of the weekend but even that, to this very day, has yet to break even. This was a year when, financially, we desperately needed things to go our way so the air show was a major disappointment.

The *Warriors* single did well, though, peaking at 20 and the album reached number 12 a few weeks later. I'd actually been quite unlucky with the single and felt it could have gone much higher. In its second week we released a particular version, a picture disc I think, to help keep the interest in the record alive and active. Unfortunately for us, for that one week only, the chart compilers decided that picture discs were not allowable and so discounted our sales. The record, which had gone up prior to that, was repositioned and so dropped two places. A week later they reintroduced the picture disc as allowable again. This manoeuvre killed the single dead in its tracks. What little radio play there was fell away completely and the single plummeted. It seemed as though this streak of bad luck was a pay-back for all the good fortune that I'd had in '79 and I was sure that it would be over soon.

I also did a record signing at HMV in Oxford Street and 3,000 people turned up, stopping the traffic for a while. This was a great boost for me. I hadn't been on a British stage for two and a half years and, with the 40-date *Warriors* UK tour now announced, I was very unsure as to how the fans would react. Would they turn away, would they forgive me turning away? I was more than ready for the grief that the press were going to give me, I knew they would have a field day with this change of heart, but I was worried about the fans. The HMV session made me feel much more confident that things would be okay. The press was one of the reasons for coming back with such a long tour, the other was my desire to show the fans that I was back to stay.

The *Warriors* stage set was intended to have a slightly apocalyptic feel, to go with the image. It was built, at great expense, by the set designers of a film studio and had a very life-like feel to it. Two towers, damaged and war weary, stood either side of a central riser, itself made to look like the top of a third tower. Along the front of this riser a grille was incorporated, with lights and a smoke machine behind it, to give the impression of air-conditioning units that you see on top of American skyscrapers. Inside these buildings stood the keyboard players, the drummer was positioned on top of the central column, in front of a back drop. The bass player and guitar positions were at the foot of the two tall towers. It was very large and required a lot of people to put up every night and made it a very expensive tour to put on. The cladding of the set alone cost well over £50,000. Chris Payne and my brother John were the two keyboard players and John also added the saxophone to his list of live credits. Ced Sharpley was back on drums, Russell on guitar and Joe Hubbard was on bass. Tik and Tok, whom I'd last worked with at Wembley when they were part of the dance group Shock, were the support.

On the first day of the tour rehearsals the lighting operator went down sick. This was a big, big problem. It could have been a lot worse as I had spent so much of my time working the lighting consoles I knew more than enough about it to carry on without him for a while. I programmed the lighting rig for the entire show, fully expecting him to be back each day. But each day came and went and still no word. I was there until three or four in the morning every night for four weeks, programming and rehearsing the lights, which was a tremendous added pressure. Although I was able to get the show together I obviously wouldn't be able to run it on tour. We needed to find out what was going on and, if our man wasn't coming back, to find a replacement. He wasn't and so, with only a day or two of rehearsals left, James Dann stepped in to take over lighting duties. James had been around light shows for years but by now I had everything where I wanted it. James' job was to learn my cues, understand what light pictures went with what song, learn the music and then hope for the best. Even without the main task of programming the lights themselves it was a lot to take on at such short notice. This was not the start to my big comeback tour that I had been hoping for.

The set looked amazing but our main lighting adviser, whom we had relied on totally since day one was, as it turned out, less than genuine. He cost us hundreds of thousands of pounds before we realised. One of his ideas was for me to use a new form of moving lights which were, at the time, supposed to be cutting edge technology. Instead of renting, as we should have done, we were encouraged, by our lighting expert, to buy 16 of them. By only four gigs into the tour we were down to three working models. They cost a lot of money and were a complete disaster. I think it was well known that I had a 'spare no expense' mentality when it came to putting on shows, and so people just plucked figures out of the air whenever I arrived on their doorstep. I was always looking for something different and unique, all the latest technology, so it left me open to frequent rip offs.

I was a little disappointed with the attitude of the band during rehearsals. It wasn't hostile but it had a very definite 'Only here for the money' feel to it. They were only being asked to play two sets a day. That was about three hours of music, a bit of tidying up loose parts, which they should have had together by now anyway, plus a little bit of hanging around. I was getting there at eight or nine in the morning and working through till three or four, sometimes five, the following morning. It was my show so I had no problems with working those hours, but it made me tired and irritable and I expected the band to work hard at least for the few hours they were there. The pressure of a comeback tour, of sorts, was already heavy, and the lighting problems made it twice as bad. One day they played a part very badly and I lost my temper. It was one of

184

the very few times I've ever lost my temper in rehearsals. They had been rehearsing for well over a month, it was a song most of them had been playing since 1979, and it was just sheer bloody laziness. Joe Hubbard argued that they were tired and overworked. Fucking overworked! It took me some time to calm down. Joe was naff throughout the tour. Good player but such a prima donna. He would complain about everything. We rented him the most expensive bass gear you could get, because that's what he had to have, and he would insist at running it flat out. Number 10 on the dial night after night. He would be blowing up speakers, amps, whatever he touched and then complain about the sound. I suggested to him that he should just turn it down a little but it fell on deaf ears. Unsurprisingly, I overheard him at the Dominion Theatre, London, saying to the tour manager that if it blew up again he was leaving the tour. He didn't realise that I was standing behind a partition and heard every word. I was so angry I could've killed him. I found his attitude and behaviour on tour to be the most unprofessional of any musician I've ever worked with. It was such a shame because he could really play.

The tour itself felt like a holiday compared to the rehearsals. On stage I was a lot more confident, although I nearly suffered a disaster at the Edinburgh Playhouse, which has quite a steep slope up to the stage. During one song I used to stand on top of the grille in front of the drums and I would just walk off it. This was quite a drop, about seven feet, but after doing it a couple of times I got more confident. The crowd would always let out a gasp as I fell, so it was good fun. At Edinburgh the angle of the stage got the better of me and I shot forward, completely out of control, with my arms windmilling like a mad thing. I grabbed hold of the microphone stand as I wobbled past and managed to stop myself from going off the front of the stage. Just. It was not cool.

I had to bleach my hair nearly every night on that tour as the new transplants, from the second operation, were growing so quickly. At one point the surgeon rang up. He'd just seen me on *Top Of The Pops* and was horrified to see that I'd bleached it at all. I didn't dare tell him it was now a nightly exercise.

Paul Gardiner joined us on stage at one of the London gigs and the crowd went completely crazy. Paul did nothing more than walk

185

on to the stage and wave and they just loved him. It was one of the last times I saw him alive. The first few weeks of the tour were hard. It seemed to be taking a lifetime. After about three weeks I got into my stride and I would happily have stayed out on the road for the rest of my life. When we reached Stoke I remember walking out of the restaurant as Joe Hubbard complained, yet again, about the size of his sandwich or something equally life-threatening, when a huge bang ripped through the hotel. I ran down the corridor as Tik and Tok came out of their room, slightly dishevelled but laughing their heads off. Somehow they had blown up their toilet. A few days later we had a band battle and spent time firing fireworks at each other. It was in the top floor of a hotel and we had rockets going from one end of the corridor to the other. Didn't think much of the smoke detectors. Not a single alarm went off!

I have done many things that were the worst kind of male excess that you could imagine. My feelings about groupies, or fans that sleep with you, whatever you want to call them, changed progressively over the years. When I first became famous I would feel guilty about just leaving them behind. That went away very quickly. After a while I became suspicious of everybody, everyone had an ulterior motive for being there, or so it seemed to me, and so I became quite cold and mercenary about the whole thing. I just took what I wanted and couldn't care less. I became fascinated by the way that these perfectly rational women would become desperate for it, they would sleep with me if I so much as pointed at them, or anyone connected to me for that matter. I found this total loss of self-esteem vaguely unappealing on the one hand but very difficult to say No to on the other.

After a while I realised that all of that was crap and I began to admire the honesty of it. If they wanted something they just asked for it. No harm was done, no one was hurt, no one was deceived or betrayed, everyone had fun, hopefully. I stopped thinking of them as fans I was using, or fans who were using me, and more as casual friends I happened to be sleeping with. So much of life is wasted through procedure and etiquette. Doing the done thing.

I had periods though when I just slept with every girl that passed my way. I tried to keep count for a while but couldn't. It was great fun at the time, appalling to think back on now. How I didn't catch a disease was a mystery to me. We had band competitions, for who had the best looking girl, the worst looking, the most in one day, the most at one time, the most unusual place, the most public place, the most in total. I won everything. I had not a shred of concern about what I was doing. I was young, had money, had popularity and I was going for it. At one point sex was my primary reason for touring. I was lucky to get out alive.

There were a lot of groupies around on the *Warriors* tour. Strangely enough I met the girl who I was to spend the next nine years with on that tour, Tracey Adam. I went back to my hotel room after the Blackpool show and there she was, with a friend no less. I thought I'd struck it particularly lucky but she actually wanted nothing more than an autograph. She was very pretty. I was 25 at the time and she was just 18. I didn't meet her again until the end of the tour and it was some time after that that we began to see each other more regularly.

Anyway, at one point on the tour the groupie competition was going badly for me. I had been stuck on the same number for two nights running, and I was being caught up by one of the band. In the morning I was woken to find that everyone was on the bus and waiting for me. I hadn't heard the wake up call so I leapt out of bed and, still fumbling with my zip, launched off down the corridor. As I ran I heard a girl call out. I peered into one of the rooms and found her, trying her best to look seductive and failing on all counts. She made me an offer but I just didn't have the time. Still, an opportunity to unstick myself so to speak, so I reconsidered, apologised up front for the brief nature of what was about to follow, explained that I was late for the bus, leapt onto the bed and within a minute, two at most, was leaping on to the bus with a cry of triumph. I had no class, no pride, no sense of decency, no morals, nothing. I was a wandering prick, devoid of heart and brain and I'm glad that those days are behind me.

I was also seeing Vivian Neves, the former Page Three model, around this time. I was deeply infatuated with her but I think she had much better sense than to take it too seriously. She was about 12 years older than me, still beautiful, and I enjoyed every minute that I was with her.

We played to more people on that tour than any other, about

80,000, which helped *Warriors* do better than *I, Assassin*, despite the fact that WEA didn't put much into promoting it. By this time Beggars Banquet were just the men in the middle, taking their percentage for finding me in the first place, but we had no real working relationship at all. WEA again declared their satisfaction with sales, which left me frustrated. I didn't want to be selling 50,000 albums in the UK. I wanted to get beyond the 300,000 I'd been selling with *Replicas*. It would take effort, push, money. We put out a single, 'Sister Surprise', and did a *Top Of The Pops*, but there was no other promotion put into it by WEA. No video, virtually no advertising. One TV programme on its own doesn't really do much good. It's a bit like finding a glass of water in the middle of the desert, it'll keep you going for a few more hours but really it's just postponing the inevitable. I decided, and my dad agreed, that we had run our course with the Beggars/WEA deal. Given the bad luck that had come to plague our every move, our leaving couldn't have been at a worse time – as we walked out the door, a new managing director and team walked in. They spun WEA around and, in no time at all, had turned it back into a huge success story. Meanwhile, we were on our own.

We looked around for another deal for a while but I had yet to start recording any new material and everyone wanted to hear new stuff. I was convinced that we would be better off starting our own label because I had lost all faith in the promises of the big record companies. At least on our own we would know where we stood. So, instead of waiting for the new material and signing to a proper label, we started our own, Numa Records. At this point I made another major blunder. What I should have done, having decided to start Numa, was focus on my own career and put all of what money I had left into my own future. What I *did* was try to run Numa as a conventional small label. I signed up acts, Hohokam, Grey Parade, Steve Braun, Larry Loeber and Caroline Munro. That mistake in itself was bad enough, but I compounded it by trying to be fair. If I couldn't afford a video for all the bands on the label I wouldn't have one either. I gave myself the same budget as that I gave to all the others. Stupidity beyond belief. I was told and told over and over again, this is not the way to go. I was equally convinced that it was and so, as usual, I got my way.

1984 started very badly. Paul Gardiner was found dead on a park bench on 4 February after taking his own life with a heroin overdose. He was supposed to be coming in to see my mum at our Rock City studio a few days later. She had been on the phone to him just a day or two earlier and he seemed to be doing okay. He had big problems with heroin but he was reasonably together and looking forward to visiting the studio. There was no indication that Paul's drug problem had reached such a point, or that he was suicidal. I don't think anyone suspected. I always imagined that, sooner or later, Paul would sort himself out and back he'd come. There was always a place for him in the band if he wanted it, a fact he was aware of. I found out about his suicide from a girl I was seeing who lived not far away from him. His family hadn't rung us because they'd obviously got their own problems. It just seemed strange to me that I wouldn't somehow know in my bones, as soon as it happened. I thought I would sense it, yet nothing changed. I hadn't seen much of Paul because I'd been away for a long time and then I'd been busy with the tour. To be honest the horrible reality of what had happened didn't really sink in until the funeral. I remember looking at the coffin and thinking, 'You idiot. What a waste.' It was so sad, just being aware that he was in this wooden box. My anti-religious feelings all but boiled over when we were asked to praise God's kindness and heavenly mercy or some such nonsense. He'd died so young and too much of his life had been unpleasant. I hadn't seen a great deal of God's kindness or mercy around him. Paul had been making some recordings at Rock City before he died, a cover of the Velvet Underground's 'Venus In Furs' and a new song, 'No Sense', and they became our first release on Numa as a tribute to him. He left behind a wife and young son, Christopher. I had never been too keen on his wife and I lost count of the number of times Paul had been late to the studio or rehearsals because she'd had yet another tantrum and smashed things up, or thrown his engagement ring out of the window. She was the last thing he needed, in my eyes, since he found life hard enough as it was. He needed someone to lean on, to help him, and what he got was nothing but aggravation.

By early '84 the money situation was worrying. The Ferrari was becoming increasingly troublesome and expensive to run so it had to go. It would go through a gearbox every two years, a clutch every 8,000 miles, a set of rear tyres twice a year, fronts once a year. It's a car for very rich men and I was not a very rich man any more. On the last service I had driven it out of the Ferrari workshop, the weather was snowing gently, put the car into second and it spun round like a top – the gearbox had reverse where second should have been. When I sold it that problem was back, the heater had stopped working, the doors wouldn't lock, the paint was peeling, the numberplate had fallen off, the bonnet catches had both snapped and the interior light had fallen out. The time to let it go was upon me. Anyway, I still had the Corvette. Another machine to leave for pastures new was my beloved Navajo. I sold that shortly after the Ferrari. I felt like a traitor. It had taken me safely around the world and here I was getting rid of it. But it had to be done. I was very upset as I watched it fly away.

By way of compensation, and for a fraction of the money we got for the Ferrari and Navajo, I bought a World War Two aeroplane called a Harvard. The Harvard is a wartime two-seater combat trainer which did then very much what the RAF Hawk, the aeroplane used by the RAF display team the Red Arrows, does today. It taught new pilots how to use the aeroplane as a weapon. It was Dizzy Addicott who persuaded me to buy one, saying that if you can master the Harvard, then pretty much everything else is downhill. When I told people I knew in the aviation world what I was buying I had mixed reactions. I was told that they were dangerous and unpredictable. One man even said that it was the only plane he'd ever flown that was still trying to kill him when he pushed it into the hangar. Other people I knew had had friends killed in Harvard accidents. All this made me a tad nervous but Dizzy was the voice of experience and reason and so I went ahead and bought it. I was left with a strong sense of trepidation, though, as the time to fly it drew near.

The first flight was interesting. I was with a man called Peter Hoare, a friend of Dizzy's and another excellent pilot, who was to guide me through those first few nervous trips. The engine quit momentarily, due to debris in the tanks which had been picked up after we'd stalled it for the first time, so we took it back and had the tanks flushed out. The usual pre-flight fuel check hadn't shown any signs of rubbish in the fuel. We guessed that, as the aeroplane had been in the hangar for several years with only a brief check flight by the seller before handing it over to us, a lot of crap may still have been lurking in the tanks. After that it was fine. I did a few trips with Peter and then went solo on 8 March, my 26th birthday.

The Harvard is fairly big for a single-engined aeroplane. It weighs about two and a third tons and has a wingspan of around 40 feet. With 600hp it has enough power to give you most of the problems associated with high performance piston-engined aeroplanes, but not enough to get you out of trouble. As such, it needs to be flown carefully, until you've really got the hang of it. I have getting on for a thousand hours on Harvards and am now about the highest time Harvard pilot in the UK. I know it well but, even so, there have been four fatal Harvard crashes involving people I knew within the last 24 months. That sort of accident rate keeps you on your guard. It is not an aeroplane you can get too relaxed in or take for granted and it demands your full attention at all times. As 1984 progressed, I was to suffer a major confidence crisis that almost took me out of aviation completely.

Not long after I bought the Harvard someone I knew quite well, a top display pilot, was killed in a crash. On that same day somebody from the airfield I flew from also crashed and, along with two passengers, was burnt alive. They were trapped, with people trying to pull them out, when it blew up just a few miles from the runway. That started my crisis. The display pilot was, arguably, one of the best display pilots we've ever had and I thought, oh, Christ, if it can happen to him it could certainly happen to me. I became progressively more frightened of flying my aeroplane. It had such a terrible reputation for killing people and I couldn't shake off a feeling of dread. I went through a period where, unless the weather was absolutely perfect, sunny, 5 mph wind straight down the runway, I would find some reason not to fly. Then I would hate myself for being gutless and I got grumpy and horrible to people around me. I just had to work through it; It was either that or get out of flying altogether. I would fly the plane for five minutes, terrified the whole time, land it, feel all right because I'd managed. Bit by bit five minutes became ten – ten became fifteen and so on. I got through it, I started to enjoy flying again and my confidence soared. It took me several months to work through whatever had been going on in my mind.

While I was going through this I was also making the *Berserker* album and some of those fears fed into the recordings. The track 'Cold Warning' describes the feelings of a victim. A man is sitting, scared and alone, because he instinctively knows there's something cold and horrible outside. He can't quite see but it's there, and it's been waiting for him for a long time. 'My Dying Machine' was about the feelings that you go through when you are in a machine and you know that something is wrong. I felt I had a very good understanding of genuine fear – fear for your life rather than fear of your favourite football team losing. For a long time I didn't think I would get past 30. It wasn't a desire to make my life more dramatic, I was being honest. The things I was doing, around aeroplanes mainly, seemed dangerous enough to kill me because of my lack of experience and maturity. So many other people, good pilots, were dying every year that my own demise seemed more or less inevitable. I thought for years that I would die in a plane crash sooner or later, and for a long time the idea didn't bother me too much. It would be quick, spectacular, and as good a way to go as any. I don't think like that any more. I've seen too many crashes, seen too many friends die horribly. It isn't always quick.

I started working on the album in the second half of 1984 and previewed one of the new songs, 'This Is New Love' on Leo Sayer's television show. I'd met him once before on *Top Of The Pops*. He was a very bouncy, likeable sort of bloke. He had his own TV series where he would go out and get involved in various people's hobbies. Mine was obviously flying so in addition to filming my new song in the studio, a crew came up to Duxford Airfield and filmed me flying an old DC3 around. I was always keen to do anything that involved aeroplanes, not just because I enjoyed the flying but because I was forever trying to undo, piece by piece, the damage done by the accident. A lot of my fans said that Leo Sayer wasn't credible enough and that I shouldn't have done the show. I thought that was a crap thing to say but I knew what they meant. There are certain things I've said no to over the years because I felt they were wrong for me, but when it's a show by someone whom you know and like as a person, to not want to go on because they're not credible enough would suck. We also performed a version of 'On Broadway' together which I recorded at Rock City. Leo came up with the idea that we should perform the song as though we were drunken tramps. I was saying, Yeah OK, and thinking, Oh no. I'd never been drunk, for one thing, and it had an element of acting about it which I'd always tried to keep well away from. Anyway we did it and it wasn't too bad. Before I went on there was a warm up comedian who was getting a lot of laughs at my expense because I'd dyed my hair bright blue. He kept going on about me borrowing my granny's blue rinse. Tik and Tok were with us, dressed up as coneheads. They wandered over to him and, without saying a word but using mime, they managed to make him the butt of the joke. It was brilliant, very clever, and I was grateful to them.

The *Berserker* album doesn't have a central character or a story as such. I was writing about being something, or part of something, fictional. Something that was dreadful, powerful, unstoppable. Something almost alien from what you're used to which is coming your way. I was trying to create a feeling of only half-guessed-at menace. The songs had bits which were specific to me but they were mostly weird fictional stuff about being cold, playing games with people, using people in very unpleasant ways, without ever saying what they were, exactly. Whatever this thing was, it was big enough to change how you lived and strong enough to do with you whatever it wanted. One of the things about being a pop star is that we are the ultimate ships in the night, especially when on tour. We arrive, we're very important to the people who are there, we touch people's lives and then we're gone. The experiences are fleeting. For a while you're a big fish in a small pond, and knowing how small the pond is is what keeps the ego in check but while I'm the big fish I enjoy it. The *Berserker* lyrics are another aspect of that vibe. The exception is a song called 'A Child With The Ghost' which I wrote for Paul Gardiner.

I got the idea for the *Berserker* image from a photograph in a magazine of a woman who'd been painted to look like marble. I wanted to do something that was very different from the black clothes or the gangster look. So, for the cover, I dyed my hair blue, painted my face white, wore blue eye shadow, blue eyeliner, blue blusher and blue lips. The clothes were white leather, again as a total contrast to my earlier black image. The name *Berserker* came from the Saberhagen books I'd read at school. I was very happy with the album, which was aggressively produced with hard, electronic bass replacing some of the more fluid, fretless playing of my previous albums. I started to use sound as percussion rather than using conventional percussion instruments. *Berserker* was also the last time I used a real drummer in the studio. Although a lot of musicians layered their individual styles over the electronics, including Zaine Griff who sang backing vocals on 'The Secret', the album was less conventional than *Warriors*. This was due in part to a new synthesiser, the PPG Wave, which gave me access to sounds that I hadn't had before. I started to work with Mike Smith and Ian Herron, who called themselves The Waveteam. they were PPG experts and would fight with it day in, day out, to get the best out of it, since it was not the easiest machine to operate. The PPG gave me my first real chance to get into sampling and so I went out and about dragging drains and manhole covers across the ground, hitting anything I could find in search of the perfect sound. At one point we even tried to sample the carburettor on the Ferrari. You could hear it sucking in air, which I thought was a fantastic effect. I thought we were being very inventive, running around doing this weird stuff and turning it into music.

Berserker was the first Numa-released album and we had very high hopes for it. Too high in fact, because we massively overpressed. It was easy to see why, though. We released the title track of the album as a single. It went into the chart at 36, we did a *Top Of The Pops* and it moved up the chart a few places. We assumed, reasonably based on our previous history, that the radio, always slightly reluctant to play Numan stuff, would now pick up on the song and start to play it. It was a chart single, after all. Expecting the airplay to boost the sales of the record we printed thousands more of the single and album. The pre-release orders on both album and single had also been good, so with the radio plays, we felt we were on to a sure winner. The radio didn't play it. It was as though the number in the chart where *Berserker* sat was in a void. The song was totally ignored by Radio One, the UK's national station. For us it was a disaster. Not only was it a crushing disappointment to see the song ignored but it also left us with a huge

194

amount of stock that would remain unsold. We lost so much money on that first release it all but ruined us. We had put a lot of time and money into Numa, we had put most of what little we had left into the label, and it was gone. We were in trouble. Without the support of radio my career was going to have a hard time moving forward. For the first time ever I began to think that it was all over. I began to realise that every decision I made wasn't instinctively right. I used to think I had an unnatural grasp for certain things which nobody else around me had and I believed it for a long time. Someone would ring up and say, 'the *Daily Mirror* want to do an interview with you' and I would say Yes or No based on instinct. I genuinely believed I had some weird sixth sense about these things which was, obviously, nonsense. Eventually I got it wrong so many times that it slowly dawned on me I wasn't instinctive at all. I had just been very, very lucky. And now the luck appeared to have well and truly run out. It was yet another price to pay for having known success too early. I had a very false picture of what my abilities were and now I was learning hard lessons, hard truths, almost daily. I was moving into a period of ego adjustment.

In October we played a 20-date tour around the country with Andy Coughlan on bass, complementing the ex-Dramatis regulars. I wanted the *Berserker* stage set to look like a high tech version of a Roman temple, with big columns at the back. I had five 20-foot-high towers with light panels from the 'Teletour' built around the main set in an arc. It was large and bright with lots of cold colours to complement the white leather and blue hair. However, large and expensive it was, it was not the sort of extravagant show that I'd put on before. I felt I'd dropped down a level. It had been necessary, because of our growing money worries, but it still hurt. In reality I should have cut back even more for I hadn't fully grasped just how bad things were financially. In fact, for the next ten years, I would remain slightly behind the speed of our decline. Each year we would cut back, always trying not to let it show of course, and each year we had slipped further into trouble and so should have cut back even more.

The tour went okay, the audience was down on a gig to gig basis compared to the previous year but I was already blaming that on Radio One. The image, however, turned out to be a nightmare. It took me about two and a half hours every night to get the make-up on. I had to dye my hair almost every day and the blue would stain, permanently, everything it touched. I ruined sinks and bedding the length and breadth of the country.

At the end of the tour Tracey moved into the Wentworth house with me. She was probably too young to live with someone like me who was very erratic and immature, so our relationship was doomed from the start. I was horrible at times: no patience, self-righteous, arrogant, rude. Unfortunately, by the time I'd started to mature we were already years into a very confrontational relationship which continued to go from bad to worse. We stayed together for about nine years but, in truth, it shouldn't have gone on for anything like as long. Until very recently I've been quite useless at relationships.

Towards the end of the year Beggars Banquet dug out some of my oldest recordings, all previously unreleased, and put them out under the title *The Plan*. The album actually went into the Top 30 which came as something of a surprise.

CHAPTER 10

The 'Airwave' Police, 1985-87

Initially 'Change Your Mind', the song I recorded with Shakatak's keyboard player and songwriter Bill Sharpe, was going to be a one-off single. He was recording his debut solo album in my Rock City Studio. I was there one day playing on the Battle Zone game machine when Bill came out with Nick Smith, an engineer I'd worked with in the past, and asked if I'd be interested in singing on one of the tracks. I'd met Bill before and I also had a vague Shakatak connection through the singer Tracey Ackerman, who first sang backing vocals for me on the *Warriors* album. He gave me a cassette of 'Change Your Mind' and I liked it immediately. We went in a few days later and I recorded my vocal in about two takes. It suited my voice well and it came very easily. Bill and Nick were happy, as were Bill's record company, Polydor.

When 'Change Your Mind' was released in February '85 Radio One immediately play-listed it. That, along with a *Top Of The Pops* performance, helped it up to number 17. I was still using a variation of the white face, blue hair *Berserker* image. We made a video for it which was shown in its entirety by the BBC and there was a lot of press interest in the collaboration, which on the surface was fairly bizarre. Our musical backgrounds were vastly different. The song also did well in Europe, charting at number 12 in Holland. The whole experience was great fun and Bill and I left the door open for more work together.

In March I did a promotional tour for the *Berserker* single and album in Germany. I was also developing a fairly unusual roster of

197

new acts on Numa. One of the earliest releases was by a New York performance artist called Larry Loeber who had a quirky, bizarre personality. The Numanair racing driver Mike Machonochie also recorded a single for the label called, 'Stereo Headphones'. The last thing I heard, he was the manager of one of the big New York airports – something I would never have expected him to do. Another act on the label was the model/actress Caroline Munro. She covered a song from *Berserker* called 'Pump Me Up'. She didn't understand the title's innuendo, which gave me a childishly sly giggle in the studio. Caroline was keen to try and develop a recording career but, to be honest, I was probably the wrong person to come to. She had previously been the woman in the old Navy Rum advert and she was an ex-Bond girl. At the time she was a hostess on the *3-2-1* TV programme. She actually sang a lot better than I thought she would.

My brother John Webb also released his 'Experiment Of Love' single on Numa. John is very creative, he has the ability to see and hear things which are peculiar to him but they work. I have a tremendous amount of respect for John. His life has been affected because of what's happened to me and not always for the best. He was 14 when I became famous and often got beaten up as my sole defender at his school. Eventually my parents were forced to take him out of school early and so he left with no qualifications. His education was effectively hindered by me. Not only that, but everything he was interested in, I'd already done. I was into music before him; I was flying before him. He struggled, I think, to find his own way and yet he never gave me a moment's grief about it. From 1982 onwards he was in the band and he was brilliant, never a note wrong. He chose, many years ago, to take up a career in aviation and he has shown incredible determination to succeed ever since. And he has succeeded. In many ways John's achievements far outweigh my own. John's success has been down to pure effort and skill, whereas mine has also involved good luck. He's now holder of the highest level flying licence it's possible to get, having started out as a flying instructor and worked his way towards those vital commercial licences. He is now a captain on the BAC 111 jet airliner and has already been a training captain on Viscounts, where he taught other captains how to master the aeroplane. He is also a top air display pilot, and one of only two people cleared to fly the historic Bristol Blenheim bomber, the only flying example of the type in the world. On top of that, he is a keen archer and has won several gold medals in archery competitions. I admire him enormously and feel proud to the core that I can call him my brother.

With the exception of John, I wish I hadn't signed other artists to my label because I ended up losing pretty much every penny I had left. Numa hastened my big financial downfall. I launched Numa partly because I liked the idea of helping young bands.

I've always tried to assist bands that are just starting out and I've also helped out fans with their songs in my studio. I sell my retiring musical equipment to fan club members at low prices so they can get good gear at a more affordable price. Numa records was an extension of that and I thought we would do all right out of it. I saw it as a way of developing another area of the business so I didn't have to rely on my own success. I expected my career to fade away in time but I hoped I would have a record label established which would keep me in the business. I told the bands that I saw it as a stepping stone for them. You come here, do a couple of singles, maybe an album and when the majors come along, we won't stand in your way. I wanted Numa to be a starting point for them. I would get my payback when the majors took them to bigger and better things because I would own at least one of their early albums. It seemed like a fairly good idea on paper.

The fact that I owned my own studio, Rock City, in the Shepperton complex, was also part of the package. We'd started buying into it as far back as 1980 and I had done a lot of recording there. With our own studios, and Rock City had two 24-track rooms, recording costs would be minimal. The studio would be profitable simply through our own bands using it, and when they weren't recording we would make it available to other bands as we had before. Sting used the studio whenever he was filming at Shepperton. He would finish a scene, come to the studio to work, and then go and film another scene. Cliff Richard used it, along with all kinds of other people. When Thin Lizzy were there they broke open my games machine and tried to steal the money out of the back.

Our offices were also in Shepperton. It should have been a very efficient, all under one roof, operation. However things didn't work out. The people who owned the Shepperton Film centre, and our studio building, decided the place should be only a movie centre, so they made it increasingly difficult for us to stay there.

We should've pulled out much sooner. My dad kept saying to me, 'We need to get out of this fast, it's all going wrong', but I insisted we hang on. I was convinced that we could make it work and, if we could, we were going to be set up for life. Part of the trouble was I had no idea the radio problem would be quite so bad and, as I mentioned before, I wouldn't allow myself a larger budget than the other bands. That was very stupid since it was the money from my sales that was needed to fund the operation, but I was so determined to make sure that we all got the same treatment that I cut off the money supply.

It has to be said, though, I was shocked by the egos in some of our acts. We did an all-day photo session for the bands, including me, with one of the top rock photographers in the country. Towards the end of the day we were running about an hour late – which wasn't bad considering how many different set-ups we had to get through. The last band, Grey Parade, threw a tantrum, smashing up light bulbs and a drinks machine because they'd had to wait in a pub for that hour, at my expense I might add. I'd been waiting just as long and I was paying. They said they wouldn't be treated that way. What fucking way? They behaved as if they were big stars and earning me a fortune in sales, when in fact they had only made one single that no one had bought. We dropped them the next day. We told them, 'You don't behave like that when you're famous. You certainly don't behave like that when you're not.'

On 27 April I released a double live album, *White Noise*, taken from the *Berserker* tour. It slipped quietly into the Top 30 along with a four-track Live EP which peaked at 26. We also enjoyed a flash of success when 'White Noise' reached number two in Belgium. A concert video from the *Berserker* tour was also released.

I was already working on my new album, *The Fury*. Mike Smith and Ian Herron, The Waveteam, were now working with me as co-producers. I had been going to team up with Colin Thurston but, after assisting on one track, he was called away to help on the new

Human League album. When Colin left, Mike and Ian asked if they might be given a try instead. For me it worked well. They made me work much harder on my vocals, pushing me constantly.

We released the first single from the album, 'Your Fascination', in late summer '85. I, as I still tended to do in those days, had high hopes for it. Once again a total lack of radio play was to surprise and disappoint me. 'Your Fascination' climbed to 46 but, without any real promotion, it just died and faded away. The next single 'Call Out The Dogs' another song about the press, only reached as far as 49. A third single, 'Miracles' also went into the top 50. We were sliding into the lower reaches of the charts but we weren't making any real impression. It began to dawn on me that the radio situation was not a temporary problem, not just one or two records that they hadn't liked. They were not going to play Numan stuff, full stop.

The album went straight into the UK charts at 29 and then rose another five places the following week. Without those singles, though, it had nothing to lean on and began to slide back out of the charts over the next five weeks. We had no money to promote anything we released. Financially we were sliding into debt as quickly as my records were sliding out of the chart and there was nothing we could do about it.

The Fury possesses a very metallic, industrial feel. It's rhythmic and funky using a wide range of staccato sounds built up throughout our experimental time with the PPG. In fact it was the first time I'd written a complete album in the studio. Until then I sat at home working out the melodies on the piano. On *The Fury* we went into the studio and worked on the grooves first, which are all electronic. There are no real drums, very little conventional bass playing and virtually no guitar on the album. It was more spontaneous in many ways than how I'd worked before. *The Fury* was also my most expensive album to make. I was in Rock City for about 90 days, usually with The Waveteam. It still only cost £12,000 to make which I mostly spent on hiring Dick Morrissey, Tessa Niles and the producers. Their contributions complemented each other brilliantly, but I still spent many hours alone working on my own ideas which is why I think I must be one of the cheapest studio acts in the business. I know bands who spend ten times that on demos. In fact, one of Numa's acts, Hohokam, spent £60,000 on an album that never came out. That's a ridiculous amount as they had free studio time at Rock City.

The album cover was a bit of a mistake. If I was young I would-n't have bought an album with a man in a white suit and red dickie bow on the cover. I had always thought to use album covers as a guide to what was inside and now I had forgotten what I was doing. The cover was completely inappropriate, said nothing about the music and probably did the album a great disservice. Lyrically, there are some bizarre things on it and the album is quite aggressive in its stance, but I look like the man who lost it all at Monte Carlo.

On *The Fury* I often started off with just a title for a song, such as 'Tricks', 'Your Fascination' and 'Creatures'. I then tried to find lyrics that suited. A lot of the time I ended up writing about myself, pop stardon, crisis points, failure, sex and the seedy side of life. These were recurring themes for years come, now I think of it, I became totally preoccupied with the career struggle and it coloured my writing for far too long. I had recurring themes when I was at school too. I was often being told off in English for writing yet another war story as part of my essay homework. On one occasion our English teacher said, the essay title is 'A flower in the morning sun'. I wrote a long story about a man at war who died horribly. As he fell, mortally wounded, into the bottom of a muddy trench, he opened his eyes and the last thing he sees was a flower in the morn-ing sun. I really got into trouble for that.

The song 'This Disease' is written from the perspective of some-body on drugs who is in desperate trouble. There are little refer-ences to bisexual women finding me other girls, and for a while I'd only go out with bi-women. 'The Pleasure Skin' is about male pros-titutes in a horror story kind of way. I was trying to create images of dark alleys and seedy little doorways where these horrible old creatures hide, inviting you to do things to them. 'God Only Knows' draws on some of the experiences I had flying over the Pacific, where you're sitting, relatively helpless, and waiting for bad things to happen. Those feelings have stayed with me forever. 'I Still Remember' was another love song. The last line, 'this could be my last song/Everything must end some day,' was a wind-up for the fans. I thought to myself when I wrote it, 'this will get them going'. Those are the final words on the album.

For *The Fury* shows in September I brought back the square 'Teletour' light panels again. The band stood atop a wall of light panels eight feet high and forty feet wide. From the roof three motorised gantries, also clad in light panels, could be lowered down to form tall towers. At the back of the stage a hydraulic lift carried the band up onto the stage. Jane Spiers, a lighting designer I'd not worked with before but who'd done a lot of work with Depeche Mode, helped to make it one of my most spectacular shows. Jane also pointed out my tendency to go bright with the verses and tone things down on the choruses which is, conventionally at least, the wrong way round. I'd never thought about it before: I lit the verses bright because generally they're longer. I record my music back to front as well, with verses often bigger than choruses. *The Fury* tour was one of the best of my career, the audiences were great and we didn't have a single bad night. I was also pleased with my own performance. I thought I was starting to get the hang of it.

1985 was also a breakthrough year for flying. I joined the Harvard Formation Team, which was to grow into one of the leading display teams in Europe, and I also had my aeroplane painted in Japanese colours. I had found it very difficult getting display work for the aeroplane. I was new with a poor, albeit press-created, reputation as a pilot and a number of other people were already established on the display circuit with Harvards. I needed to work the aeroplane. With my money all but gone, and the Harvard costing up to £15,000 a year to operate, I had to find work for it. I decided to paint it Japanese because I noticed that, although the UK display scene had a number of British and American combat aeroplanes, with a few Germans to fight, there were no Japanese planes. We had the Allied Pacific fighters but no enemy. The Harvard bears a passing resemblance to a Japanese World War Two fighter called a Zero and Harvards were used to represent Zeros in the famous war film *Tora, Tora. Tora.* I thought that if I painted my plane like a Zero I might get some work for it as the enemy who gets shot down at all the air shows. Joining the Harvard Formation Team in some ways took away some of the need for that paint job but, in general, it worked a treat. It worked so well, in fact, that we added a 'shoot down' routine to the HFT's normal display, which proved very popular.

I had been working hard on my flying skills and was slowly introducing an aerobatic element into the team's display. My own formation flying skills were also improving rapidly and I soon found myself a regular display pilot. I had a way to go, but I was one of them now, and that in itself was a major achievement in my eyes. I kept every display programme that I was mentioned in, and flying became everything to me. It was such a breath of fresh air that I threw myself wholeheartedly into aviation. I found that I had a way with aeroplanes, I picked things up easily. I had a natural leaning towards display flying, since the challenge of it drew me like a moth to a flame.

Although flying had, almost certainly, taken over as my main interest for a while, music was still a driving passion. Through the end of 1985 and early '86 I worked on new material. The first to be finished was a relatively dark ballad, 'This Is Love'. It was released as a single on 19 April 1986. I loved it and there was some especially beautiful playing by Dick Morrissey. Once again, our hopes were raised. It climbed to 28 in the chart, our best position for some time. One day someone rang me up and said, 'Your new song is on Radio One'. I couldn't believe it. I rushed to turn on the radio and I thought, 'This is it, everything's going to be all right now'. Then the DJ, Steve Wright, apologised for having played it. He said the track was utterly depressing and that he had been forced to play it. Radio One single-handedly built a brick wall up in front of my career and now they were adding to that by rubbishing me to an audience of millions. It was a key moment for me. My confidence began to fail, as I contemplated being killed off by radio. The incident hit me very hard and, creatively, I began to lose my way. I started to listen to advice, and what a horrible can of worms that is. Everyone knew what I should and shouldn't be doing, or so it seemed. Write this, write that, do this, do that, work with him, work with them, write a dance track, write a funny track, collaborate, collaborate, collaborate. Every single piece of advice I got said more or less the same thing, I should be doing something else. But that mysterious 'something else' was different depending on who you spoke to. It took away all my belief in my own ability and left me bewildered and very, very confused.

At the end of June we put out another new single, 'I Can't Stop', which was a more up-tempo track. It followed an all too familiar pattern. We had a reasonably good opening chart position at 34, then it went up another seven places and I performed it on *Top Of The Pops* and *The Wogan Show*. *The Chart Show* was also playing the video, made for a hard to find £5,000 by a Shepperton-based company. However, without that crucial radio support by the third week it was on its way back down. It's hard when you're so close to having a genuine Top 20 hit, time and time again, only to see radio ignore the song and for it to fall away. While every other song in the chart was picking up plays, even those below mine or going down, my singles were never played. The amount of sales we needed to push us that little bit further was relatively small but as an indie, and especially as a broke indie, we couldn't afford any meaningful promotional budget. We did our best to employ pluggers to try and get the records on to Radio One but, eventually, one man was told that he was not allowed to enter the building if he intended to plug a Gary Numan record. There was a serious 'anti' vibe. All the time I was very aware that the longer I went on without the big breakthrough the harder it would become. Soon the singles would stop even creeping into the Top 30 and I would have no stick left to bang on doors at the radio stations. Despite all our efforts we were still going backwards.

At one point my dad had a meeting with the senior producer at Radio One who said that, 'Gary's problem is, all his songs sound like 'Are "Friends" Electric?' That meeting was cut short for some reason and so, the following week, my dad had another meeting with the same man who then said, 'If Gary would write another song like 'Are "Friends" Electric?' we'd play it.' My father said, 'But last week you said that all his stuff does sound like 'Are "Friends" Electric?'. The man replied, 'No I didn't.' And that was that.

Eventually my fans decided to express their frustration directly to Radio One. On Saturday 9 August, they organised a Day Of Protest outside Broadcasting House in central London. Quite a large number of people turned up, although we decided to stay away. The station always blamed us for organising it but we didn't – we had no hand in it whatsoever. It was almost unprecedented for fans to do that sort of thing and I started to change my mind about them at this point. They were trying to help me and offer support without asking for anything in return. It was no longer a 50/50 deal between us. I really started to appreciate just how much they were trying to do for me. Their protest didn't change Radio One's playlist policy and, if anything, it did more harm than good. It made an impression on me though. I owed them.

In 1986 I flew at over 20 air shows. I tried to capture some of the feeling in a small piece that I wrote for one of the Fan Club Yearbooks. It was a blow by blow account of a typical air display day.

07:00. The alarm goes off and I'm instantly wide awake. Normally the waking up process takes me at least an hour and that's on a good day. Today is different. It's Air Show Day. I'm clean and ready by 07:15. My flying suit, helmet, gloves, parachute, knee board, with all the information I actually know off by heart but still write down, car keys, empty stomach and I sweep out of the hotel door. No breakfast for me. I'm not exactly nervous at this point but it's a similar feeling. Nod to the other pilots, engineers and friends on the way out, but not really noticing who they are. I'm already thinking of the sequence I hope to be flying later on, weather permitting.

07:30. Driving to the airfield, I'm still not used to being a display pilot. I feel as though people should know what I am as I drive along. Being a pop star is great and yes, I am proud but a display pilot, well that's something else again. I feel I should have a red glow around me like the porridge advert. Then the flying comes back into mind and the 'similar to nerves' feeling gets a little more similar.

07:45. Arrive at the airfield. Weather looks good as I drive in the gate. Panic for a moment, someone's stolen the plane. Jump out the car and shout, get very embarrassed and climb back in. The ground crew have moved it closer to the pilots' tent, which is very handy for me. Walking along the crowd line can sometimes take forever if you dare to stop to sign autographs. If you don't you're a 'star struck pig' so it's better to avoid the whole situation if you can.

08:00. Finally get to the aeroplane. Getting here this early is vital to me. The crowds don't start arriving for a while yet so I can take off the covers and give the aeroplane a thorough check over without the constant irritation of people stopping me to chat. Such distractions can actually be dangerous as these people make it easy for the pilot to miss something. Perhaps something vital.

08:15. Test flight time. This early pre-show flight does me a lot of good. It eases the nerves that worry about the aeroplane starting. The nerves that worry about all its different systems. It allows me to practise one more time. It calms the nerves, hopefully, that worry about my having an 'off' day. I climb into the cockpit and love the feeling. It smells good. Oil and dirt, fuel and hydraulic fluid and the sweat of 43 years of pilots all add to it. You have to love old aeroplanes to understand it. If I could bottle that smell I could sell it to pilots the world over and make a fortune. And the feeling. Remember, this is a Harvard, two and a half tons and 600 hp of machinery which demands respect. It's scary at times. It's a plane with a bad reputation for being difficult and I love it. Today is a warm summer's morning and she starts fairly easily, quickly settling into that rhythmic throbbing as I start to strap in. I never strap in before it's running on its first start of the day in case it catches fire. Call the Tower and we're moving. We means me and the aeroplane, because now it's teamwork. No nerves now. We pull up at the runway's end and I check the engine and flying controls. No problem so it's another brief, clipped call to the Tower and onto the runway. Now it gets exciting. The power is on, the tail comes up and we're away. For the next ten minutes I wring out the aeroplane and myself. I put the wheels gently back onto the tarmac and smile. We're both working well. It should be a good day.

08:45. Shut down the engine and prepare to hide. The crowd are beginning to arrive and the nerves will be back soon with a vengeance. I decide to watch the other display planes arrive and so head off to hide in the pilots' tent.

09:00. Spot the refuelling truck arriving and make a mad dash to snare the crew chief before the other pilots can get to him. I'm lucky. In the next fifteen minutes I'm refuelled, re-oiled, re-dieselled and wiped down. Over to the fence to sign a few things before the main crowd arrive. I don't really hear the conversation, the nerves are back already. Nothing too bad, just a steady gnawing feeling that will grow and grow until we fly again.

10:00. Other pilots drifting in and out of the tent. Everybody is very friendly but the conversation is a little bit forced. Especially mine. Even the air show veterans seem a little uptight. Everybody

207

shows an unusual interest in the time. Everybody looks at the sky, back to the watch, back to the sky. I would bet that to a man they are mentally flying their display again and again. I know I am.

11:00. The briefing. Everyone necessary and several who aren't magically materialise in the tent within seconds. Today is predominately a Warbird show, which means a lot of war scenes or what they call 'set pieces'. Each set piece is briefed separately after the main brief so the whole thing is a rather long-winded but vital affair. We are told about the weather, the airfield and the condition of the runway. We discuss the running order of displays and the associated problems it may give to various pilots. We synchronise watches and then go to our set piece brief. At this display I have two set pieces. The first at 13:00 and the second at 13:40. The first is a surprise, a nice one. I am to perform a three-minute low-level aerobatic routine and then position to be shot down by the Corsair. We run through everything, from call signs and signals to start times and radio frequencies. A lot of things to think about as I head off to the other end of the tent for the next set piece briefing. This time it's with the Harvard Formation Team. I am to shoot down the Beech 18 and then become the Aerobatic Singleton to fill in the time gaps in the Formation Team display. This one is difficult. Positioning for accurate timing will be the problem. The nerves gnaw harder than ever. Also,because the two displays are so close together, I will stay airborne after the first and wait at a safe distance for the second one to begin. No rest for the wicked.

12:00. Briefing finally ends. Already the first few displays are underway and the air show is up and running. I have 30 minutes to go before 'strapping in time'. I try to eat a burger but I'm still not hungry. I try a drink but it's no good. Gnaw, gnaw they go. Worse than any stage fright except for the old punk days when I had it bad. Surprisingly the time passes quickly and suddenly I find myself strolling to the aeroplane. A quick wave to the fans. Too much to think about now.

12:30. Climb in. The world outside seems strangely quiet even though the hood is open. I strap in almost in a trance of concentration. I feel weak. I feel sick. I desperately want to be here but at the same time I wish my hobby was stamp collecting. The gnawing of nerves becomes a voice.

What if the engine fails?
What if the controls jam?
What if the wing breaks off?
What if you make a mistake?
What if you burn?

Mercifully I get the signal to start. Fuel on, pump, prime, electrics on, mags on, brakes on, starter engaged. The engine roars into life, a cloud of smoke and the nerves vanish. Now it's down to business. Over 100,000 people here today. I worry a lot more about what the handful of pilots will think than I do the crowd. Taxi clearance from the Tower comes though crystal clear. Good, radios are working well. The engine runs up perfectly again and so we wait. Five minutes to go. I will be taking off five minutes before my display slot time to give me enough time to climb to the right height. I check the engine again and tell the Tower I'm ready. The Spitfire display ahead of me is wonderful and I remember I still have an awful lot to learn. I'm pleased with the feeling. Over-confidence is perhaps the biggest killer of them all in this game. 'Harvard clear take off.' You can almost feel your body change into top gear. Everything is 100 per cent. I acknowledge the Tower and line up on the runway. Power on. The noise is incredible, exhilarating. We roll forward, keep it straight, already working hard. 80 mph and she flies. Keep it low, gear up, no higher than ten feet. Accelerate to not less than 120 mph and then pull hard right. Back to climb power and climb as hard as we can behind the crowd. Up to 2,000 ft and clear of cloud. Good. Don't want to go into cloud upside down. Not experienced enough for that yet. Do a roll, just to make sure everything is OK. Better to go wrong now when it's possible to jump out than at low level when I've got no chance. 'Harvard clear to display' comes the Tower. I acknowledge. Deep breath and go.

This is the thrill of it. Pointing towards the ground, up to almost 260mph. Compensate for the wind, ride the bumps. Position is everything, must hit the mark. Speed good, 500 ft and pull. Four G comes on and I feel the effect pushing me hard into the seat. The blood begins its evacuation from my brain and vision blurs slightly. Ease off the pressure over the top. Speed is very low now. Be careful or she'll flick and that will be that. Nose down again, speed coming on. G back up to four. New position and pull. This time I roll her upright over the top and dive for the far end of the runway. I need at least 190mph or I'll have to throw away the manoeuvre. Speed is good. Height and position are okay so PULL. Roll out again. It's going well. Check the gauges.

The Harvard's in good shape. I see the Corsair in the distance moving into position. Thirty seconds to his attack. Pull hard left and up and then roll to the right to reposition for the Slow Roll. Down to 300 ft with deliberate excess speed. Pull to just above the horizon and let the speed bleed off. 190 mph. Aileron limit speed. Roll it NOW. I look out the side and notice the pilot's tent go past as I reach the inverted position. Spot on. I can't help grinning. Pull right. The radio chatters and the Corsair is on my tail. For the next few minutes we wheel around the sky until it's time for me to turn on the smoke and prepare to die. This part is great fun. Down to 100ft or less. Looking to all the world like an accident waiting to happen. Roaring low over bewildered people in cars, on bikes, on foot. I can see their upturned faces. Mouths open. But back to business. Smoke off. Check the plane. Gauges show no problems. Throttle back. Climb, change fuel tanks etc. Another 15 minutes and I'll do it again, but there'll be no more nerves today. I look forward to the party this evening. To the excited conversation. The bar filled with stories and flying hands describing different exaggerated stories. Tomorrow morning at 07:00 and it all starts again. Ten minutes to go now and I love it.

After all the success of 'Change Your Mind' a year earlier, I was very unhappy the second Sharpe and Numan single, 'New Thing From London Town', didn't do much when it was released in the autumn. Numa only managed to get the song to number 52. On the B-side was one of my favourite ballads, 'Time To Die'. It was inspired by a scene in *Blade Runner,* one of my all-time favourite films. My Aunt Charlotte had just died when I saw the film for a second time. She was 82 and I thought how terrible it is that old people have all these memories and experiences which are lost with them. Even though some of the stories stay within the family, most of it is gone. 'Time To Die' was about the sadness of our memories dying with us.

The title for the new album, *Strange Charm*, came from a conversation I had with Mike Smith. He told me about quarks which are, or were, the smallest things known to theoretically exist at the time. They were called Up, Down, Strange and Charm. There may be more but that's all I can remember. I read that scientists had theoretically weighed the universe and found it to be a little light and they claimed that the existence of Black Holes could explain the weight discrepancy. How on earth do you weigh the universe?

It was a hard album to finish. The career problems created a dreadful atmosphere to write in because it felt like everything I was doing was for nothing. I also aggravated the situation because I wasn't writing at home any more. Like *The Fury*, the new album was written in the studio. I knew I wanted a very dark and dreamy sound for *Strange Charm*. However, I didn't quite know which direction I wanted to take my songwriting. I was also running out of things to write about. There were quite a few arguments and the studio atmosphere was unusually tense and bad-tempered. At one point I had three different versions of a song on the 24-track and I couldn't decide which way I wanted it to go. I kept saying, 'Let's decide later' but everyone else wanted a decision there and then. I was becoming less and less creative because I was relying too much on the PPG. It was like a Pandora's Box. Everything I wanted was in there but then the bastard thing wasn't giving it to me. Instead of going off and developing ideas I just grew more frustrated with it. There are only eight songs on *Strange Charm*, which says it all really. It charted very poorly, only just inside the Top 60. In reality it didn't sell much less than *Berserker* and *The Fury* but with no promotion and not even a tour, the sales trickled in over a period of time, rather than being focused in the first week or so. I also left the release so late in the year it ended up being lost in the Christmas market. To be honest, apart from the hardcore Numan fans, I don't think anyone even knew it was out.

Lyrically *Strange Charm* was very disjointed. I was more concerned with creating atmospheres than threading together a common theme. The songs are a mixture of my non-religious feel-ings, insights into fame, fictional horror scenes, a love ballad and Vietnam imagery also crops up in a couple of things, in particular 'My Breathing'. I read a great book, *Phantoms Over Vietnam* by

John Trottie, a pilot who flew two tours in the Vietnam war. Another song, 'The Need', is about an old film star, a sad, druggy relic who likes young girls. He makes his own porn movies by filming himself with his girls using hidden cameras. The title track is about some form of personal, sexual invasion. For a long time I'd written about sex in a very oblique way, but from 1984 onwards I added a layer of sexual tension and seediness which was more upfront.

In December we put out a new version of a song off *The Fury* album, 'I Still Remember'. I re-wrote the lyrics so they read from the point of view of an abused animal, and all my royalties from the single went to the RSPCA. I thought it was such a great cause and a lovely song. It could have done a lot of good but once again Radio One wouldn't go near it. *Blue Peter*, the children's TV programme, wouldn't show the video because it showed mistreated animals. They said it was too depressing for them but that was the whole point. It needed to hit home or nothing would come of it. I visited a lot of RSPCA homes and refuge centres while I was promoting the single. It was very upsetting. The level of cruelty was savage and it existed from one end of the country to the other.

Clearly we weren't going to make any progress by soldiering on with Numa. We had started actively looking for a major record deal when a new label, GFM Records, made us a fairly big offer for me to do a guest vocal on a song called 'Radio Heart'. They were lovely people but the music wasn't really my cup of tea to be honest. It was fairly lightweight, happy pop music, which is fine, but it wasn't what I did or wanted to do. I would've turned down the offer if we hadn't been so badly in debt. However my dad persuaded me to do it and, to be fair 'Radio Heart' picked up airplay and went into the Top 40 in spring 1987. I didn't feel that improved my overall artistic and commercial situation because the radio was playing a song I hadn't even written. But I couldn't argue with its short term success so I agreed to sing another two Radio Heart singles, 'London Times' and 'All Across The Nation' but they didn't do as well. Perhaps this was a good thing in some ways. They wanted me to sing on a whole album but I managed to get out of that. I wasn't ready to sell my entire soul just yet.

I began to have constant arguments with my father. The way I saw it, I was being made to feel as if I was letting the family down because I wasn't doing all the things I could've been doing to get us out of financial trouble. I felt almost bullied into singing 'Radio Heart' because of our poor money situation. My dad's argument ran along the lines of, 'It might sell millions, get us out of trouble and then you can do what you want.' My argument against it was that it could force away the few fans I had left. It was a very difficult period for us both. On my father's shoulders sat the job of trying to keep things going. I was the creative one, Dad did everything else. The pressure on him was enormous and I think he saw my reluctance as stubbornness and, possibly, even arrogance. For my part I felt that he should have been behind me more, giving me the confidence to stick to what I did best. Even so I went with his argument as far as I could, reaching a point where I was not enjoying music one little bit. Going into the studio started feeling like a job instead of a joy. I became lazy, I didn't want to be there.

The flying had a nasty shock in store for me as well. The first time I saw a man killed in an plane crash was at a display at Coventry in 1987. Something had obviously gone wrong and his plane hit the ground and blew up. I was completely unprepared for that. I started crying. Some idiot in the crowd shouted at me for an autograph as the smoke was still rising from the explosion. I was badly shaken and sat under my aeroplane with my head in my hands for some time. But we had to fly our own routine a short while later. During that display I came from very close to having an accident of my own. I was in formation behind one aeroplane and alongside another, a formation we called Card, when some wake turbulence rolled me upside down. I was thrown up close to the plane next to me. I had full opposite controls in, but it was as though my machine was gripped by a giant hand. I was 95 per cent out of control and the turbulence was much too powerful for me to correct. Then suddenly it snapped back and I slipped straight back into the formation again as if I'd done it on purpose. That was right at the beginning of the display, when we were still flying through the smoke of that fatal accident.

This didn't change my feelings about my aeroplane and the risk of mechanical failure. I love my machinery for lots of reasons, but a key one is it never lets me down on purpose and that is something

213

that can rarely be said for people. It has no spiteful intent when it fails me, it has no vicious motive. It's absolutely honest and that is why I have always felt more at ease around machinery than people. I trust machinery. An aeroplane will very rarely fail without giving you some kind of warning first; you just have to be sharp enough to spot that warning. I still find that I relax more in the company of machines than people and I'm very happy to sit in a machine on my own and develop a relationship with it. It's not quite as weird as it sounds. I think anyone who's involved closely with machinery lends it a personality. I don't have any of the behind the scenes worries and anxieties that I have with people – I don't have to entertain a machine, for a start, I don't have to talk to it on the phone. As soon as I'm finished I can just walk away and it doesn't get offended.

In September 1987 Beggars Banquet released the E-Reg version of 'Cars', remixed by ex-John Foxx producer Zeus B. Held. I didn't even know that was being done and it was a nice surprise when it put me back in the Top 20. I performed the song on *Top Of The Pops* and got a lot of press out of it. I was proud of the fact it was a hit eight years after its original release, but I really did think that was the last of it. Reliving old glories was not something I was in favour of but, then and there, I needed that recognition badly. It was a gamble though, since it could have fixed me firmly as a relic, pumping out the same old song. It didn't quite do one thing or the other actually; it neither helped a great deal nor did any real harm. A double CD compilation of old material also did quite well on the back of 'Cars', climbing to 43 in the UK.

I adopted the title 'Exhibition' for my autumn tour because I didn't have a new album ready. *Exhibition* was the name of a Beggars-Numan album of back catalogue material and it seemed an acceptable compromise to me. Theirs was the only album currently available, so why not? It wasn't an ideal thing to be touring, though. Back catalogue album, old single in the chart, it all had a slightly sad ring to it. A year later Numa released a mail order only double live album, *Ghost*, from the tour – our last release for many years on the label. Visually, we used light tubing architecturals on the set and there were lots of different levels and moving stairways, as well as a man pod which descended from the roof. Although the shows were still big, some of my more ambitious concepts had to stay on the shelf. The ideas were there but the money wasn't. We were touring to survive. Not from a money point of view, we still struggled to even come close to breaking even, but to keep the fans interested. To let them know I was still there and trying.

CHAPTER 11

This is New Anger, 1988-91

1988 started with a new Sharpe and Numan single, 'No More Lies' which came out on 30 January. It got to 34 but that wasn't enough really. Polydor noticeably pulled back on it when it didn't go Top 20 and radio didn't pick up on it. I did a TV show for 'No More Lies' that I found to be another key moment. On the same programme were Bros and Sinead O'Conner. I felt like a fossil. I thought I looked shit, I was out of touch, I didn't want to be doing the song, nothing wrong with it but it just wasn't me, and I all but walked off at one point. I felt about as down professionally as I thought it was possible to go and I was not coming up with a suitable answer.

I had other things on my mind as well. When I'd been making *Strange Charm* it dawned on me one day that, without Mike and Ian, I would find it virtually impossible to make an album. I'd allowed myself to lose touch with technology. I had leaned on the PPG so much on the previous three albums that I didn't have a clue how to do certain things. I'd been using samples but didn't really understand sampling. I had no idea about computer based sequencing, even though those albums had been sequencer-based. I was also out of touch with the way synths in general had moved on. Soon, we were going to be leaving Rock City and so I felt that I needed a better understanding of how to sound engineer music in a studio. I couldn't afford to write albums in the studio, so I would need some kind of basic recording set up at home, and I had to get new equipment and start to teach myself how all this stuff worked. I was surprised at how much I'd backed out of things. I had been a studio boffin, I'd known everything, had a hand on every dial, every button. Now all I could do was open the door, Although I still did the occasional interview where people would talk about me as this high tech whizz kid, with a firm grasp on the cutting edge of music technology, I didn't have a clue about any of it.

Trouble was, we didn't have the money for any new gear. We took out a loan, trying as much as possible to not let anyone know that it was for me. When people found out I blamed my imaginary accountants and said it was part of some clever tax dodge that I didn't fully understand. I said I just did as I was told when it came to tricky financial wheeling and dealing. I got away with that blag for years. Everyone just assumed I was rich, but by then we'd already taken out a second mortgage on the house to try and keep going. Anyway, we got the loan and I bought a very simple sampler, a sequencer and a little 4-track cassette recorder. Over the next few months I got to grips with the basics of what I needed to know. Then I moved up to slightly more complicated equipment, via another loan, and so got on top of the technology once again. At last I began to apply myself. It felt, in a small way, as though I was taking charge again. I intended to become my own cottage industry, but it would take a little time.

As the year progressed the tax man came back to haunt me. He wanted £200,000, mainly from the big money years, so it had taken him a while to catch up. I had nothing, in fact I had a few hundred thousand less than nothing. We were up to our necks in red statements. What to do? We put the Wentworth house up for sale. It took a while but we managed to sell it barely months before the bottom fell out of the housing market. It was one of the few times we'd struck lucky since the career had taken off. We were now able to pay off the tax man and a few other things, but we were still in trouble. Still, it was yet another slight easing of the pressure, another breathing space.

While all this house selling was going on we were approached by Miles Copeland, former manager of The Police and still manager of Sting. A rich, powerful and influential man. We had been talking to an American for some time and were close to signing a deal for my Numa stuff to be released in America. It wasn't a great deal but at the time it was better than nothing. Miles offered us a much better deal, worth a million pounds over the next five years in advances alone. I thought we were saved, we all thought we were saved. Miles' operation was worldwide, his labels IRS and Illegal weren't majors but they had finance and could certainly do a far better job than we were doing. Also since I would be the most expensive signing they had, naturally enough we expected to be the priority act for the label. Great things were promised in regard to re-establishing me in America and Europe. Because of this optimistic turn in our fortunes I went out on a limb slightly with my new house in Essex and took out a hefty mortgage. I now realise I should have played safe, and got us out of trouble before taking any kind of risk whatsoever. I moved into the new house in August. It sat in several acres, had lots of rooms, perched on a hill and I thought it was perfect. I thought everything was going to be perfect.

Before I moved in, though, Tracey and I managed to grab a six-day holiday to Skiathos, one of the Greek Islands. Garry Robson and a few other friends had rented some rooms in a hillside villa so Tracey and I were able to join them. It was my first holiday in 12 years so I actually found a few things awkward for the first day or two. Simple things like sitting on the beach in my bathing costume were slightly embarrassing. I was desperate to learn how to water ski but I had to press on as we had so little time. By day six I was able to mono ski, although I still had to start with two. Tracey spent most of her time on the water with her skis tied together and her backside in the air.

When the holiday was over we arrived back at Heathrow and left immediately for Biggin Hill where the Harvard Formation Team were waiting to fly to Europe. It was the 50th anniversary of the Harvard and the team, along with many other Harvard owners, were to spend the next week displaying in Belgium, Holland and back in the UK, collecting other European-based Harvards along the way. It was a fantastic trip, not without its hairy moments, but thoroughly enjoyable all the same. To look out of my cockpit and see seventeen World War Two aeroplanes crossing the white cliffs of Dover on their way back to Biggin Hill was a surprisingly emotional moment for many of us.

When I signed to IRS I'd pretty much recorded most of the next album, which I intended to call *Cold Metal Rhythm* at Rock City and another studio operated by Tim Summerhayes. Tim was a great engineer whom I'd worked with off and on since 1979. The Waveteam were still with me, although I was back to producing the album on my own by now. Much of the work had been done at home, which saved more than enough money to justify buying the new equipment. Before deciding on what studio to finish the album in I worked briefly in a small room near to my parents' house. The control room had been shown to us and did indeed look very impressive, with racks of equipment all over the place. It didn't go quite as well as I'd hoped though. On one occasion the big two-inch 24-track tape recorder developed a fault which sent my precious songs spooling all over the floor. I looked in horror at the engineer, who was standing next to the machine, but he just froze and stared at it. We had to stop the reels before they locked and stretched or snapped the tape, ruining all the work done on those songs so far. I shouted at him and leapt around the mixing desk. By the time I'd got to the machine and slowed the reels, about 400 feet of delicate tape was lying on the grubby floor. No harm done though, thank goodness. When the time came to use some of the impressive equipment they admitted that most of it didn't actually work and wasn't even wired in. It was just there for show, to look impressive.

I decided to finish the recording of the album at a studio called Black Barn in Ripley, Surrey. We were there for two weeks and, at the end of it, came up with what I considered to be my best album for quite some time. Miles and some of the IRS people came along once or twice, but the album was essentially finished and so they had little opportunity to get that involved and make changes. Miles had a bit of a flare up over one track, 'Devious', as he thought we'd lost the 'magic' of the demo. It was at times like this I wished I had more diplomatic charm. I know people who can twist the ugliest situation around and come out with exactly what they want. Apparently there are certain social interaction skills that we learn as we're growing up. If someone offers you a drink, for example, there are certain appropriate responses. If someone holds a door open, that kind of thing, we respond in certain, and correct, ways. These skills get progressively more complicated as you get into more and more diverse social situations. The thing about eye contact, what you should and shouldn't be doing for example. It becomes incredibly complicated but most people pick the responses up automatically. I worry that I lack some of these skills. There are certain sorts of interaction between people which most find easy and natural and a very few find stressful and difficult. That's me. I'm told that I sometimes respond to certain everyday things in ways that could be interpreted as unfriendly, even hostile. I have no idea what I do wrong and I mean nothing by it, but am well aware of the problem.

I think IRS expected to have success with me straight away. I remember the managing director of the UK division, Steve Tannet, leaping around his office when he played the first single from the album, 'New Anger'. I was happy about his enthusiasm but a little embarrassed at the sight of such a tubby man dancing around. IRS had chosen the track after listening to the finished album and had thought it particularly strong from the very beginning. Steve was full of it, the song was going to be a big hit, it would do this, that and the other. He forgot all about that in October when it reached 46 in the UK charts. We were up in his office a few weeks after the release and he said, 'Of course, you chose the wrong single there, we never wanted that one at all.' 'Hello,' I thought I, 'Earth calling Tannet.' He flatly denied that he'd chosen the single and danced around his office. It was record company bullshit supreme. They tell lies so often, so convincingly that they begin to believe the opposite themselves. I'd much rather someone talk to me and say, 'Gary that song's shit, we don't want to put that one out but we like that one.' I might not agree with what they say but at least I'd know what they really thought. People have claimed they're trying to protect me from things I might not want to hear. For Christ sake, I've been around long enough. After the press I've had I think I'm hardened to it.

'New Anger' is a pretty heavy, nasty track which summed up the way I felt at the time. I must admit that one of my reasons for wanting to get back into the chart was revenge. I wanted to get back at everyone who had put the knife in. In fact the accompanying *Metal Rhythm* album is one of the most aggressive of my career. I poured out my nerves and frustration into my music, making it very psyched-up, raw and uncompromising.

The abbreviated title came about because IRS didn't want me to call the album *Cold Metal Rhythm*. They said the word Cold had negative connotations. It was too petty to even argue with and I was keen to be seen as willing to co-operate, so the album was released with the title *Metal Rhythm*. In America they called it *New Anger*, changed the sleeve a bit, for the worse in my opinion, and swapped around some of the tracks, taking several *Berserker* songs and sticking them on *Metal Rhythm*. It was an appalling move, for the entire feel, instrumentation and production style of those *Berserker* tracks was different to *Metal Rhythm*. I just couldn't see the point of that at all.

The UK album title, original and adapted, came from the percussion that Mike and Ian were adding via a new type of drum sampler. I thought the sounds coming out of it were incredible, and Ian came up with some truly amazing percussion parts. I felt the percussion on the album was a key feature and so named the album to highlight that fact.

In Britain, *Metal Rhythm* just missed out on the Top 40, as did the next single 'America'. This song expressed some of my feelings about the country which I considered relocating to in order to increase my international profile. I was hoping IRS would lift me back into a position that would make touring overseas a viable proposition again. Since leaving WEA/Beggars our overseas record sales had all but died. We had set up several overseas licensing deals for Numa but they seemed to rely totally on success in the UK to launch the records in their own countries. The venture had not been successful and I felt that it was pointless touring overseas until we had achieved some reasonable degree of success, or at least good and supportive labels. If we lost the UK sales we were finished. Concentrating on the UK meant that we abandoned the rest of the world, and so my tours became an annual UK event only.

The *Metal Rhythm* tour was good, the attendance big enough to make it acceptable, but we still managed to lose a small amount of money, which was disappointing. We played 18 shows over three weeks, including three nights at the London Astoria. I was still going way over the top on the light shows but I'd put myself into a corner in many ways. I'd said so much over the years about big shows, and I'd become well known for always putting on decent light shows, so I found it impossible to abandon them. I didn't want to, creatively, and I thought the loss of face would be unbearable. I couldn't admit that I'd run out of money so I tried to cut back in ways that wouldn't show too much. At the end of the day, though we were still spending far too much money on the shows and that was helping to drag us still further down.

Metal Rhythm actually did much better than any of the albums that Numa had put out so IRS were obviously doing something right. I was desperate to tour the States but I needed IRS to fund any monetary shortfall. They dithered about, came up with a few dubious suggestions but never came across. One idea they had to minimise the costs was to use a girl band that Miles managed as the support act. Then, I would go on stage and this girl band would come back on as my backing band. I couldn't see the advantages. I would need to rehearse them for at least three weeks to get them up to speed on my material, and the cost of that far outweighed flying my own band over. Not only that, but the girl band didn't have enough people, or the right players, to play my sort of music. It was a very silly idea. Not being able to tour America undermined my enthusiasm a great deal. One of the prime reasons for signing to IRS, apart from the money, was being ignored and forgotten.

Miles had a few strange ideas. IRS became adamant that I should record a cover version of something 'because everyone's having hits with covers'. I hated that way of thinking. I see myself first and foremost as a songwriter and I found the idea of recording other people's songs insulting. I don't think I'm the best songwriter around by any means, but I still prefer to sing my own songs. I felt as though they were writing me off as a songwriter and I took that very badly. Miles wanted me to cover an old song called 'Sixteen Tons Of Number Nine Coal', the one with the line 'I was born one morning when the sun didn't shine, I picked up my shovel and walked to the mine'. It's an old American miners' song, I think. He kept saying, 'Do it in the Numan way'. I don't think so. The other one he wanted me to do was 'My Baby Just Wrote Me A Letter' or whatever it's called, the old 60s pop song. In the end we compromised and I covered a couple of Prince songs, '1999' and 'U Got The Look'. Prince was an influence on my music in the late '80s but I did not want to do it. When I'd finished recording them Miles said they sounded too much like the originals and he didn't want to release them anyway. '1999' appeared as a B-side and 'U Got The

Look' cropped up later on one of my next batch of Numa albums, but we never released it as a single. I only put it out on my own album because I had other creativity problems – but I'll get to that later.

People around me, as well as IRS, kept saying to me, 'Look Gary, the dance scene is happening. Why don't you get some dance drum machine type things and do what you do over the top of that.' I thought that was an over-simplistic way of looking at things. You can't go out and do a dance track unless you really know what dance is all about. There's much more to it than sticking on a drum machine at 130bpm and then doing your song on top. I don't know enough about dance music to write a track that would be credible for people who are into that particular type of music. To have done that really would have been selling out and anyway, I didn't want to make dance music. I wanted the label to get behind and push my music.

After the third Sharpe and Numan single we decided that we should make a Sharpe and Numan album. My dad talked about it as a 'second string to our bow'. I like Bill very much, he is a very gifted player and writer, but I didn't really want a second string to my bow. I was concerned, as I had been from the start with all the collaborations I was 'encouraged' to get involved in, that it would alienate and drive away the few fans I had left. Loyalty could only be stretched so far. I had nothing against the Sharpe and Numan album. I think it's a good album actually, well written and beautifully produced. If my own career had been going well I would have had no qualms whatsoever about making that album, because my own status and musical direction would have been solid and successful. It was because my own career was taking on a slightly aimless feel that I was so concerned. IRS were wanting me to change almost everything I did. They seemed to want me to be anything but what I actually was, which was frustrating to say the least.

We recorded the album at a studio near Chertsey. Nick Smith was engineering and the three of us always had fun whenever we were together. My only part in it creatively, was to write the lyrics and sing. Another Sharpe and Numan single 'I'm On Automatic' came out in June, closely followed by the *Automatic* album in July.

Bill and I were far from impressed with the way Polydor worked the album. It had that 'throw it out and see if it sticks' feel to it. It didn't stick, sadly, and it would have taken Sherlock Holmes himself to discover that *Automatic* was even available. So much for the power of major record companies. They *are* powerful, but only if they focus their considerable expertise and financial capabilities on you. Without that attention they're no better than the smallest independent. Worse possibly.

In 1989 I also put together my own 24-track studio in the new house. Although the IRS advances were good, it still wasn't enough to get us fully out of debt, and so having my own place meant I could carry on recording albums for next to nothing. We needed another loan to buy the equipment, athough I'd hung on to some of the stuff from selling off Rock City. I started to work on my next album *Outland*. I found it difficult for a while, for I was now not only writing and producing everything, but I was also the engineer – and the maintenance engineer as well. I spent many a long night surrounded by manuals and a soldering iron, trying to repair things. Our choices were simple. Either I got to grips with the technical side of things, as well as the creative side of things, or I ceased to function as a recording artist. I had to become that cottage industry I'd talked about. So I did. With a few lies here and there, we borrowed the money to buy the gear we needed, then I figured out how it worked and I actually wired the bulk of the studio myself. It was almost like being back at school except that this time I worked all hours. At one point I was reading 17 different manuals. It began to feel like us against the world in a sense and, although I would have preferred things not to have been that way, I did get a strange kind of buzz out of the challenge.

Briefly, for a few days only, IRS sent me to America for a promotional visit. It was pretty cool, actually. I did a lot of press while I was there and had an enjoyable trip. The only strange thing was on my first day in Los Angeles. I went to the IRS offices, which were situated in a fantastic Mexican-style white building; they gave me a telephone and some phone numbers and told me to start ringing people up. They were the phone numbers of various retail outlets around the country, record shops basically, and I was supposed to be firing up the various shop managers' enthusiasm by calling them up in person and having a chat. I would ring up and say, 'Hello, I'm Gary Numan', and a voice at the other end would go 'Who?'

Before getting down to work on the next album, I had mixed a live album called *The Skin Mechanic*. It had been recorded during the previous *Metal Rhythm* tour and was released on IRS in October '89. The tour itself was great fun. The light show was still bigger than we could afford but I thought it looked great. One night I hyperventilated back at the hotel for reasons best kept to myself. I ended up wapped around the toilet seat, completely naked with vomit dripping off my chin. I had to be picked up by big Gary Layton, my long-suffering security man, and dropped into bed, still firmly locked in position. A doctor came and gave me an injection in my arse to relax me. I had pulled most of the muscles in my neck and my hands and feet were completely blue. The band went on ahead and I had to get a car to take us on to the next show which was in Oxford that night. About three hours before it started I still couldn't stand up but it worked out okay.

Once the tour was over it was straight into the studio. Mike Smith was once again a major help on the album. Ian Herron, the other half of The Waveteam, had gone on to build and run his own studio by now, so I worked ever more closely with Mike. He was a constant source of bizarre information and brilliant ideas. It was the first album that I had ever engineered and so I had a lot to learn but, all things considered, it wasn't that big a deal. The only major problem occurred during a lightning storm. It was a weekend, the studio was shut down and I had gone out for the evening. When I came back the house was in darkness and I realised that the house's main earth circuit breaker had tripped. I reset it and everything appeared to be fine, until I went into the studio the next day and found signs of burning. It turned out that I had accidentally left some of the gear plugged in. Although all the power had been off the lightning had travelled around, through the plugs and into the studio, doing phenomenal damage. Some of the two-inch master tapes had been scorched and were ruined, and a great deal of the equipment, including the main console, was all but ruined. I eventually had to replace the console with another. We finally finished the album in early autumn. Miles and Steve came to the house to listen. It was a nerve-racking hour for me. They had taken up my second contract option, which meant another big chunk of money, but I was deeply suspicious of what other plans they might have for me. I just wanted them to like the album as it was and release it with a minimal amount of interference.

They said it was brilliant, exactly what they were looking for, shook hands with Mike and me and left. I was over the moon and felt as if a huge weight had fallen off my shoulders. Dad was delighted, we patted each other on the back and waited for things to happen. About a week later we got a phonecall from them saying they'd changed their minds and it wasn't what they wanted after all. They wanted to change the word 'infected' to 'affected' in the song 'Confession' because I had another song called 'From Russia Infected' on the album. They said it looked as though I'd run out of ideas. I tried to explain to Miles that I'd always linked the title of one song with the lyrics of another, because it was fun to see if people spotted stuff like that. It was a kind of trademark. He wouldn't have any of that so I had to get the girl backing singer back in and completely remix the track. Not only that, but since the album was put together so that the songs merged into one another, I had to recompile the entire album and that necessitated hiring in specialist equipment again. It cost me several thousand pounds to re-do that one word. I couldn't believe that changing the word 'infected' to 'affected' was going to make the difference between *Outland* being a big selling album or not. They were happy with that change for another week or two. Then they asked for other minor stuff, a tweak here and there. We tweaked, and they were happy for a while. Then they asked for some more little tweaks. We tweaked again. They finally accepted the fourth version of the album on 19 November and by then I was sick to death of it.

I'd been having a few other problems with Miles during the making of the record. Nothing major but annoying nevertheless. He suggested I bring over from America the session guitarist, Steve Hunter, to play on the album. Steve Hunter used to play with Alice Cooper, Lou Reed, any number of big acts. I'd seen him play many times and I was a big fan, but I couldn't possibly afford someone like him. Miles was unhappy with me because he said I was particularly uncooperative about Hunter. That was unfair, because I had no idea that it was anything more than a suggestion in the first place and I decided not to because I had a brilliant young guitar player already whom I *could* afford.

I have no wish to criticise Miles Copeland. He has an ear for things that other people miss and he is no fool. Often though, I got the impression that he signed me as someone whom he intended to mould into something else. That inevitably caused conflict, since I thought I was being taken on as a viable artist in my own right, and that the music I was writing and recording would be sold aggressively by the label. I didn't expect that music to be a mere starting point for their other Numan ambitions. I didn't want 'dance' remixes done, I didn't want to fly over expensive American guitar players to play on one track. Now, with the benefit of hindsight, I see exactly what he was trying to do, and it made sense. If I had grasped his ideas then, I could have helped more and contributed something. His suggestion for the 'dance' remixes was horribly wrong but another team might have done an excellent job.

He was convinced that remix of a song called 'My World Storm' could be a hit single. He put me together with some people who, in his opinion, had their 'finger on the pulse'. They came to my studio and for the first twenty minutes lectured me on how I'd fucked up my entire career. I took their advice with as much dignity and calm as I could muster and then I watched them go to work. They began twiddling knobs and enthusiastically complimenting each other with cries of 'Wicked', 'Kicking', 'Crucial'. I stood there for a full ten minutes until I felt I had to point out to them that the button that actually turned on the knobs they were so brilliantly twiddling was still in the 'off' position. Nothing had been happening at all.

The American producers Jam and Lewis were a big influence on *Outland*. I thought their grooves were extremely clever. In particular I loved what they did on the Janet Jackson album, *Rhythm Nation*, which featured some of the most inventive use of rhythm and technology I'd heard in years. Perhaps I should've taken the percussion thing and added something else to it, but my songwriting followed the black funk/dance/rock style as well. It wasn't entirely what my fans had been hoping for, although some thought it was one of my best albums. Being so involved, and responsible, for virtually every aspect of it, from writing to production to engineering, I felt it was a very personal record. By mastering the technology I was able to get closer to the sounds in my head.

After its release in March '91, *Outland* sold over 30,000 copies in Britain, so things still looked promising. However IRS only released one single off it, 'Heart'. They were still upset that I hadn't wanted to go the remix route.

We went out and toured the UK with *Outland* in March, a 14-date tour that saw some new people in the line-up. Mike Smith at long last joined us on keyboards, my brother John was still firmly established, as was Cedric on drums, but I had a new guitar player, Keith Beauvais. Keith had played on *Metal Rhythm* and *Outland* and was a cool musician.. We also had Jackie Rawe on backing vocals, who was an outrageously good singer.

The album was released in America but I wasn't entirely convinced that IRS had done a decent promotional job. I did an interview with an American journalist one day, who was also a big fan, and she didn't even know it was out. If a fan in the media didn't know, what chance did the rest of the population have? Despite that it still sold 20,000 copies, presumably by word of mouth.

Another project that Mike and I had worked on throughout the year was a soundtrack for a fairly low budget American horror film, *The Unborn*. The director of the film, Rodman Flender, was a fan of an old B-Side, 'Asylum', which he felt evoked exactly the right mood for the movie. Mike and I saw it as a 'door opening' opportunity, as writing music for films was something I'd long wanted to do. We wrote well over a hundred pieces of music which we would regularly send off to Rodman in California. At first we didn't even have a script, so we just wrote things that we thought sounded a bit creepy. Then we got a very rough cut of the film, which helped a lot. Finally, Rodman came over and stayed for a while and helped us shape the final pieces of music. The film was released later that year and came to the UK on video about a year or so later. I was very proud of the music and I was surprised IRS didn't seem the slightest bit interested in releasing it.

Towards the end of the year we heard that a large number of people were being dropped from the label. Yen, an old support band of mine were gone, others soon followed. Rumours began to circulate that it was going to be sold to EMI. All this began to sound a bit ominous. The next advance was the crucial one to us, since it was the one that was going to wipe out all our debts and put us back on our feet. Many phone calls were made over the next few weeks to try and clarify the situation and then we received a letter from the company saying that EMI were indeed buying into them, but that we were a key ingredient and featured prominently in their future. Two weeks later another letter arrived saying that we were out. No money, no deal, no apology.

We immediately relaunched Numa, only this time with no other bands on the rosta, just me. We quickly put out a single, 'Emotion', and on 14 September went out on tour yet again. This tour was rather grandly called a European tour but, in truth, we did one gig in Brussels and then came straight back to the UK again. It was also different in that I had decided to play in clubs, since I thought it would create an excellent, personal vibe with the fans. I kept the same band, went out and played 19 shows and didn't worry too much about things for a few weeks. When we came back, though, we had a lot to think about.

CHAPTER 12

A Question of Faith, 1992-94

The financial situation was crippling. The bank threatened to take away my house and my parents' home. Mine was put up for sale for a year and we even talked about the possibility of doing up my dad's garage and letting me live in that for a while. The only thing that saved the house was that no one offered us enough money. The best offer we had was tens of thousands less than the mortgage. By now the country had slipped deep into recession, so no one had the money to buy the house, yet the interest rates were so high that keeping it was all but impossible for us. Everything went up for sale, including the aeroplane, but it was clear that we didn't have the assets to get us out of trouble. Instead, we completely overhauled the way we operated. Tracey, a qualified graphic designer, had already started doing all of our artwork and we now had a small home studio that was good enough to record albums in. We looked at everything we did, cut away anything that wasn't absolutely essential, lied, begged, borrowed some more and just lived from one day to the next. But we did start to turn things around. For the first time in years we earned a penny more than we spent. We started to run telephone info lines, which brought in money and gave us a good way of relaying information to the fan base without expensive mail outs. The second line was used to play demos of new songs, as they progressed from rough idea to the finished article. This was very useful to me, as the feedback was often brutally honest. The third phone line was for competitions. We tried to arrange for prizes that would allow a large number of

fans to spend the day with me doing something reasonably interesting. We had days out karting, at paint ball centres, laser dromes,
flying, dry slope skiing, all manner of things. We tried to further
improve the relationship between me and my fans. They had been
running Numan discos for over a decade but their support was all
the more important at this point because it was the only positive
thing we had going for us. They were keeping the whole thing alive
in the absence of any chart success. I grew even closer to them
during this period, perhaps too much. The competitions began to
have a slightly detrimental effect since I was becoming too accessible. I think fans often prefer the people that they follow to be
slightly hard to get to, a little mysterious. I knew it was time to back
away when people started to call me, 'Gaz, mate'.

We had made a video for 'Emotion', the first directed by my girlfriend, Tracey. She did an amazing job, keeping costs down to less
than £2,000 and producing something which was a significant
improvement on many of the promos I'd done in the '80s. Tracey
desperately wanted to get into film work so it seemed like a good
place for her to start. She rang around, bragged this and that,
pulled in favours, talked sweetly and softly and made things happen.

The next album couldn't have been more important. I felt only my
best would lift us out of the situation we were in. I was so anxious
for it to be special, so obsessed with what I was doing, nothing
sounded quite good enough. I'd go into the studio, come out with
dozens of ideas and junk them all. After a while your confidence
starts to slide and then you don't come up with a dozen things, you
come up with two and they both seem dreadful. I was working 12
hours or more nearly every day for months, half hoping the music
would find its own way, but it didn't at all. I had no idea how I wanted
the album to sound, either collectively or with the individual songs. I
didn't know what it should be about, I didn't know how to sing it. I
was lost from the very beginning. The more I threw out, the more
depressed, worried and critical I became. I could have written the
greatest song ever known and I would probably have junked it,
mumbling trash under my breath. I'd always dreaded writer's block,
always talked about it a lot in the past but I'd never experienced it
before. I was aware that we desperately needed the money from the
album quickly so the pressure intensified.

I had other problems too. Tracey and I were getting on worse than ever before. Hardly a day would go by without petty little tit for tat niggles creeping in. Even the relatively friendly bits were worthless, because we both had so much anger under the surface. We nearly split up so many times I lost count, yet somehow, the thought of not being together seemed worse than the way we lived. Something had to give sooner or later.

Another tour was scheduled for March '92. The original idea was to have the album ready for that tour but it was a long way from being finished. We decided to take a leaf out of the Beggars Banquet book and put out a Numa compilation album, *Isolate*, and tour that instead. It was not an ideal situation but, at the time, it was the only thing we could do. Keith Beauvais couldn't do the tour but he recommended a friend of his, Kipper, as his replacement. Kipper turned out to be not only an excellent guitar player but also a man with a personality that seemed to overflow more than merely exude. Kipper had a friend, Suzie Webb, who came in on backing vocals at very short notice and went on tour with us instead. Suzie was great, had a personality on a par with Kipper, and between the two of them provided most of the off stage entertainment for the next two weeks.

We had released another new single, 'The Skin Game', as well but the sales of that and the *Isolate* album fell well short of the what IRS had been achieving. During the tour I had had many conversations with Kipper about the problems I was having with the album and we decided that, when it was over, Kipper would see if he could help me out. He took four songs away to his home studio and I went round to his house one night with Tracey to listen to what he'd done. He played his new versions and they were considerably more musical than my own efforts. I realised that it wasn't the way I should be going but, to be honest, I didn't really have a choice. What else could I do? I couldn't afford to hire a heavyweight producer and that route was no more guaranteed to come up with the goods than anyone else anyway. I'd completely ground to a halt on my own and it had been weeks since I'd even thought of an idea, let alone liked one. So Kipper started coming around the house and we finished off the album together. I convinced myself it was all right, that it was a 'clever' mixture of funk, pop, rock and electronics. I almost convinced myself that I liked it. Not long after it was released though, I had to admit, only to myself for a while, that it was not what I'd hoped. There was nothing wrong with it as such, it just doesn't have much of me on it – not playing-wise, but emotionally. It is the most 'non-Numan' Numan album I've ever made, for my style, sound and character are completely missing. Whatever people think about my music, it's always been very personal. So, at a time when I was experiencing extreme lows in my career and private life, the last thing I felt like making was a shiny, polished pop record. But that's what I'd done.

The album was called *Machine And Soul*, and it went into the chart for one week at 42 then dropped out. Sales fell woefully short of even a half of what IRS had achieved. Where were all those thousands of people? They were wondering what the hell I was doing probably. The sales were crushingly disappointing, but because of our cut-backs we earned reasonably well from it. The sales of the next single 'Machine And Soul' fared even worse and it peaked at number 72. Somehow Tracey managed to make a video for the song for £900, which MTV Europe played. I was impressed with how she'd managed to get that one together for so little money. Generally, though, our relationship continued to deteriorate.

Although the musical side of my life was struggling, the flying side had gone from strength to strength. The Harvard Formation Team had become one of the most successful and sought after teams in Europe and we were very busy. Pilots came and went but the core was always Anthony Hutton, the team founder and leader, Norman Lees and myself. The team had not been without tragedies of its own. A few years earlier one of the first team members had been killed when an impromptu aerobatic manoeuvre had gone wrong, on his way home after an air display. Another friend of ours was killed at an air display near to where we lived. The truth of what had at first seemed glamorous danger became increasingly apparent as the years went by, and the number of friends who'd died crept ever upwards. Nevertheless, it was a risk that everyone who took part knew, understood and accepted. Those 'hairy' moments were all good, character-building stuff. One time, the team were travelling to an airshow at RAF Cosford one year. Four Harvards accompanied the team's mother ship, a twin-engined Beech 18, also of World

War Two vintage. The weather was acceptable but far from pleasant and for much of the time we flew in rain. As the miles passed
the weather became worse, and we flew lower to stay below the
cloud. Legally we weren't allowed to fly in cloud and few of the
aeroplanes had suitable equipment for that sort of thing anyway.
Eventually it became almost impossible to go forward and so the
Beech led the formation around. We intended to head back a few
miles to an airfield we knew and sit out the weather there, hoping
we would be able to continue to Cosford later. It was already too
late since the weather had closed in behind us. What, only minutes
before, had been reasonably possible was now a grey wall of cloud,
even darker and more hostile-looking than what lay ahead. We now
had no choice but to continue onwards to the nearest airfield,
Coventry. Without a word being said the aeroplanes pulled together
into a tight formation. Normally we travelled cross country in a
reasonably spread-out fashion but not in this sort of weather. The
Beech had the navigation equipment and two pilots to operate the
aeroplane. The rest of us were all in single-engine, single-crew
machines with little or no nav gear. We would follow the Beech.
During our displays we flew within 4 to 6 feet of each other,
depending on what formation we were flying. That was extremely
close, but nothing compared to how close we flew now. The
weather just kept getting worse and, what's more, the Beech
seemed to be slightly unsure as to exactly where we were. Too
many heading changes.

It was tense. I couldn't take my eyes off the Beech for even a
micro second, so close were we. We were so near to the ground I
could clearly see, even though I stared at the other aeroplane, cars
moving along a road underneath us. We had to be at 200 feet,
probably less. Even at that ridiculously low height we were still in
and out of cloud and constantly in heavy rain. At times I could
barely make out the Beech, which was little more than a faint grey
outline. We flew even closer. Suddenly the Beech turned sharply to
the left and I thought that was the end for some of us. The turn was
essential, for we had almost flown into a massive array of tall masts
and aerials which soared up into the clouds – if we had gone into
them we would all have died. Turns like that were almost impossible to stay with, but fear certainly sharpens the reflexes. Every

single aeroplane went with the twin as though they were glued to it. If I hadn't have been so terrified I would have been highly impressed. As we turned I looked, from my high and safe position on the outside of the turn, along the formation and saw the plane on the inside, and the lowest, pull up to clear some trees. I was amazed he'd been able to see them at all. The situation was very grave, and then we popped out of the cloud into a hole in the weather. It was about a mile across, a circle of no rain and no cloud, like the eye of a hurricane. We took a small breather and eased away from each other about a foot. I looked down and saw a stationary police car, the policeman making notes in his little note-book, no doubt taking our registration numbers for the low flying complaint. It made me smile, for he was lucky he wasn't picking up pieces of us from all over the countryside. Coventry wasn't far and we were able to raise them on the radio. They were in heavy rain with very low cloud, in effect they were closed. Just as that news came in my engine began to misfire, which was almost more than my poor frazzled nerves could stand. We set course for Coventry and plunged straight back into the weather. We knew the airfield was close but it seemed to take an age before we flew low across the runway. It was impossible to make nice textbook approaches, we couldn't afford to lose sight of the vague outline of runway that we could barely see at best. We slid into a loose, but very close, trail formation and just followed the man in front. When his wheels went down, mine went down, when his flaps went down, so did mine. I didn't see the runway until I was almost on the ground, our forward visibility was virtually non-existent because of the rain. We all got down safely, got out and kissed the ground and did all those silly things that frightened people do when they get away with some-thing life-threatening. The man in the back of my aeroplane who had come along to help out had no idea that anything had been amiss. He'd unplugged his headset to take photos and hadn't heard a word I'd said to him. Just as well really. . .

Sometimes things got quite surreal. We arrived at a military base near Dublin once to find that Customs had pinned a note to their door saying, 'Gone home, hope you had a nice flight, see you tomorrow'. I always enjoyed our trips to Ireland. Once we were on our way back home with four Harvards and a Russian aircraft, also from the war, travelling with us. Our route on that occasion took us across the Irish Sea towards South Wales. The weather, as was so often the case, was rather grim and we were travelling at about fifty to a hunded feet across the water. This was very low, to be honest, but we were all experienced display pilots and it kept us clear of the cloud, which was only a hundred feet or so above us. In the distance we saw a dark shape loom out of the mist. I could see the other pilots picking up their maps and studying them intently. I did too but I could find no island in this part of the Irish Sea. We rushed ever closer. A few radio calls went back and forth but no one could figure out what it was doing there: either we were hopelessly lost or we were witnessing a freak of nature. Suddenly it became clear and we pulled up rather sharply to avoid flying into the side of a huge cargo ship. I've often wondered what those sailors must have made of us. Picture the scene. You are standing on your ship in a misty, murky sea when you hear the loud but distant throbbing of several motors. All of a sudden five aeroplanes from World War Two hurtle out of the gloom, straddle your ship and then disappear. They must have thought we were some ghostly apparition from the war.

Another time two of us were flying towards Londonderry. My friend Lee Proudfoot was in one Harvard and I was in mine, with Tracey in the back. Not long after take-off, but already over the sea, Tracey decided that she had to have a wee. We carried small bags for just such an emergency but getting your tight jeans down low enough, especially in the back of an old military aeroplane, was not easy. The first I knew of impending doom was when the aircraft began a gentle dive towards the sea. I pulled back on the stick, my heart thumping like crazy, but it wouldn't budge. Suddenly Tracey shouts from the back, 'Don't pull it I've got my jeans past my knees.' Her struggles had proved successful but only by pushing the stick forward to make way. I urged her to hurry but, to my horror, she was stuck. I tried my best to instil a sense of urgency into her without inducing panic but it was no good, she'd started so she had to finish. Meanwhile the aeroplane increased its downward momentum and the sea started to look a lot closer than I wanted it to. It felt like the longest pee in history but she made it before we became a submarine. Actually, a little later, and safely high up in the air once again, she threw the bag out of the aeroplane. This is strictly

236

forbidden but I thought, what harm can it do, we're about 30 miles from land at least. I banked the aeroplane over and couldn't believe my eyes. Way down below us was small sailing yacht. I hoped Tracey's gift from heaven missed, but if it didn't, I made sure we were long gone before it arrived on deck.

The return trip had its own little drama, but of a very different kind. We were on our way back from the display in Londonderry. The weather had begun to close in and so we tried another route, only to have the weather beat us again. We could see the Isle of Man in the distance and so made our way there. Lee was leading, which I was pleased about as it meant the navigation responsibility fell on his shoulders. As we approached the eastern end of the island the weather was looking more and more unfriendly. For the first few miles it was sunny but then, like hitting a wall, we came upon the bad stuff. We dropped off the side of the island and followed the southern coastline, out over the sea. So bad were conditions that we were forced to fly below the height of the cliffs because the cliff tops were already lost in cloud. The rain was appalling and forward visibility was poor. We twisted and turned, keeping as close to the cliff face as possible. We hopped over jagged rocks that reached out to sea, banked over the tall masts of sailing boats, fighting their own battle with the elements. The rain was so heavy water streamed into my cockpit. We flashed along, staying close to each other. To lose sight of each other now would be a disaster. I would have to break away, out to sea, to make sure that we didn't collide in that horrendous weather and the aeroplane did not have the instrumentation I needed for flying blind. Suddenly we came to a rising hill, it looked as though the top was clear of cloud and so we hurtled up it. We thundered over the crest, the noise of our passing scattering sheep as they grazed, and the airport loomed dead ahead. We were safe.

Over the last year or so with the Harvard Formation Team Norman Lees and I had decided that, for it to continue, it had to become ever more exciting to watch. It was becoming increasingly difficult to find work at air shows. Because of the large number of aeroplanes in it, the team was an expensive item for an air show organiser to consider. Competition was fierce, new and more exotic aeroplanes were being added to private collections every month, and organisers and the public were becoming spoilt for choice. Our collection of noisy trainers were beginning to lose their appeal. Norman and I wanted to add more dynamic manoeuvres to the teams routine. For the past few years I had designed the team displays, changing and stretching them with each new season. I had also been adding solo aerobatics for some time and, over the previous few years, had also incorporated formation aerobatics for just two of the aeroplanes within the team routine. In 1992 Norman and I decided to start The Radial Pair, a two-ship display act that concentrated on close formation aerobatics.

I was also made a display pilot evaluator by the Civil Aviation Authority, the governing body for all things aviation in the UK. This was a great honour and a major endorsement of the high standard of flying that I had reached. For me it was the aviation equivalent of being number one in the charts. Because of new legislation in the wake of the horrific accident at Ramstein, where the Italian display team collided and crashed into the crowd, it was now a requirement for all UK display pilots to have a DA. A DA was a Display Authorisation which said what type of aeroplane you could fly, what type of manoeuvres and at what minimum height. The DA scheme was designed to make sure that only the best, and/or the safest, pilots flew at British air displays. To get a DA you had to fly for an evaluator who had the authority to say yes or no. The evaluators were recognised as experts within their various disciplines. So you see, for me to be made a DA Evaluator for formation flying and aerobatics in warbird aeroplanes was a big deal. Nothing to do with money, or who I was, it was purely on proven ability. I couldn't have been more proud.

The Radial Pair had a very successful first year. Our display was virtually unique and we flew the length and breadth of the country. I had already become better known to some people as a pilot than as a pop star. In fact some aviation fans didn't even know I was a singer, they had only ever seen me on TV with the aeroplane. The Harvard was a big attraction to the media. For several years I could almost guarantee getting TV exposure if I mentioned the plane was available for rides and it must have earned me several times its value in media exposure over the years.

To help promote their own airshow the Crunchie Aerobatic

Team offered me and Norman a go at wing-walking on their Stearman bi-pianes. This was a once in a lifetime experience, and as soon as the wheels lifted off the ground I knew that I was going to love it. The only problem was I let out a scream of delight. It was such an epic moment, it was so exhilarating to be standing on the wing of an aeroplane as it flew off the ground, I just let rip. The trouble was the wind was forced into my lungs at 80mph, and I couldn't get it back out again. I was suffocating, I didn't know how to breathe against the airflow. After about two minutes I still hadn't drawn a proper breath and I was close to passing out. I was about to give the pilot the signal to land when I figured out all I had to do was keep my mouth shut and breathe through my nose. We were up there for 20 minutes, flying upside down and going through a whole range of acrobatic manoeuvres. At one point we turned upside down and Norman's aeroplane came along below us. I was looking up at Norman, which actually meant I was looking down at the ground, if you see what I mean. We could almost shake hands. I was waving my arms like a lunatic and laughing my head off. It was a truly awesome experience, one of those things that live with you forever.

Musically,though, things were on the grim side. I worked myself into such a state I had my second weird mental experience. Someone else watched the whole thing in my living room. They said I was screaming my head off but as far as I was concerned the sound of my own voice was somewhere in the background. It sounds a little overly dramatic now but I felt a blackness in my soul. I'm not spiritual, but it felt like my whole life essence was being sucked into a black void which I could see as much as feel. I felt I was dying, I fell over, couldn't move properly, it was as though my whole body was just giving up. I was so frightened by that, I honestly believed I was fighting for survival. I started to scream louder so I could recognise something to hang on to. I also grabbed at an object, I still don't know what it was, hard enough to feel pain to try and bring me back. Bit by bit I came out of it, but I was in a really bad way for a while. I think all the worries and pressure of the last few years just chose that moment to come out.

The year 1993 got off to an awkward start. Tracey moved out and went to live in London. She had already been spending time away and we were getting on as horribly as ever. It was the best thing for both of us. I think we'd both known for some time that it was over but neither of us quite had the courage to see it through. When you've been together such a long time you feel as though too big a part of your life is tied up in the other person to let go easily. Officially we were still going out with each other but I don't think either of us expected things to work out. It was just the first step to ending it.

In June we had decided to make a documentary of The Radial Pair. Tracey was going to direct it and we were hopeful that we could put it together fairly cheaply, as she had proved herself adept at doing just that with the two promo videos. The filming was the curtain call on our relationship. I, for my part, had already begun to look elsewhere and Tracey had clearly taken a shine to the cameraman on the film crew. We did not work together well during the making of the video and it was a very nasty experience, but at least it brought the relationship to an end, which was ultimately a relief. We've seen each other since once or twice and, as so often happens it seems, we now get on much better. The documentary came out very well, edited superbly by my old friend Nicky Robson. I wrote the script and the music (we eventually put out the soundtrack as a separate mini album) and Tracey directed it with great style and the end result was a professional film.

With Tracey gone to pastures new and happy with her man I picked up my relationship with a girl called Gemma O'Neill. I'd known Gemma for some time, she'd been a fan since day one, but on the previous tour in '92 I'd got to know her a little better. Her mother was in hospital, ill with cancer. I spoke to Gemma off and on throughout the tour but her mother's condition worsened and, sadly, she died. Many months later I called Gemma to see how she was coping and took her out for the day. She was very sad and was having a hard time of it. In '93 we began to see a lot more of each other and I began to realise that she was everything I'd ever wanted. She was beautiful, thoughtful, kind, and as mad as a hatter. She had so many lovely ways about her that I could spend all day reading them out. In a word, she was special. Everyone around me loved her and she began to bring about a change in me that was unprecedented. I still found it hard to commit to someone after being with

Tracey for so long. To have so much time with someone come to nothing was hard and I didn't want to step straight into another 'exclusive' relationship. I wanted to float for a while in my personal life and see where things took me. I saw other people as well as Gemma for a while, which was very hard on her. I wasn't deceitful, I was honest about things, but that didn't make it any easier. I was lucky she managed to put up with it just long enough for me to see sense.

I started work on the next new album with Kipper. It was a disaster. I still didn't have a clear idea of where I wanted to go with the record but I knew where I didn't want to go. It was a very strained and difficult few weeks but when it was over I knew that Kipper was not the man. In fact I was beginning to realise that I had to fundamentally rethink the way I went about making albums. Gemma was a huge help. It took her a long while, and I argued and fought back every step of the way, but bit by bit, she was able to make me see where my strengths lay. She gave me the confidence to step back into the studio and let whatever was inside me come out. I would play my own guitar, I would do everything myself. For good or for bad I would make this next album the most Numan of them all. I felt as though I was stepping into a studio for the first time and I felt inspired. My mind began to wander and to see things in that slightly off the wall way that I'd always been so proud of all those years ago. I felt as if I had gone full circle and I began to enjoy making music again. I remembered why I had always wanted to be a musician and everything just clicked back into place.

In August 1993 Beggars Banquet released a new dance version of 'Cars' remixed by Native Soul. Native Soul was actually two men, Charles Pierre and Francis Usmar. Getting involved with yet another re-release of 'Cars' was not the way I wanted to be going but, as before, it was about the only thing around that had a chance of success and I needed some of that success. My new stuff was taking shape nicely and I needed to let people know that I was still alive. I would do my best to minimise the damage that being seen to live on old glories could do for me. The song only got to 53 in the chart, so those credibility problems didn't really come into play, but I did get a chance to play around in some excellent cars. Part of the Beggars Banquet promotion involved a tie-in with McLaren, the famous racing car team. They had a new road car about to be unleashed upon the public and Beggars had been able to use the car for the sleeve artwork. On 9 August I had a go in this new 230 mph super car. To be honest, as I climbed in behind the driver I was slightly blasé about it. I'd had a Ferrari Boxer, I was used to quick cars, I'd take all this in my stride. When that McLaren took off down the straight at the MIRA test track the only word that came from my mouth was 'FUCK'. Three times in a row, in fact. It was stunning. Savage and raw it pushed like the giant angry hand of God. It stopped quick, too. I had never been in something so fast and yet still connected to the ground. I asked how much they were going to be sold for, in that nonchalant way that implied I could afford anything. They said half a million, plus VAT. I said the F word again, three more times. That was about the same amount as my debt. I also had a go in the prototype Aston Martin DB8. To be sitting beside the driver of that car as he drifted all four wheels around tight little lanes at over a hundred miles an hour was something not to be missed. Later that day we went to Silverstone where I had a chat with Formula One driver Mika Hakkinen. I was allowed to watch the F1 cars practise from the pit lane, something akin to getting an Access All Areas pass to your favourite band.

In September I had a run in with the CAA during an air display at Rendcombe. It was a small show that needed local support to keep going. The weather was appalling and all the pilots there felt a desire to do what they could for the organiser and the poor bedraggled public that had bothered to turn out and support it. The Radial Pair flew when the weather was at its most dire. To make matters worse, the commentators had asked if Norman would talk through our display from the cockpit. The CAA offical present knew of this slightly unusual practice but said nothing to oppose it and so we went ahead. At one point, while flying through heavy rain and avoiding low cloud, I called to Norman to change from one formation position to another. Norman missed that call and so, when it came time for me to lead us in a tight turn to the right, Norman was in the wrong place. I did what I thought was best to avoid an accident and turned as tightly as Norman could accept and climbed slightly. This took our flight path over the very end edge of the crowd line. Flying over the crowd was not allowed, but in this particluar case it seemed the safest alternative. There was no danger. When we landed the CAA representative banned me immediately from further display flying, and did so in the presence of local press who sent the story to the nationals. The headlines next day read 'Flop Of The Props'. I was made out to be a wild idiot who had recklessly endangered lives, which was absolute rubbish. Many other pilots came to my aid and the ban was lifted within minutes, but not before the local press had already hurried off to ring the nationals. My action was seen by the other pilots present as the right decision taken under great pressure and in very difficult circumstances. The CAA later apologised.

Our lowest day financially came soon afterwards. We were having a bit of trouble paying off a few of the old tour debts. My dad took one of the men concerned to one side and explained the situation. This man had been around us for a long time, had earned very well from us over the years, and my dad considered him to be a friend. He was told that we were deeply sorry that we hadn't been able to pay him, it was not our way, but that we would as soon as we possibly could. He said he understood, shook hands and left. A few hours later his partner rang up and said that he would force us into bankruptcy if we didn't pay him by midday. So much for honesty and friendship. I have no idea how my dad got us out of that one, but he did.

From that day on things began to go our way a little but it has been hard. We had a long way to go but little sparks of hope can give you a lot of strength. Now that Tracey wasn't around any more we had no one to do the artwork for us. We couldn't afford to pay for it to be done so I got a Desk Top Publishing programme for my computer and taught myself how to do it. I learnt how to do the album covers, posters, backstage passes, T-shirts, fan club newsletters, tour programmes, everything. I called myself NuFederation so people wouldn't still think that outside companies were doing the work. I found that I enjoyed every minute of it and so I still do it all, funnily enough. Between the three of us, Mum, Dad and me, we took on the workload of a small corporation. Debt put an incredible strain on all of us and no matter how efficient we became as a company I knew it was only through new music that we would recover – and that was down to me. No matter how excited I was about my new writing, after *Machine And Soul* I wasn't exactly confident about my artistic future. I went to sleep worrying and when I woke up eight hours later it was as if I hadn't slept at all, my thoughts just picked up where they'd left off. My dad was equally troubled. He hadn't had a good night's sleep for so long my mum lost count. At times he was unbearable to be around and so stressed that we worried about his health. He was in his mid-50s, so was my mum, and by now they should've been looking forward to a quiet retirement and a fat bank account. Instead of enjoying an easy time they almost lost their house, everything they'd ever worked for. And I felt responsible.

On 23 October 1993 a two week UK tour, *Dream Corrosion*. opened. For years fans had been asking for more old stuff, but I'd always taken that as an insult to the newer material. Gemma was able to explain to me, for the first time, what they meant by it. I began to see that it was not an insult but that the early music was more Numan in its style and content than much of what I'd done in more recent years. They had been trying to tell me for years that my attempts at improving the musical quality of my albums were taking away the thing that they actually wanted the most, my style. It was a strange thing to realise but it dawned on me that I needed to become more of a Numan fan if I was ever to understand what they saw in me. We rehearsed a long set, over two hours. I'd replaced Cedric on drums with Richard Beasley who was unbelievably good. The excellent T.J. Davis came in on backing vocals and Ade Orange made a welcome return on keyboards. I'd met Ade when Hohokam brought him in as an extra producer on their album and he had played in my band a few times before in the late '80s. Although we played a lot of old material during the two hour show, I changed it by adding huge, industrial percussion loops to tracks such as 'Films' and 'I'm An Agent'. The grooves evolved out of the instrumental music for the Radial Pair, which inspired me to follow a heavier, darker, less polished direction. I was also pushing heavy guitars to the front, injecting yet more power into the music.

I loved being onstage. After the 1991 *Emotion* tour I felt comfortable slipping in the odd club date, including a good night at The Marquee in London. I felt that I could play anywhere; I'd finally come of age as a performer. The last gig of the tour at

Hammersmith was one of the most exciting moments of my life. I've never been so vibed up, never so enthusiastic and solid an audience reaction. I really didn't want the tour to end. It's normal to feel a bit low after the incredible lifetyle and excitement of touring but the days after the *Dream Corrosion* seemed empty. When Kipper rang up and said that OMD were looking for a support for the arena tour I said yes before he'd finished the sentence. So, about four weeks after my tour finished, we were back on the road. I also made a commitment to Gemma. From now on we would be exclusive.

Over the previous year or so on two separate occasions, I'd been to a clinic in London and had more work done to my hair. The OMD tour seemed like as good a time as any to go for a change of style. It was the first time in years that I'd really had enough hair to do anything different. The tour kicked off in Scotland. I hadn't supported anyone for about 15 years so it was a bit unusual walking out on to a stage without my huge light show firing up all around me. OMD were looking for a name support because the tour hadn't been selling as well as they'd hoped. For me it was an ideal situation. The number of Numan fans who came to each show was impressive and made me feel more at ease. The two bands and crews all got on very well, wiping away any lingering bad feeling after OMD's tight-lipped attitude towards me the moment they finished the 1979 tour. I was under no pressure whatsoever: the lights weren't mine, the PA wasn't mine, the worries weren't mine I just turned up, did my bit, had fun. Apart from my three Wembley shows in '81 I'd not played in arenas. The atmosphere was incredible and it gave me more incentive to want to get back to that level than money ever has. Meanwhile we had also filmed and recorded that Hammersmith show and put it out later as a double CD and video. It did well and things began to look much more comfortable financially.

Shortly after the tour finished I went to Italy to make a video for a song called 'Like A Refugee'. It was put together by the same people who had been involved with 'Radio Heart' and once again I was the guest vocalist. It was a lovely song, loosely based on the Yugoslavian refugee situation. I'd recorded the vocals for it a month or so before. We flew to Bergamo to shoot the promo with a bizarre robotic marching band called Da Da Dang. They dress up in striking constumes that glowed in the dark and we all paraded through the old part of the walled city at night. The song didn't do anything unfortunately, although I did a fair amount of promo work around it and was actually made 'God For The Day' on Radio One. However, they *still* didn't play the song.

In January 1994 I visited Silverstone again, to watch Michael Schumacher testing the new Benetton Formula One racing car. I also started pursuing my own racing interests, in a very minor way, by getting involved in regular competition in the Club 100 karting series. I love anything to do with controlling machines. Speed is a by-product really, a bolt-on extra that comes with the real challenge. I like to go into something I know very little about and try to figure out how it works, adapt to it. I get completely absorbed by things. Gemma says I get a bit obsessed, but it's not that. I just derive great enjoyment from studying, understanding and improving whatever I'm interested in. With the karting I went to the track every week and spent the day with an instructor taking me round and round, doing hundreds of laps. Each time I'd try to find out how I could do every corner better than I'd done it before, come back, get out of the kart, talk about it, think about it. Then I'd go back round again. This went on for months until I could post times as fast as anyone. To study and analyse things and make them work is one of the most pleasurable things I can do. To watch myself improve at something, whatever it might be, by my own efforts, study and application is very rewarding. If they go fast so much the better. Some people down at the track slagged off their kart or blamed someone else if they lost, but I'm not like that. If I'm beaten I go straight to the winner and say, How on earth did you go around that bend so quickly? and then immediately try to learn what he did, go out and do it too.

My aeroplane had been taken apart. It was in need of serious maintenance work and we still couldn't afford that, so we had it stored in a hangar for the next year. I stayed flying by hiring a friend's aeroplane and using the air display money to pay for it. It was quite a good arrangement. The Radial Pair had another productive season, although even we were finding it harder to get work. I also flew a Russian Yak 11 warbird owned by a friend of mine. I loved the aeroplane with a passion, since it was blindingly fast and incredibly manoeuvrable. It made the Harvard seem like an old tank in comparison. The Yak gave me my fair share of heart-stopping moments though. It caught fire on me one day as I returned to the airfield after a display. Another time, the undercarriage wouldn't come down. I flew it in many air displays until the owner got his own DA and started displaying it himself.

Meanwhile the new album, *Sacrifice*, was almost done. I'd read a couple of Clive Barker books, *Weaveworld* and *Imagica*, and after them I started to think differently. I also started to read horror stories, and became interested in tales from the Bible and supernatural imagery. Horror stories had never appealed that much before, for I'd always found them too disturbing. I'd been to see *The Exorcist* when I was young and had to walk out before it even got going really, jeered all the way to the door. Anyway, the Clive Barker books inspired me to start a novel of my own entitled *Pray, The Final Treachery Of God*. It's to do with God abandoning us, dissolving Heaven and Hell and everything inside, bringing creatures to earth that live on the energy of dead things and the raising of demons to fight back against these creatures. It's a long way from being finished, but I hope to get there one day. Some of the lyrics for *Sacrifice* came from my initial book outline, or at least certain themes and images. The most direct steal is the opening speech on the album, which is also how I imagined the book would start. In the story God is real, but he's nothing like we thought. He creates life for the fun of seeing what happens and when he gets bored he moves on. We're the first planet he's come to where some people have seen heaven for the lie it is when they've died. They've resisted and become ghosts, still attached to the earth. Human ghosts enjoy a state of being which he's unable to reach and he more or less has a cosmic tantrum.

Although *Sacrifice* isn't directly related to the book, many of the songs obviously come from the same mindset, the same thoughts. On 'Pray', the opening speech is a ghost talking to other spirits, telling them that something bad is coming for them and they've got to wake themselves up and fight it. The singing part is more like a chant, which represents a side of many religious people that I find disturbing. I consider even the concept of belief in a super being bordering on the fanatical. I think religion fosters hatred and prejudice, because of misinterpretation. People look to the Bible, to religious doctrine as the truth, as examples of God's wisdom, but so much of it is interpreted in ways that promote intolerance and violence. I don't believe in God at all, but I wonder how those who do can justify some of the opinions that they cling to based on their belief? How can they believe that God is all forgiving, all merciful, if they believe it's okay to kill and to persecute those who don't believe, or live their lives, as they do? I don't understand how generally normal people come to the conclusion, for example, that homosexuality is a wicked perversion. To me that belief is evil.

'Deadliner' is about the darkest nightmare of my life, which has stayed with me to this day. I'd gone back to my room after a show and, as I went to bed, I began to feel uneasy. It was as though something dark and brooding was watching me, a very scary, uncomfortable feeling. I lay down on my bed and went straight into a dream. In the dream I was aware that I was dreaming yet I was absolutely convinced there was something in there with me. Everything in my dream was dark, every room, every street. People were swearing at me and being very aggressive. At one point I was in a room and I could feel the same presence that I'd felt before I'd gone to sleep, only now it was much stronger. This sounds a bit strange but it had a hand missing and it pushed the stump through me and smashed me against the ceiling. It then spun me around, grinding me. I was trying to wake up because it felt if I didn't I could die in the dream. When I finally opened my eyes the bed was saturated with sweat. I'd only been in the room about five minutes so I couldn't have been to sleep more than two or three. I tried not to, but I fell asleep again and went straight into another nightmare similar to the first. Eventually I got out of that one, and each time I came out I was half screaming and unable to breathe properly. It was as if a door had been opened on to my dark subconscious.

'A Question Of Faith' is about obsession, where you become so obsessed by the influence of someone you start to do things that would otherwise be completely beyond you. It ends with a line about the little boy, Jamie Bulger, who was killed by two other children. How could that happen? It asks if that murder made people question their faith. 'Bleed' is about demonic possession and things that go bump in the night. When your mother says you're safe tucked up in bed but you know better. It talks to you and tells you what it's going to do when it comes for you. 'Desire' is the equivalent of me standing in the middle of a field looking up at the sky and saying to God, 'Come on then, what have you got?' I don't think God's coming, I don't think it's even there, but if he does I will be humble, believe you me. I'll be the first to admit I was wrong. I have actually stood outside looking at a particularly beautiful sunset and said to God, 'Prove it. Turn the sky green, just for a second. You can't, can you?' 'Walk In My Soul' describes my feelings for Gemma. 'Magic' is about my beliefs in anything but God, I would sooner believe in fairies and goblins. I want to believe in Tolkien's world. I have found other authors to be more inspiring and helpful when it comes to writing songs and lyrics but none has ever come close to Tolkien's ability to make me feel as though I were part of the story, of another reality almost, albeit as a silent onlooker. I want to believe in the Third Age, in Elves and Hobbits.

I wanted the sleeve to give a clear indication that this album was a much darker affair than anything I'd done for a long time, possibly ever. The cover was black with my face just ghosting in from the right-hand edge. The vinyl sleeve was finished in matt but they couldn't do that on the CD for some reason. The overall packaging gave a clear guide as to the music. With the music and the packaging I felt I was back on course. The album logo, the pictures, the artwork, the sound of the record, the lyrics, everything – was all moving together. I had my big machine back again, all the pieces turning perfectly together.

We released 'A Question Of Faith' as a single in October and followed up with the album two weeks later. Neither charted but, nonetheless, *Sacrifice* sold significantly more than *Machine And Soul* and it was generally regarded by fans as one of the best albums I'd ever made. The fan club membership soared. I had a long way to go to get back as a mainstream chart act, but the fans were coming back in their thousands. *Sacrifice* turned me around in more ways than one. Financially, we had now recovered and, although we were a million miles away from the multi-millionaire days of yesteryear, we were all right. Creatively, I felt like I'd come home. I was enjoying it all again, I was thinking better, my mind was wandering like it used to. Most importantly, it was fun again.

An extended version of the album which followed in early '95 enabled me to make more of a show of the instrumental elements

249

and grooves than had been possible on the conventional version. I felt vindicated with that release because many fans were more into it than I'd expected, preferring it to the original version. In fact a Numan Internet site ran a survey that showed the extended *Sacrifice* to be the favourite Numan album of all time.

The autumn *Sacrifice* tour was another two-hour show. This time though we cut it back to just ten dates, in what we felt were our strongest regions around the country. I was disappointed in that it made the tour far too short, but as a strategy it worked very well. We actually made money – which was almost unheard of. The new album tracks went down brilliantly. For the tour I dropped backing singers, no female vocals, and tried to emphasise the harder sound of the new material. I brought back a lot more of the older songs as well and added much of the feel and sounds from *Sacrifice* to them. This gave much of the older material a new lease of life.

I met Menswear and Shampoo when they came backstage at the last Hammersmith show. I kept feeling like a dad as I heard myself giving advice to Menswear and I kept thinking, 'What the fuck are you doing?' These people were just at the start of something amazing and I'm going, 'Oh, you've got to be careful about this that, and the other' and they were looking at me as if to say, 'Shut up, Dad!'

As the tour progressed I got ill. Before going on stage at Bristol I was very sick. In fact I walked from the toilet on to the stage and since I couldn't stand properly I spent most of the gig hanging on to the microphone stand. In Colchester we had a power cut when the smoke from the on-stage smoke machines drifted to an upstairs part of the building and set off a smoke alarm. I sat on stage in the dark for a while, chatting to some of the fans at the front. It reminded me of so many tour horror stories. Once, at Portsmouth, we had been seconds away from walking on when a bright flash alerted the crew that the entire stage structure was live. It had mains voltage running through it. If we had touched any part we would have been zapped to the moon and back. There was also a show on a pier, where the stage was made of crates and at one point I looked down and could see through the floor to the sea below.

The final show on the tour was at the London Astoria 2. When we booked the venue I mistakenly thought it was the bigger Astoria where we'd played before, so it was a bit of a shock to find we were in the rather dingy downstairs room instead. We had also agreed to come back after that show and play four songs for the gay club, G.A.Y., that took over the building after our main show was over. Kipper caused some ill-feeling by saying he wanted more money to play those extra four songs. It seemed very tight, very unfriendly and reminded me a lot of how mercenary my earlier band had become. I have always tried to operate a give and take atmosphere with the band members and this seemed more like all-take no-give to me. I suppose it was a good example of how people can fall out with each other. I'm sure Kipper saw it as fair, I just saw it as greedy. I don't know who was right, we all have our own standards by which we live our lives. The gay gig went okay, although we had been billed as a nostalgia act from what I could make out. A 'Songs from the '80s', vibe. The promoter nearly had a heart attack when he listened to the soundcheck for the main show. 'Can't you play the songs like you used to?' he enquired. 'It's a bit heavy, I don't think the gay crowd will go for this.' I couldn't change things, wouldn't actually, and the crowd went for it just fine anyway.

The introduction of a new Numan logo seemed very popular. I was used as a merchandise stock controller throughout the tour. We had two T-shirt designs and each night I would wear one of the them under my jacket. Whichever T-shirt I wore sold about three times as much as the other. If the stock of one design was getting a bit low they would tell me and I would wear the other shirt for a while until things balanced up again. We also recorded the Hammersmith show once again and later released another double live CD called *Dark Light*. Even though both that and the *Dream Corrosion* CD had been two-hour shows, only a handful of songs were repeated on both albums. I thought that made them especially good value for money and I was very pleased with the end result of both releases.

In 1994, for the first time in years, possibly since Robert Palmer, other artists started covering my songs at their own gigs. The Smashing Pumpkins did a version of 'M.E.' from *The Pleasure Principle* album and when Beck came over to the Astoria, London in '94 he played an instrumental version of 'Cars' It was another chink of light as we continued to recover financially and take each tiny step forward. I had always thought that to have your songs

251

covered by other artists was the ultimate accolade for a songwriter. To have my songs covered by other people, especially artists of such high standing, was a great honour.

I also discovered a new interest at the end of the year, motorbikes. When we were rehearsing for the November *Sacrifice* tour, Kipper turned up at my house on a cool motorbike. This thing looked like a bullet. It was the frst time I'd been interested in them and I decided there and then that I had to get my licence and buy a bike. I got almost obsessed about the idea and by the time the tour started I had piles of magazines and I'd even made myself a little booklet of the various bikes that I liked with all the different prices. When I came back from the tour my brother, who had also decided to get one, rang me up to say that he'd seen the bike I was looking for, a Yamaha Virago 535. I met him at the shop and it was exactly what I wanted. I bought it and it was delivered a few days later. I still hadn't had a lesson. A week after the tour finished I had my first lesson, a week after that I had my licence. I passed first time, which was a huge relief. I didn't know how I was going to stand waiting a month for another test if I'd failed. Some bike riders seem to have a slightly snotty attitude about what bikes are cool and what aren't. I don't care. I love my bike, I love all cruiser bikes. So far I've fallen off it once and been knocked off it once. That seems to be about normal.

CHAPTER 13

New Dreams for Old, 1995-97

At the start of 1995 I wrote a new song, 'Absolution'. I'd gone out and bought some new keyboards and was just putting a track together as a way of learning a few things about the equipment. I started at about ten in the morning and by five in the afternoon the song was written, recorded, mixed and finished. I thought that was quite cool. Lyrically the song looks at the dangers of blind faith, and gets progressively more extreme as it unfolds. The style of writing, using heavy synth drones under huge drum loops, was an extension of what I'd done with 'Sacrifice' – only far more powerful and anthemic. I thought it was close to being the best song I'd ever written, still do. With my confidence already beginning to soar I had had a few moments of doubt after 'Sacrifice', I wasn't sure that I would be able to come up with anything better, but with 'Absolution' I pushed those doubts aside and gave myself a new, even darker, style in the process. I began to put the next album together almost immediately.

We released 'Absolution' as a single on 20 March. The sales were poor, but that didn't surprise me considering our previous 12-year-blank with radio. Nothing had changed, they still didn't play it. I did have to make some decisions about singles, though. I was now selling something like four times as many albums as singles and so, apart from tradition, why was I still putting out singles? I decided to give up on them for a while and concentrate on the next album instead, which I gave the working title, *Exile*.

In the spring I remixed a version of my own 'Are "Friends"

Electric?', which had been covered by the American group Nancy Boy, led by Donovan's son the singer/model Donovan Leitch. There was talk of another collaboration when I met Wayne Hussey from The Mission at one of their gigs in Rock City, Nottingham. Over the next few months I saw them a few times, including The Mission's farewell gig, and became friends with Wayne who is an excellent man.

I have always wanted to be outrageous but never had the courage. I love outrageous rock stars, people with no clear sense of right or wrong, who have the money to indulge themselves and don't seem to care about anything. I've never had that in me. I watched Wayne on the *James Whale* TV show once, drunk as a skunk and taking nothing from James Whale at all. I would have been polite and answered his snidey questions as best I could. Wayne called him a 'wanker' and then fell over.

We still plan to write together at some point in the future. It was mainly Gemma's doing that I went to the gig in the first place. She was working hard to get me out and about more. My hermit existence kept me away from the business and she thought I should be more involved. She was quite right. We started by going to see most of the people that she was into, The Mission, Siouxsie and the Banshees, the Sisters of Mercy, The Cure, Björk, Suede, people that I'd not taken that much notice of before. I enjoyed much of what we heard and elements of that began to creep into the work I was doing on the new album. Other favourites, such as Depeche Mode, Nine Inch Nails and Jesus Jones, also began to make their mark. I was not only enjoying making my own music again but I was also becoming a fan of the whole business. I began to roam far and wide, checking out bands. Unfortunately we missed Hole who were playing 'Cars' every night on their world tour. I would've liked to have heard that. 'Cars' was also covered by a rock band, Headswim, on their 'Years On Me' single and Molly Half Head released a version of 'Are "Friends" Electric?' The latter was also revamped by a Tool spin-off band, The Replicants, and another American band, Weezer, opened their shows with an old instrumental of mine, 'Random', and played 'M.E.' at some of their US gigs.

While I worked on new songs in the studio, Numa released

Babylon 1-7, a series of half-hour mini-albums made up of B-sides, previously unreleased material and remixes. The fans had repeatedly asked us to put our old vinyl stuff on to CD and so the *Babylon* series gave us the opportunity to do that and re-release some of the more obscure things that had previously slipped out unnoticed. *Babylon* was quite successful for us but I felt a little uneasy about the whole idea. I really worry about milking the fans, and I have no wish to put out anything that isn't good value and what they want.

On 3 June '95 we put out the *Dark Light* live double album, taken from the *Sacrifice* tour. We also released my first instrumental album, *Human*, which consisted of 36 tracks that had been written, but largely unused, for the *Unborn* film. The music was written with Michael R. Smith of Waveteam fame in early 1991. It was an hour-long collection of musical ideas, each with a specific mood or atmosphere in mind, not a conventional instrumental album.

Meanwhile I began to get ever more deeply involved in the Internet. I had read so much about its potential I began to see it as possibly an important part of our future. I went on-line in the summer and immediately set about finding out how it could be of benefit to us. In November I launched my own web site, NuWorld. I thought the cost of employing people to design sites was incredibly over the top, so I figured out how it worked by studying the code of sites I liked the look of. Bit by bit I built up my own knowledge and carefully put NuWorld together. The site was hosted by a company called County Internet who have been incredibly helpful in answering my desperate questions. I'm no expert, keeping up with the rapidly advancing technologies is a full-time job for anyone, but I enjoy working on the site. I run it from home, without any outside help, and I hope to keep it that way for as long as possible. The number of visitors coming to the site more than tripled in the first half of '97 and NuWorld is now averaging about 1,500 a week. The rate of increase is quite phenomenal and we have to be extremely careful about how we progress so that we don't get snowed under. Our operation is still very small and would struggle to accommodate too big a rush in demand. The Internet-generated business is already stretching us. In many ways I believe that the days of record shops may be numbered. As technology progresses we may see an entirely new way of manufacturing and selling music developing. I can envisage a time when I finish an album in my studio and send it as a file to a main server computer, where people can download the music at home for a given fee on to whatever format they choose.

Around this time people started asking me about some new '80s clubs in London, such as Cell, Arcadia and Club Skinny. I think they were associated with the New Romantic thing and I wasn't ever a part of that; I'm not putting it down but didn't want to get involved in a nostalgic '80s revival. As the year progressed I was frequently asked to go on TV and talk about the '80s. I didn't want to be seen as an '80s act. I wanted to be seen as a '90s act who had also been around in the '80s, and the '70s for that matter, and that is an entirely different vibe. I remember going on the TV programme *Pebble Mill* once talking about punk and punk fashion. I only did it because I hadn't been on the TV for ages and I had no idea what I was talking about. I didn't want to get into that sort of thing again.

One Thursday evening in October Beggars Banquet rang up to say Carling, the brewers, were thinking of using 'Cars' on a new commercial for their Premier lager. I'd heard this sort of thing so many times in the past that I really didn't get that excited about it. They had always come to nothing. The American giant corporation General Motors were going to use the song once and then went with something else, something strangely similar I might add, so I'd long since stopped getting my hopes up whenever TV commercials were mentioned. Then, on the following Saturday, my brother rang to say, 'There's just been an advert on the TV using your music.' Apparently the agency who put the advert together played it to Carling quite late in the day, having already commissioned their own music, which wasn't quite finished.

While they were waiting they played the advert with 'Cars' as the soundtrack and told the Carling executives, 'Don't take too much notice of the music, we're having something else.' Carling said that 'Cars' suited it perfectly and so they kept it. The agency needed a quick decision from Beggars Banquet, who went for a rather high figure and got it. The advert ran for eight months on the TV and it also had a fairly long run in the cinema.

The knock-on effect was that 'Cars' became a Top 20 hit again in March '96. There was also an underground dance 12" released by the XL label, featuring 'Cars' remixes by Astral Body and Witchman – I'm told the latter became a regular in The Orb's DJ set. A compilation of my singles, *Premier Hits*, was licensed to Polygram who TV-advertised the album, which went straight in to the UK album chart at number 21. It's subsequently come out on Beggars Banquet all around the world, and has timed nicely with the emergence of Electronica music I'm now labelled, amongst other things, as the Godfather of Electronica. Not bad for a twenty-year-old song and a lager commercial. It also meant that 'Cars' has been a hit in three different decades.

It was great being on *Top Of The Pops* with 'Cars', but the feeling was slightly clouded because it was an old song. I was still running with that double-edged sword, exposure with the wrong material or no exposure. With my public profile beginning to climb on the back of the fourth re-release of 'Cars' I was more desperate than ever to try and make sure that I brought attention to my new stuff – which was very difficult to do. *The White Room* was a cool TV show to be on but I was upset when we recorded three songs for the programme -'Cars' 'Are "Friends" Electric?' and 'Prophecy'- and they didn't show the new one. They had told me, prior to filming the show, that they only broadcast two of the three songs from each artist and of the three that I could do, I had to play 'Cars' and 'Are "Friends" Eilectric?' or else I couldn't go on. I knew which one was going to be dropped. No one watching the TV knew I'd been told to play old songs. It just looked like, Numan's on the TV again and he's trotting out the same old hits he always does. I turned the *Big Breakfast* down because they wanted me to do 'Are "Friends" Electric?' and the presenter, Zoe Ball, was going to join us and sing along. Bollocks to that. I did manage to sneak in 'Scar' from *Sacrifice* on Bob Mills' *In Bed With Me Dinner* programme, but even they still made me play the other two. I love those two songs, I owe so much to them, but they have become a giant cloud that I constantly struggle to escape from under. I accepted the logic of playing 'Cars' on *Noel Edmonds' House Party*, however, because it was pointed out to me there were 14 million people watching. Those sorts of viewer figures are worth the risk.

It was clear to us that Numa was not capable of capitalising on this new higher profile. We decided that *Exile* had to be given a better chance. *Sacrifice* had been one of the best albums I'd ever made and yet it had virtually sunk without trace. We could not allow that to happen again. I put the new album on hold while we got ourselves together and began to look around at bigger and better labels. In the meantime Beggars were releasing the *Numan Premier Hits* back catalogue album and so we hung our March/April tour around that album instead of *Exile*.

On this tour I had the idea of suspending a big cross in the roof. The audience wouldn't see it until it swung down. It was going to be 20ft high, with all the edges lit in strip lighting. I'd be posing like a dead Jesus as it was lowered down. That was just one of the things that couldn't happen because of the expense, but we had a good set nonetheless. It was supposed to look like the inside of a dark cathedral and while I don't think it quite reached that lofty aim, it still created the effect of dark, gothic mystery.

For many years I had used Andy Keightley as my lighting designer and John Barnes as the moving light programmer. Both man were brilliantly creative with lighting, and we worked together long into the night on every show. All three of us are passionate about making each one as spectacular as possible. With the *Premier* show we worked ridiculous hours programming the lights, almost up until the doors opened on the first night. I was getting three hours' sleep per day at the most. I was there all day for the music rehearsals and all night for the lights.

I came up with a more mature style of clothing for that tour as well. Gone was the leather image of old and in was a smoother look I felt more appropriate for the new *Exile* material, and my age. I also felt as though I'd found something much more in keeping with my personality. I was now 38 and I was beginning to feel a little awkward leaping around the stage in leather, and perhaps more importantly it really didn't suit the new music. I took a gamble with the song list for the tour and I played four of the new *Exile* songs. The fans had only heard 'Absolution' of those four and so the others were completely unknown to them. I know other acts do it all the time but it made me nervous.

We cut the show down to 80 minutes this time, so it didn't take quite as much out of me, the band or the fans. I hate exercise. I'm lucky in that I have a naturally slow heart beat, so my internals think they're fit but in reality I'm not. The first nights of tours have always nearly all but killed me. Over the 14 dates the audiences were definitely on the increase. The ticket sales were the best they'd been since the early '80s. A lot of people came up to me at the after-show parties and said it was the first time they'd seen me in years. I felt good about that, it was nice to be reclaiming old fans, but the thing I found most rewarding was when people came up and said they'd never heard of me before. Now we were starting to make an impression.

In April 1996 Castle Communications released an album of Numan covers by a studio-based duo, Techno Army. I agreed to re-sing the tracks, but it wasn't quite the cutting edge dance music I'd been led to believe it would be. I thought the album was going to sound like the Chemical Brothers with my voice layered on top but actually Techno Army were more Euro-pop with hints of Shakatak. The album disappeared almost instantly, overshadowed by the re-release of 'Cars' and the *Premier Hits* album, except for two German remixes of 'Cars' which did well in the club charts.

I was very impressed with The Foo Fighters' version of my 'Down In The Park' track that I'd written in '79. They recorded it for inclusion on the album *Songs In The Key Of X-Music From And Inspired by The X Files*. I knew they'd been playing it live for the last year or so but this was very cool. Coincidentally Marilyn Manson also released a cover of 'Down In The Park', and their version was very different from my original but I thought it was excellent.

On 26 June my grandad died. He had been in hospital for some time after having suffered a series of multiple minor strokes. His name was Frederick James Lidyard, but everyone called him Jim. Except for us grandchildren, for we all called him Poppa. Poppa was the most gentle of all gentlemen. I never saw him angry, I never heard him complain about anything or anybody. I loved him very much and yet I found it hard to believe that he was really going to die. I didn't even start to visit until near the end, and by then I don't think he even knew I was there. I had never faced death in the family before and reality would not sink in. I carried on as though nothing was wrong, assuming he would get up one day and walk out of that hospital with his round belly and friendly smile. But he didn't, and I miss him. Poppa fought against the Germans in World War Two and earned several medals. I only ever heard him talk ahout it once or twice but, when he did, he talked all night. As usual, he mainly told us about the funnier moments but every once in a while you could see him turn over something unpleasant in his mind. How terribly final death is for those who are left behind. I wish I believed in heaven. I expressed feelings for him through a new melody but so far I've been unable to find the right words.

In August we played the UK's V-96 Festival, headlined by Pulp. This finally gave me the opportunity to play alongside some of the best new bands around, and to play songs of my own choosing. Actually, I was strongly 'advised' to play my old hits, but I thought that would have been a waste. Most of the people in the audience weren't even embryos when my early songs were in the chart and they would have meant nothing to them. It was the new stuff that held my future and so that's mainly what I played. It was cool, things went well and I had the chance to play in front of something like 70,000 new people over the two days. We did one show at Chelmsford and one at Warrington. I was on the same bill as Cast, The Longpigs, Stereolab and Supergrass, as well as Pulp. I had never even been to a festival before, let alone played at one, so it was a big step into the unknown for me. Walking out onto a stage in front of 35,000 people each day was an experience not to be missed. Jarvis Cocker also said some nice things about me in the press which was kind of him. I met him in the toilet before we went on but I forgot to say thank you since I was a tad nervous of how the crowd would react. As we walked to the stage I could hear chants of 'Numan, Numan' so I knew I had a reasonable number of my own people there. That calmed me down a lot.

In the summer I spent a week working as an instructor at a special training school for already qualified pilots who want to learn the rather demanding art of formation flying, aerobatics, and formation aerobatics. I had spent some time over the years teaching people how to do various things with aeroplanes but I had never been an 'instructor' before. The level of flying skill required was considerable and of the 14 instructors I was one of only two civilians, the rest were all current or ex-military pilots.

It was a good week, but it certainly had more than its fair share

of high-anxiety moments. The students are asking a lot of themselves and, as an instructor, you need to allow mistakes to be made
so that the student can see and learn from them. The skill is knowing how far to let things go before taking over. When you are upside
down, only a few feet away from another aeroplane, you only have
tiny fractions of a second to judge a likely outcome and react appro-
priately. You are often left in control of an aeroplane that is trying
to do anything but go the way you want it to. It is very demanding
work but, because of that, very satisfying and enjoyable. One week
at a time is enough, though. I had a problem with my own aeroplane as I was descending over an airfield near the south coast. The
motor suddenly coughed and spluttered and I lost virtually all power.
A quick radio call to clear the runway and a tight curving approach
saw us safely on the ground, but it reminded me that you can't relax
in these old aeroplanes for a second. Gemma was in the back and
it was, I think, the final straw for her.

I had already lost another four friends to crashes in the previous
twelve months, one of them a former Harvard Formation Team
member and another my old acrobatic instructor, Hoof Proudfoot.
Hoof's accident hit me particularly hard. Gemma had never
thought too much about the danger of display flying until Hoof. He
was the first person to die that she had met and talked to so it
brought the realities of the dangers home to her and she did not
want me to do it any more. Over the previous two years I had had
the Harvard rebuilt from top to bottom and it now looked as
though it had just been made. Somehow, though, my heart wasn't
in it the way it had been and I had even put the aeroplane up for
sale. I decided to fly at fewer air displays and actually only flew in
five all year. It may have been Hoof's accident, it may have been
a culmination of all the friends who had died, but whatever it was,
something was missing in me. I used to eat sleep and drink aeroplanes but now, well I didn't even think about flying very often.
Nothing has changed. I still don't know how I feel about it, so I'm
just letting the decision make itself. I pulled out of air displays
completely in '97. I look at photos of my flying friends at home
and it saddens me to realise that I barely have a single group photo
where all the pilots are still alive. I don't know how I feel about
that. I don't know how I feel about any of it. I think it's going to

take me some time to put my aviation thoughts back into order.

At the end of 1996 I accepted a leading part in a forthcoming British movie called *Kinsmen*. It took me many months to come to a decision because I have never really harboured any serious ambition to be an actor. I might well fall flat on my face, but how much more stupid it would be to have not even tried. I will also be writing the music for the film, which is another cool aspect of the whole project. The film may or may not happen, since getting the finance for these things seems to be a very difficult and long battle. If it does I hope that I will at least come out of it with some experience and since I may never get to have another go I'll try to enjoy things while I'm there. Towards the end of '96 I started acting lessons in a bid to be more prepared. They went surprisingly well but it was more nerve-racking than losing both engines over the Pacific Ocean.

On 12 December I asked Gemma to marry me. I had wanted the moment to be very special but the time was never right. I had plans to fly her to Paris; I had plans to do all kinds of things. What we actually did was have a meal in our local pub. It was not the way I wanted it to be but she is the person I want to be with for the rest of my life. I am very happy. In Gemma I have my best friend and someone that I cannot imagine spending even a day away from. She has enriched my life in more ways than I can count. She is, and will remain always, my reason for breathing.

And so to 1997. Up until then I had no idea that I had been an influence on anyone, certainly not other artists. I was genuinely amazed when I heard that an album of Numan covers called *Random* was nearing completion. I seem to have spent most of my career fighting the odds, my credibility factor rarely appearing to climb above zero. I even took a perverse kind of pleasure in my isolation at times. When I heard that other people were playing my songs live I was staggered. When I then heard that the *Random* album featured 26 covers by some of the biggest acts around it became one of the most impressive things that has ever happened to me. It was released on 9 June and included reinterpretations of my songs by St. Etienne, Matt Sharp (Weezer) and Damon Albarn (Blur), Gravity Kills, Kenickie, Jimi Tenor, Moloko, The Orb, Dave Clarke, Bis, Sukia, Towering Inferno, Jesus Jones, Dubstar, Pop

Will Eat Itself and Republica. The latter's version of 'Are "Friends" Electric?' was my only direct contribution to the album. Tim Dorney and Saffron from Republica came to my house and we spent a day working on the song, which we later finished off at their London studio.

I've now met many of the people on the album and had the chance to thank them for their kind words and for taking the time to be involved in the *Random* project. I appreciate the trouble they've taken to give a very public nod of approval towards my work. As a songwriter I couldn't have asked for a more flattering or meaningful endorsement and I am truly grateful to them all. Many of the bands were people I also admired. I first came across Gravity Kills earlier in the year at The Falcon in Camden, London. I'd been told that they had done one of the tracks on *Random*. I was already a fan after having seen them on MTV a few weeks earlier. They were brilliant, and are probably my favourite band at the moment. Some of the band came down to our house for an afternoon a few weeks later and their keyboard player/producer Doug Firley is remixing my new album, *Exile*. 1997 will also feature an album of techno remixes, *Random 2*, with DJs such as DJ Hell, Robert Armani and Dave Angel revamping some of my older songs for the clubs. To be honest I'm completely bewildered by all this fresh attention. At 39 years old, it's the last thing I expected after decades of going it alone.

During a promotional week in New York at the end of March I spent some time with a couple of other *Random* acts, Peck Slip and Deadsy, as well as meeting the techno artist Moby who interviewed me for *Ray Gun* magazine. Another new band Trans-Am also wrote a piece on me for *CMJ Monthly*. I was supposed to do some recording with Girls Against Boys but we didn't have time in the end.

In June 1997 I finally finished *Exlie*, after taking a reasonably long break from it. Since my experience with *Machine And Soul* I have inherited a legacy of trepidation whenever I go into the studio. Even though I now enjoy the process of making records again I still have feelings of dread at times, feelings that another dry spell may be just around the corner. Whenever an idea doesn't come together quickly I have to work hard not to panic. I am very proud of *Exile*, but I can't deny that it was also a difficult and stressful project. Still, this album came more easily than the last, so hopefully things will continue to get better.

On *Exile*, just as on *Sacrifice*, I wrote, played most instruments, produced and engineered everything myself. I'm not being possessive; I just work better on my own. I worked hard on the rhythm structure of the songs, developing huge rhythmic grooves and as big a stereo picture as possible. I wanted the production, the sound of the album, to be huge. The music is very aggressive and yet almost dreamy at times, cathedral-like, with flowing melodies and ethereal textures.

Lyrically, from the snippets they've heard, the album has already causes some ripples of upset amongst my more religious fans. I expect it may cause considerably more offence when it's released. *Exile* takes the point of view that God and the Devil, Heaven and Hell are one and the same. It then looks at certain aspects of the Bible and reinterprets things accordingly. Mary, for example, is raped by the three wise men. Angels urinate on the graves of children. God laughs as Jesus burns on the cross.

As I grow older, my attitudes to life and death are changing. I was always more worried about age than death, my only concern was how I died. Now I don't want to die, I want to live forever. There's so much more to see. I want children but I'm unlikely to live long enough to see them reach the age I'm at now. I would love to watch my grandchildren grow up and see what they make of themselves. I hate the idea of missing what the universe has to offer, the amazing things out there, secrets to uncover. I want to see the new technology. I'm going to miss so much because I'm going to die a few decades too soon: before starships fly and aliens visit the White House. We're so close to the start of it all. I dread getting old, I have so many things I want to do before I die. I have much to prove, much to accomplish and much less time to do it in. I feel the need to move faster, to try harder.

For me the future is far from certain but I look forward to and accept whatever challenges may come my way. My standing is much improved and my credibility has rarely been higher. I've had millions, lost everything, and am now clawing my way back up again. I've been one of the biggest stars in the world and then all but forgotten, and now it seems I am rediscovered. Creatively, I lost my way for a while but then found it again, clearer than ever.

I am soon to be married and that's a whole new adventure in itself. I also have a new record deal with Eagle Records. I have been both extremely fortunate and desperately unlucky. I have been up, down and sideways more times than I can remember. Faced death in many different ways and got away with it every time. And I'm still in my 30s. I can't wait for tomorrow.

Discography

TUBEWAY ARMY

SINGLES & UK CHART POSITION

Beggars Banquet

02/78 That's Too Bad / Oh! Didn't I Say (-)
07/78 Bombers / Blue Eyes / O.D. Receiver (-)
03/79 Down In The Park / Do You Need The Service? / I Nearly
       Married A Human II (-)
05/79 Are 'Friends' Electric? / We Are So Fragile (1)

ALBUMS

Beggars Banquet

08/78 Tubeway Army (14)
Listen To The Sirens / My Shadow In Vain / The Life Machine /
Friends / Something's In The House / Everyday I Die / Steel & You
/ My Love Is A Liquid / Are You Real? / The Dream Police / Jo
The Waiter / Zero Bars (Mr Smith)

06/79 Replicas (1)
Me! I Disconnect From You / Are 'Friends' Electric? / The
Machman / Praying To The Aliens / Down In The Park / You Are
In My Vision / Replicas / It Must Have Been Years / When The
Machines Rock / I Nearly Married A Human

GARY NUMAN

SINGLES

Beggars Banquet

08/79 Cars / Asylum (1)
11/79 Complex / Bombers (live) / Me! I Disconnect From You (live) (6)
05/80 We Are Glass / Trois Gymnopedies (5)
08/80 I Die: You Die / Down In The Park (piano version) (6)
12/80 This Wreckage / Photograph (20)
08/81 She's Got Claws / I Sing Rain / Exhibition (6)
02/82 Music For Chameleons / Noise Noise / Bridge? What Bridge? (19)
06/82 We Take Mystery (To Bed) / The Image Is / We Take Mystery (early version) (9)
08/82 White Boys & Heroes / War Games / Glitter & Ash (20)
08/83 Warriors / My Car Slides 1 & 2 (20)
10/83 Sister Surprise / Poetry & Power / Face To Face (32)
08/87 Cars (E-Reg Model) / Are 'Friends' Electric? / We Are Glass / I Die: You Die (American mix) (16)
08/93 Cars ('93 Sprint) (53)
02/96 Cars / Down In The Park (live) / Are 'Friends' Electric? (live) (17)

WITH PAUL GARDINER

07/81 Stormtrooper In Drag / Night Talk (49)

WITH DRAMATIS

11/81 Love Needs No Disguise / Take Me Home / Face To Face (33)

Numa

10/84 Berserker / Empty Bed, Empty Heart (32)
11/84 My Dying Machine / Here Am I / She Cries (66)

05/85 The Live EP: Are 'Friends' Electric / Berserker / We Are Glass / Cars (27)

07/85 Your Fascination / We Need It / Anthem (46)

09/85 Call Out The Dogs / This Ship Comes Apart / No Shelter (49)

11/85 Miracles / The Fear (49)

04/86 This Is Love / Survival (28)

06/86 I Can't Stop / Faces (27)

11/86 I Still Remember / Puppets (74)

07/91 Emotion / In A Glass House / Hanoi (-)

03/92 The Skin Game / Dark Mountain / U Got The Look (68)

07/92 Machine & Soul 1999 / The Hauntings / Cry Baby / Wonder Eye (72)

07/93 Dream Corrosion Live EP: Noise Noise / I'm An Agent / It Must Have Been Years / Jo The Waiter (-)

09/94 A Question Of Faith / Pray Like God / Whisper Of Truth (-)

03/95 Absolution / Magic (-)

06/95 Dark Light Live EP: Bleed / Everyday I Die / The Dream Police / Listen To The Sirens (-)

IRS

09/88 New Anger / I Don't Believe / Children (46)

11/88 America / Respect (live) / New Anger (live) (49)

03/91 Heart / Shame / Icehouse / Tread Careful (43)

LIMITED EDITION VINYL EPS (tracks are now added as bonus tracks to Beggars Banquet albums)

Beggars Banquet

04/85 Tubeway Army '78 Vol 1
That's Too Bad / Oh! Didn't I Say / Bombers / Blue Eyes / Do You Need The Service? / O.D. Receiver

04/85 Tubeway Army '78 – '79 Vol 2
Fadeout 1930 / The Crazies / Only A Downstat / We Have A Technical

04/85 Tubeway Army '78 – '79 Vol 3
The Monday Troop / Crime Of Passion / The Life Machine / A
Game Called Echo / Random / Oceans

ALBUMS

Beggars Banquet

09/79 The Pleasure Principle (1)
Airlane / Metal / Complex / Films / M.E. / Tracks / Observer /
Conversation / Cars / Engineers

09/80 Telekon (1)
This Wreckage / The Aircrash Bureau / Telekon / Remind Me To
Smile / Sleep By Windows / I'm An Agent / I Dream Of Wires /
Remember I Was Vapour / Please Push No More / The Joy Circuit

04/81 Living Ornaments Box Set – double live album (2)

04/81 Living Ornaments 1979 – live (47)
Airlane / Cars / We Are So Fragile / Films / Something's In The
House / My Shadow In Vain / The Dream Police / Conversation /
Metal

04/81 Living Ornaments 1980 – live (39)
This Wreckage / I Die You Die / M.E. / Everyday I Die / Down In
The Park / Remind Me To Smile / The Joy Circuit / Tracks / Are
'Friends' Electric? / We Are Glass

09/81 Dance (3)
Slowcar To China / Night Talk / A Subway Called 'You' / Cry, The
Clock Said / She's Got Claws / Crash / Boys Like Me / Stories /
My Brother's Time / You Are, You Are / Moral

09/82 I, Assassin (8)
White Boys & Heroes / War Songs / A Dream Of Siam / Music

For Chameleons / This Is My House / I, Assassin / The 1930's Rust / We Take Mystery (To Bed)

09/83 Warriors (12)
Warriors / I Am Render / The Iceman Comes / This Prison Moon / My Centurion / Sister Surprise / The Tik Tok Man / Love Is Like Clock Law / The Rhythm Of The Evening

09/84 The Plan (29)
This Is My Life / My Shadow In Vain / Critics / Mean Street / Thoughts No. 2 / Bombers, Basic J / Ice / Something's In The House / Friends / Check It / Steel & You

09/87 Exhibition – double album compilation (43)
Me! I Disconnect From You (live) / That's Too Bad / My Love Is A Liquid / Music For Chameleons / We Are Glass / Bombers / Sister Surprise / Are 'Friends' Electric? / I Dream Of Wires / Complex / Noise Noise / Warriors / Everyday I Die (live) / Cars, We Take Mystery (To Bed) / I'm An Agent / My Centurion / Metal / You Are In My Vision / I Die: You Die / She's Got Claws / This Wreckage / My Shadow In Vain / Down In The Park / The Iceman Comes

07/93 The Best Of Gary Numan 1978-83 – double album compilation (70)
Cars / We Are Glass / Are 'Friends' Electric? / My Love Is A Liquid / Music For Chameleons / Complex / Me! I Disconnect From You / Bombers / The Joy Circuit / We Are So Fragile / Films / Warriors / That's Too Bad / Everyday I Die / On Broadway (live) / Please Push No More / Cars ('93 Sprint) / We Take Mystery (To Bed) / I Die: You Die / Down In The Park / She's Got Claws / Stormtrooper In Drag / My Shadow In Vain / This Wreckage / Sister Surprise / M.E. / You Are In My Vision / Metal / I'm An Agent / White Boys & Heroes / The Life Machine / My Centurion / Remember I Was Vapour

03/96 Premier Hits – compilation (21)
Cars (Premier Mix) / I Die: You Die / Are 'Friends' Electric? / Down In The Park / We Are Glass / Bombers / We Take Mystery

(To Bed) / She's Got Claws / Complex / Music For Chameleons / That's Too Bad / This Wreckage / Warriors / Love Needs No Disguise / White Boys & Heroes / Sister Surprise / Stormtrooper In Drag / Cars (original version)

Virgin TV

11/82 Newman Numan – compilation (45)
same tracklisting as Premier Hits, excluding Warriors and Sister Surprise

Numa

11/84 Berserker (45)
Berserker / This Is New Love / The Secret / My Dying Machine / Cold Warning / Pump Me Up / The God Film / A Child With The Ghost / The Hunter

04/85 White Noise – double live album (29)
Intro / Berserker / Metal / Me! I Disconnect From You / Remind Me To Smile / Sister Surprise / Cold Warning / Music For Chameleons / The Iceman Comes / Down In The Park / This Prison Moon / I Die You Die / My Dying Machine / Cars / We Take Mystery (To Bed) / We Are Glass / This Is New Love / My Shadow In Vain / Are 'Friends' Electric?

09/85 The Fury (24)
Call Out The Dogs / This Disease / Your Fascination / Miracles / The Pleasure Skin / Creature Tricks / God Only Knows / I Still Remember

10/86 Strange Charm (59)
My Breathing / Unknown & Hostile / The Sleeproom / New Thing From London Town / I Can't Stop / Strange Charm / The Need / This Is Love

05/87 Ghost – double live album (-)
Ghost, Call Out The Dogs / I Die You Die / Creatures / I Can't Stop / Me! I Disconnect From You / I Can't Stop / Creatures / Tricks /

The Sleeproom / My Breathing / Cars / Metal / Sister Surprise / This Disease / We Take Mystery (To Bed) / We Are Glass / Down In The Park / Are 'Friends' Electric? / My Shadow In Vain / Berserker

03/92 Isolate – compilation (-)
My Breathing / Call Out The Dogs / Emotion / My Dying Machine / Time To Die / Berserker / Your Fascination / The Secret / Creatures / This Is Love

07/92 Machine & Soul (42)
Machine & Soul / Generator / The Skin Game / Poison / I Wonder / Emotion / Cry / U Got The Look / Love Isolation

08/93 Dream Corrosion – double live album (-)
Mission / Machine & Soul / Outland / Me! I Disconnect From You / We Are So Fragile / Repect / Shame / Films / Dream Killer / Down In The Park / My World Storm / The Machman / Generator / Noise Noise / Cars / Voix / You Are In My Vision / It Must Have Been Years / That's Too Bad / Remind Me To Smile / I'm An Agent / Are 'Friends' Electric? / My Breathing / I Don't Believe / Bombers / Jo The Waiter / We Are Glass

10/94 Sacrifice (-)
Pray / Deadliner / A Question Of Faith Desire / Scar / Love & Napalm / Walk In My Soul / Magic / Bleed / The Seed Of A Lie

07/95 Dark Light – double live album (-)
Pray / A Question Of Faith / I Dream Of Wires / Noise Noise / Listen To The Sirens / Everyday I Die / Desire / Friends / Scar / Magic / Praying To The Aliens / Replicas / Mean Street / Stormtrooper In Drag / Deadliner / Bleed / The Dream Police / I Die You Die / The Hunter / Remind Me To Smile / Are 'Friends' Electric? / Do You Need The Service? / Love & Napalm / Jo The Waiter / I'm An Agent

Eagle Records

10/97 Exile
Dominion Day / Prophecy / Dead Heaven / Dark / Innocence

Bleeding / The Angel Wars / Absolution / An Alien Cure / Exile

WITH MICHAEL R. SMITH

11/95 Human – instrumental (-)
Navigators / Bombay / We Fold Space / A Cry In The Dark / Manic
/ Empire / A Little Lost Soul / The Visitor / Magician / Undercover
/ Halloween / Embryo / Elm Street / Harmonos / Big Alien / Blind
Faith / New Life / Fairy Tales / Diseaes / Tidal Wave / Alone &
Afraid / Sahara / Cold? / Do You Wonder / Betrayal / Suspicion /
The Unborn / Lethal Injection / Frantic / Mother / Black Heart /
Thunder Road / Law & Order / Needles / Climax / Inferno

IRS

10/88 Metal Rhythm (48)
This Is Emotion / Hunger / New Anger / Devious / America / Voix
/ Repect / Young Heart / Cold Metal Rhythm / Don't Call My Name

10/89 The Skin Mechanic – live (55)
Survival / Respect / Call Out The Dogs / Cars / Hunger / Down
In The Park / New Anger / Creatures / Young Heart / Are
'Friends' Electric? / We Are Glass / I Can't Stop / I Die You Die

04/91 Outland (39)
Interval 1 / Soul Protection / Confession / My World Storm /
Dream Killer / Dark Sunday / Outland / Heart / Interval 2 / From
Russia Infected / Interval 3 / Devotion / Whisper

SHARPE & NUMAN

SINGLES

Polydor

02/85 Change Your Mind / Remix, Remake, Remodel (17)

01/88 No More Lies / Voices (34)
05/88 I'm On Automatic / Love Like A Ghost (44)

Numa

07/86 New Thing From London Town / Time To Die (52)

ALBUMS

Polydor

06/89 Automatic (59)
Change Your Mind / Turn Off The World / No More Lies / Breathe
In Emotion / Some New Game / I'm On Automatic / Rip It Up /
Welcome To Love / Voices / Nightlife

RADIO HEART

SINGLES

GFM Records

03/87 Radio Heart (35)
05/87 London Times (48)
10/87 All Across The Nation (-)

ALBUMS

GFM Records

11/97 Radio Heart – only the three singles feature Numan (-)

GARY NUMAN & DA DA DANG

SINGLE

The Record Label

04/94 Like A Refugee (I Won't Cry) (-)

JOHN PEEL SESSIONS

Strange Fruit

12/89 Double Peel Sessions (N/A)
Me! I Disconnect From You / Down In The Park / I Nearly Married
A Human / Cars / Films / Conversation / Airlane

GARY NUMAN COVERS ALBUM

Beggars Banquet

06/97 Random (N/A)
CD 1: St. Etienne – Stormtrooper In Drag / Matt Sharp & Damon
Albarn – We Have A Technical / Gravity Kills – Poetry & Power /
Peck Slip – I Can't Stop / An Pierle – Are 'Friends' Electric? / EMF
– We Are Glass / The Magnetic Fields – I Die: You Die / Jesus
Jones – We Are So Fragile / Posh – She's Got Claws / Earl Brutus
– M.E. / The Underdog – Films / Sukia – Me! I Disconnect From
You / The Orb – Jo The Waiter

CD 2: Kenickie – I'm An Agent / Jimi Tenor – Down In The Park
/ Moloko – Are 'Friends' Electric? / Chris Holmes – Remember
I Was Vapour / Towering Inferno – Metal / Dubstar – Everyday I
Die / Amanda Ghost – Absolution / Deadsy – Replicas / Pop Will
Eat Itself – Friends / Republica – Are 'Friends' Electric? /
Windscale – War Songs / Bis – We Are So Fragile / Dave Clarke
– Cars

GARY NUMAN REMIX ALBUM

Beggars Banquet

10/97 Random 2

TECHNO ARMY FEATURING GARY NUMAN

Castle Communications

04/96 Techno Army (-)
Are 'Friends' Electric? / Cars / We Are So Fragile / I Die: You Die / We Are Glass / She's Got Claws / Machine & Soul / Deadliner / Emotion / A Question Of Faith / U Got The Look / Cars mixes